AIPARTHENOS | EVER-VIRGIN?

Understanding the Orthodox Catholic Doctrine of the Perpetual Virginity of Mary, the Mother of Jesus, and the Identity of James and the Brothers and Sisters of the Lord

AIPARTHENOS | EVER-VIRGIN?

Understanding the Orthodox Catholic Doctrine of the
Perpetual Virginity of Mary, the Mother of Jesus, and the
Identity of James and the Brothers and Sisters of the Lord

Laurent A. Cleenewerck

First Published by Euclid University Press

1250 24th St. NW, Suite 300 - Washington DC 20037, USA

www.euclid.int and www.euclidconsortium.org

Aiparthenos | Ever-Virgin? Understanding the Orthodox Catholic Doctrine of the Perpetual Virginity of Mary, the Mother of Jesus, and the Identity of James and the Brothers and Sisters of the Lord

Cleenewerck, Laurent A.

Copyright © 2015 by Laurent Cleenewerck. All rights reserved.

Printed in the United States of America

ISBN-13: 978-1507798379 (Createspace)

ISBN-10: 1507798377 (Createspace)

Library of Congress Catalog-in-Publication Recommendations

1. Orthodox Eastern Church – Doctrines

2. Catholic Church – Doctrines

3. Mary, Blessed Virgin, Saint

I. Cleenewerck, Laurent.

For my wife Irene

His ornari aut mori.
S'en couronner ou mourir.

"Remembering our most holy, pure, blessed, and glorious Lady, the Theotokos and Ever-Virgin Mary (ἀειπαρθένου), with all the saints, let us commit ourselves and one another and our whole life to Christ our God."
(Great and little litanies in all Orthodox services)

With appreciation to those men and women whose scholarship or engagement has enriched this study, including those cited herein who may have reached different conclusions:

- Richard Bauckham
- John P. Meier
- John McHugh (+)
- Eric Svendsen
- John Painter
- Robert Eisenman
- Ben Witherington, III
- James White
- Megan Nutzman
- John Pacheco
- Robert Sungenis
- Jeffrey J. Bütz
- Tim Staples

Table of Contents

ABBREVIATIONS 11

INTRODUCTION 17

"RAW" BIBLICAL DATA 25
    1)   Old Testament 26
    2)   New Testament 27

HOW IMPORTANT AN ISSUE? 39
    1)   Dogma, Doctrine or Opinion? 40
    2)   A Different Gospel? 46
    3)   St James is popular… 48

THREE POSITIONS 51
    1)   Introduction 52
    2)   The Epiphanian View 53
    3)   The Helvidian View 113
    4)   The Hieronymian View 170

HISTORICAL DATA 181
    1)   Second and Third Century Witnesses 182
    2)   Fourth century witnesses 216

VIRGINITY 'IN PARTU' 227

CONCLUSION 235

APPENDICES	239
1) The Holy Land circa 30 AD	240
2) Epiphanian Chronology	241
3) Epiphanian Family Tree	243
4) Lightfoot's Summary	245
5) The Protevangelium of James	246
6) Orthodox Liturgical Texts	261
INDEX	**265**
SHORT BIBLIOGRAPHY	**270**

ABBREVIATIONS

Bible Book Name Abbreviations:

Book Name	Abbreviation(s)
Genesis	Gen
Exodus	Exo
Leviticus	Lev
Numbers	Num
Deuteronomy	Deu
Joshua	Jos
Judges	Jdg
Ruth	Rut
1 Samuel	1Sa
2 Samuel	2Sa
1 Kings	1Kg
2 Kings	2Kg
1 Chronicles	1Ch
2 Chronicles	2Ch
Ezra	Ezr
Nehemiah	Neh
Esther	Est
Job	Job

Book Name	Abbreviation(s)
Psalm	Psa
Proverbs	Pro
Ecclesiastes	Ecc
Song of Solomon	Sng
Isaiah	Isa
Jeremiah	Jer
Lamentations	Lam
Ezekiel	Eze
Daniel	Dan
Hosea	Hos
Joel	Joe
Amos	Amo
Obadiah	Oba
Jonah	Jon
Micah	Mic
Nahum	Nah
Habakkuk	Hab
Zephaniah	Zep
Haggai	Hag

Book Name	Abbreviation(s)
Zechariah	Zec
Malachi	Mal
Tobit	Tob
Judith	Jdt
Additions to Esther	AEs
Wisdom of Solomon	Wis
Sirach	Sir
Baruch	Bar
Letter of Jeremiah	Let
Song of Three Youths	N/A
Susanna	Sus
Bel and the Dragon	Bel
1 Maccabees	1Ma
2 Maccabees	2Ma
1 Esdras	1Es
Prayer of Manasseh	PMa
Additional Psalm	N/A
3 Maccabees	3Ma
2 Esdras	2Es

Book Name	Abbreviation(s)
4 Maccabees	4Ma
Ode	Ode
Matthew	Mat
Mark	Mar
Luke	Luk
John	Joh
Acts	Act
Romans	Rom
1 Corinthians	1Co
2 Corinthians	2Co
Galatians	Gal
Ephesians	Eph
Philippians	Phi
Colossians	Col
1 Thessalonians	1Th
2 Thessalonians	2Th
1 Timothy	1Ti
2 Timothy	2Ti
Titus	Tit

Book Name	Abbreviation(s)
Philemon	Phm
Hebrews	Heb
James	Jam
1 Peter	1Pe
2 Peter	2Pe
1 John	1Jo
2 John	2Jo
3 John	3Jo
Jude	Jud
Revelation	Rev

Note: PJ is an abbreviation for the *Protevangelium of James*

Formatting: Scriptural citations are formatted with a different font and should be easy to distinguish from other citations.

Footnote references: this book uses simplified footnote references, with mention of the author, abbreviated title and page number. Please consult the short bibliography (at the end of the book) for more details. Citations from the Fathers (and ancient authors) may be given without reference to a particular edition, (e.g. *Commentary on Matthew*) except when this is deemed important.

INTRODUCTION

This book has been long in the making. I never thought I would take the time to dedicate so many hours to what seems like a 'minor' issue. For the sake of clarity, the issue should be narrowed down here and now: **Did Mary have marital intercourse with Joseph after Jesus was born, thereafter giving birth to several sons and daughters who are the people called "brothers and sisters" (in the sense of half-siblings) of Jesus?** Some Christians are not even aware that this topic is subject to any debate, and that there are 3 major views on this question (1) that the "brothers and sisters" are Joseph's children by a previous marriage (adoptive siblings) as well as other close relatives, or (2) that the "brothers and sisters" are in fact cousins, or (3) that the "brothers and sisters" are indeed Joseph and Mary's children born after Jesus (half-siblings).

Over the years, I have come to realize that 'minor' issues can in fact be related to very critical ones, like the emerging tip of the proverbial iceberg.

In January 2015, I had the privilege to participate in a well-formatted, two-hour long debate with the following thesis: "Mary remained a virgin her entire life."[1] As far the proposition was concerned, it could (or maybe should) have been the opposite, for instance "Joseph and Mary had children of their own after Jesus was born." In this case however, I accepted to present and defend the affirmative, a task I did not wish to take lightly, mindful of the warning of that James who was called "the Brother of the Lord:"

> Let not many of you become teachers, my brethren, for you know that we who teach shall be judged with greater strictness. For we all make many mistakes, and if any one makes no mistakes in what he says he is a perfect man, able to bridle the whole body also. (Jam 3:1-2)

---

[1] See http://www.theopologetics.com/category/laurent-cleenewerck/

Only a couple of months before, I had written a letter to a very prominent Evangelical mega-church pastor citing this very text. To be specific, I had written a letter to Pastor Mark Driscoll of Mars Hill fame, after coming across his new sermon series based the Epistle of James, which was titled:

JAMES: JESUS' BOLD LITTLE BROTHER

The description began like this:

> *"James grew up as Jesus' kid brother…"*

It then really dawned on me that a vast number of Christians can read a sentence like that and think nothing of it. For some strange reason (considering how nefarious James is to the 'saved by faith alone' doctrine), several of the most prominent Evangelical mega-church pastors have likewise preached series on the Epistle of James, and all of them see nothing amiss with such elaborations (if not elucubrations) on how these poor kids (children born the sexual union of Joseph and Mary) must have a hard time measuring up to their big brother the sinless Jesus. Amazing situation indeed! And obviously, their listeners don't seem to mind either.

On the other side, when hearing such ideas put forward so casually (and as if the existence of uterine half-siblings of Jesus was a plain matter of undisputed fact), Orthodox and Catholic Christians shake their heads in dismay. How absurd! How offensive! It is not just an intellectual shaking of the head but something that goes deeper, some kind of piercing of the heart and soul.

In the case of Mark Driscoll, I took the time to compose and fax a letter dated 15 January 2015 which was an attempt to share in a couple of pages compelling reasons to think twice about being so emphatic about James being "Jesus' kid brother" born from Joseph and Mary. After all, in typical fashion, Driscoll had dismissed the ancient Orthodox view in these words:

> But there are three positions regarding Jesus' relationship with this man, James. The first is that they were step-brothers, and it is

> taught that Jesus' father Joseph, his adoptive earthly father, Joseph, had a marriage prior to Mary and that he had children including James. And then perhaps his wife died, and he became a widower, and then he married Mary. That was his second wife. Therefore, James would have been from the first marriage and was a step-brother to Jesus.
>
> There's no evidence for this in the Bible. I think it is speculative at best. It doesn't seem to fit with the preponderance of evidence that we receive in God's Word. Every indication is that Mary and Joseph were a young, poor, rural couple, that they were getting married for the first time. There's no mention of any prior wife; there's no mention of any prior children, so let's dismiss that position.[1]

It is surprisingly common to see the Orthodox (Epiphanian) view misunderstood and so casually dismissed. Another example is found in Eric Svendsen's doctoral dissertation dealing with Mary's status in Scripture and Christianity:

> The view that the "brothers of Jesus" are children of Joseph by a previous marriage remains, by and large, the least popular of the three. McHugh notes that virtually no one holds it today except some supporters in the Eastern Orthodox Church (1975:209). If it were not for Bauckham's recent defense of this theory (1994), we may have safely disregarded it from further consideration.[2]

It is somewhat surprising that Svendsen's doctoral committee failed to call for a correction on this paragraph, and it shows the danger of relying on secondary sources (in this case McHugh who is a Roman Catholic), an endemic problem in Christian theology. The fact is that the Epiphanian / Orthodox view is the most ancient, the most

---

[1] Mark Driscoll, *Sermon Series on James*, retrieved from the following URL: https://marshill.com/media/james-jesus-s-bold-little-brother/james-1-1
[2] Eric Svendsen, *Who is my mother? Rhe role and status of the mother of Jesus in the New Testament and in Roman Catholicism*, 54

widely held position during the formative centuries of the Christian faith, and that it remains the official position of the Orthodox Church to this very day. Considering that more than 150 million people – perhaps as many as 300 million – hold to this view by virtue of being Orthodox Christians, it is amazing to read that "virtually no one holds it today."

This convergence of factors, coupled with the fact there is to my knowledge no work entirely dedicated to this issue written from an academic and Epiphanian / Orthodox perspective, has led to the publication of this book.

Also, a number of arguments in favor of the Orthodox (and Catholic) view have never, to my knowledge, been put forward in a formal and systematic way. The debate with Robert Zins on this topic certainly provided the timely impetus and context to dedicate the necessary time to complete this study. It was not the first structured debate on this subject I might add, and my sense, in accepting to do the debate, was that the Orthodox view was not adequately defended by the Roman Catholic debater who had to face off with two fierce and experienced Protestant apologists, namely James White and Eric Svendsen.

Last but not least, there are certain new arguments put forward by the Helvidian side[1] that needed to be discussed in a formal way, notably those published by Eric Svendsen and John Meier.

My hope is obviously that both Orthodox and Catholic Christians will find this book helpful and inspiring. Roman Catholic readers will certainly deplore the fact that in spite of our agreement on the issue of the perpetual virginity of Mary, 'Latins and Greeks' do not quite agree on the identity of the brothers and sisters of the Lord. It

---

[1] In fact, several Roman Catholic scholars have also written in defense of the Helvidian view.

is my hope however that the overall approach will be helpful to those coming from the Latin / Hieronymian tradition as well.

For readers approaching this topic from what I tend to call 'the modern Protestant Evangelical view,' I would be content if they could conclude with their fellow-perspectivist John P. Meier:

> [Absolute] proof of the Helvidian view is impossible and that the Epiphanian view could be upheld with intellectual integrity.[1]

---

[1] John Meier, *The Brothers and Sisters of Jesus in Ecumenical Perspective*, 27

Below: Orthodox icon of St James, the Brother of the Lord, apostle of the 70, Bishop of Jerusalem (Source: Orthodox Church in America)

Below: Orthodox icon of St Joseph, portrayed as an older man (Source: Orthodox Church in America)

"RAW" BIBLICAL DATA

1) OLD TESTAMENT

Old Testament passages deemed relevant to the question of the perpetual virginity of Mary will be discussed as arguments associated with one of the three positions below. But since the topic of the Old Testament is introduced, it is important for the reader to be aware that we can almost speak of 'two Old Testament sources:' the Hebrew text (for which we rely heavily of the Masoretic Text) and the Greek text (for which we rely on the Christian codices of the Septuagint). This point should remind us (and whoever is engaged in biblical studies) that we are dealing with languages and cultures upon which we cannot impose our own modern mindset. There is such a thing as retrojection and anachronistic interpretations against which all sides in this conversation should be guarded.

Let us for now focus on New Testament passages that are relevant to the question at hand: Did Mary remain a virgin all her life or did she have children with Joseph after Jesus was born? The selection is somewhat arbitrary, but it seems useful to offer a broad selection of the passages deemed relevant.

2) NEW TESTAMENT

The following selection of New Testament passages is taken from the EOB: Eastern / Greek Orthodox New Testament with footnotes copied from the EOB, for clarifications are needed.

It is very important that the reader should start with these basic texts and read them carefully, without prejudice.

a) Matthew 1:1-11

> The book of the origins[1] of Jesus Christ,[2] the son of David, the son of Abraham. ²Abraham became the father of Isaac. Isaac became the father of Jacob. Jacob became the father of Judah and his brothers. ³Judah became the father of Perez and Zerah by Tamar. Perez became the father of Hezron. Hezron became the father of Ram. ⁴Ram became the father of Amminadab. Amminadab became the father of Nahshon. Nahshon became the father of Salmon. ⁵Salmon became the father of Boaz by Rahab. Boaz became the father of Obed by Ruth. Obed became the father of Jesse. ⁶Jesse became the father of King David. David became the father of Solomon by her who had been the wife of Uriah. ⁷Solomon became the father of Rehoboam. Rehoboam became the father of Abijah. Abijah became the father of Asa.[3] ⁸Asa became the father of Jehoshaphat. Jehoshaphat became the father of Joram. Joram became the father of Uzziah. ⁹Uzziah became the father of Jotham. Jotham became the father of Ahaz. Ahaz became the father of Hezekiah. ¹⁰Hezekiah became the father of Manasseh. Manasseh became the father of Amon.[4] Amon became the father of Josiah. ¹¹Josiah became the father of Jechoniah and his brothers, at the time of the exile to Babylon.

---

[1] Or "history," "generations"
[2] Messiah (Hebrew) and Christ (Greek) both mean "Anointed One"
[3] CT reads "Asaph"
[4] CT reads "Amos"

b) Matthew 1:18-24

[18]Now the birth of Jesus Christ happened like this: after his mother Mary was promised in marriage to Joseph but before they came together, she was found pregnant by the Holy Spirit. [19]Joseph, her betrothed,[1] who was a righteous man did not want to make her a public spectacle and so intended to put her away[2] quietly.[3] [20]But as he was thinking about these things, behold, an angel of the Lord appeared to him in a dream, saying, "Joseph, son of David, do not be afraid to take Mary your wife home, for what is conceived in her is by the Holy Spirit. [21]She will give birth to a son and you shall give him the name Jesus[4] because he will be the one to save his people from their sins."

[22]Now all this happened so that what had been spoken by the Lord through the prophet might be fulfilled:

[23]Behold, the virgin shall be with child and bring forth a son. They shall call his name Emmanuel; which means, 'with us [is] God.'[5]

[24]Joseph arose from his sleep and did as the angel of the Lord had commanded him: he took his wife to [live with] him, [25]and had no relations with her before[6] she had brought forth her firstborn[7] son; and he named him Jesus.

c) Matthew 2:13-23

[13]After they had departed, behold, an angel of the Lord appeared to Joseph in a dream, saying, "Arise! Take the young

---

[1] Or "husband"

[2] Some translations have "to divorce her" or "to dismiss her"

[3] Or "secretly/in private"

[4] "Jesus" (Yeshua) means "God saves" or in short "salvation"

[5] Isaias (Isaiah) 7:14. NT agrees with LXX against MT ("virgin" instead of "young woman").

[6] EOB footnote has been removed to avoid untimely discussion of this verse.

[7] This expression indicates a legal status, not that other siblings are implied. Other ancient manuscripts (א, B) omit "firstborn" which may have been added in Matthew to harmonize with Luke 2:7.

child and his mother, and flee into Egypt.[1] Stay there until I tell you, for Herod will seek the young child to destroy him." [14]So Joseph arose and took the young child and his mother by night, and departed into Egypt. [15]They remained there until the death of Herod, so that what had been spoken by the Lord through the prophet might be fulfilled:

Out of Egypt I have called my son.[2]

[16]When Herod saw that he had been outwitted by the wise men, he became extremely angry. He dispatched [his men] and killed all the male children who lived in Bethlehem and all the surrounding countryside, two years old and under, according to the exact time which he had learned from the wise men. [17]And so, what had been spoken by the prophet Jeremiah was fulfilled:

[18]A voice was heard in Ramah, lamentation,[3] weeping and great mourning: Rachel weeping for her children. She would not be comforted, because they are no more.[4]

[19]But when Herod died, behold, an angel of the Lord appeared to Joseph in a dream when he was in Egypt, saying: [20]"Arise! Take the young child and his mother, and return to the land of Israel; those who were trying to kill the young child are dead."

[21]Joseph arose and took the young child and his mother, and they came into the land of Israel. [22]However, when Joseph heard that Archelaus was ruling over Judea in the place of his father Herod, he was afraid to go there. Being warned in a dream, he withdrew into the region of Galilee. [23]He thus arrived and lived in a city called Nazareth, so that what had been

---

[1] Like Moses, Jesus is threatened with death by an evil ruler. The irony is that the Jewish king is Pharao and Egypt is now the land of refugee. Compare also Revelation 12:4,14

[2] Hosea 11:1 (a typological application of Christ as Jacob-Israel). In this case, NT agrees with MT against LXX.

[3] CT omits "lamentation" which may have been added to harmonize this quotation with Jeremiah 31:15 (38:15 in LXX).

[4] Jeremiah 31:15

spoken through the prophets might be fulfilled, "He will be called a Nazarene."[1]

d) Matthew 12:46-50 (also Mark 3:31-35 and Luke 8:19-21)

[46]While Jesus[2] was still speaking to the multitudes, behold, his mother and his brothers stood outside, desiring to speak to him. [47]<Someone said to him, "Behold, your mother and your brothers stand outside, desiring to see you.">[3]

[48]But to the person who had spoken, Jesus[4] answered, "Who is my mother? Who are my brothers?" [49]He then stretched out his hand toward his disciples and said, "Behold, my mother and my brothers! [50]As it is, whoever does the will of my Father who is in heaven is my brother, and sister, and mother."

e) Matthew 13:54-56

[54]Coming into his own country, he taught the people in their synagogue and they were astonished, saying, "Where did this man get this wisdom and these deeds of power? [55]Is this not the carpenter's son? Is not his mother called Mary, and his brothers, James, Joses, Simon, and Judas?[5] [56]Are not all of his sisters with us? Where then did this man get all of these things?" [57]And they stumbled[6] because of him.

---

[1] No exact match in the Old Testament. Three possible figurative antecedents for the name Nazarene are the Hebrew words *nazir* (set apart, consecrated), *nezer* (crown), and *netser* (flower, branch, from the root) which have corresponding Old Testament passages.

[2] Greek "he"

[3] CT brackets this verse. PT has "desiring to see you" while most other manuscripts read "seeking to speak to you"

[4] Greek "he"

[5] Or "Judah"

[6] Or "were scandalized" (ἐσκανδαλίζοντ)

f) Mark 6:1-3

Jesus[1] left that place and came into his own country, and his disciples followed him. ²When the Sabbath came, he began to teach in the synagogue. Hearing him, many were astonished, saying, "Where did this man get these things?" and, "What is the wisdom that is given to him, [that] such powerful works come about by his hands? ³Is this not the carpenter, the son of Mary,[2] and brother of James, Joses, Judah, and Simon? Are not his sisters here with us?" And they rejected him.

g) Luke 1:26-37

²⁶Now in the sixth month, the angel Gabriel was sent by God to a city of Galilee named Nazareth, ²⁷to a virgin pledged to be married to a man whose name was Joseph, of the house of David. The virgin's name was Mary. ²⁸Having come in, the angel said to her, "Rejoice,[3] full of grace![4] The Lord is with you! Blessed are you among women!"[5]

²⁹But when she saw him, she was greatly troubled at his saying and considered what kind of greeting this might be. ³⁰The angel said to her, "Do not be afraid, Mary, for you have found favor with God. ³¹Behold, you will conceive in your womb and bring forth a son, and you will call his name 'Jesus.' ³²He will be great and will be called the Son of the Most High. The Lord

---

[1] Greek "he"

[2] See Appendix E

[3] Or "Hail!"/"Greetings"—One of the most common Hebrew greetings is שָׁלוֹם, "peace," reflected in εἰρήνη in Lk 10:5; 24:36, but the LXX never translates שָׁלוֹם, "peace," by the imperative Χαῖρε. J. McHugh, in *The Mother of Jesus*, 38-39, notes, "The imperative form Χαῖρε, far from being a conventional greeting, always refers to the joy attendant on the deliverance of Israel; wherever it occurs, it is a translation of a Hebrew verb meaning 'Rejoice greatly!'" (or "shout" for joy).

[4] This is the traditional expression. "The perfect participle κεχαριτωμένη has the strongest connotation of the present: 'having been favored and as a result still being in this blessed condition.' The root in the verb is χάρις grace, the unmerited favor bestowed by God. The passive voice makes God the agent." (R.C.H. Lenski, *The Interpretation of St. Luke's Gospel*, 62). Many translations have "Greetings, favored one!" or something similar.

[5] CT omits "Blessed are you among women"

God will give him the throne of his father, David, [33]and he will reign over the house of Jacob forever. And of his Kingdom there shall be no end."[1]

[34]Mary said to the angel, "How can this be [happening] to me[2], since I do not know [a] man?"

[35]The angel answered her, "The Holy Spirit will come upon you, and the power of the Most High will overshadow[3] you. Therefore, the holy one who is born[4] will be called the Son of God. [36]Behold, your relative Elizabeth has also conceived a son in her old age and this is the sixth month [of her pregnancy] for her who was called barren. [37]For nothing shall be impossible with God."

h) Luke 2 (entire chapter)

In those days, Caesar Augustus issued a decree that a census should be taken of the entire [Roman] world. [2]This was the first census made when Quirinius was governor of Syria. [3]All went to enroll themselves, everyone to his own city. [4]Because he was of the house and family of David, Joseph left the city of Nazareth in Galilee and went up to Judea, to the city of David which is called Bethlehem. [5]He did so to enroll himself with Mary who was pledged to be married to him as wife and who was pregnant.

[6]While they were there, the time came for her to deliver her child. [7]She gave birth to her firstborn[5] son and wrapped him in swaddling clothes. She laid him in a manger because there was no room for them in the inn.[6] [8]There were shepherds in the

---

[1] Used in the Creed of Nicea-Constantinople

[2] Other manuscripts omit "happening to me"

[3] Greek ἐπισκιάσει—Compare Exodus 40:33-35 LXX which is the only other instance where this verb is used: "And Moses was not able to enter into the tabernacle of testimony, because the cloud overshadowed (ἐπεσκίαζεν) it, and the tabernacle was filled with the glory of the Lord"

[4] TR adds "from you"

[5] See Appendix E

[6] Or perhaps "guest room"

same countryside, staying in the field and keeping watch by night over their flock. ⁹And behold, an angel of the Lord stood by them and the glory of the Lord shone around them, and they were terrified. ¹⁰The angel said to them, "Do not be afraid, for behold, I bring you Good News of great joy which will be for all the people. ¹¹For there is born to you, this day, in the city of David, a Savior, who is Christ the Lord! ¹²This is the sign[1] to you: you will find a baby wrapped in strips of cloth,[2] lying in a manger." ¹³Suddenly, there was with the angel a multitude of the heavenly host praising God, and saying:

¹⁴Glory to God in the highest, and on earth peace, [and] good will among mankind.[3]

¹⁵When the angels went away from them into heaven, the shepherds said to one another, "Let us go to Bethlehem now and see what has taken place, which the Lord has made known to us." ¹⁶They came with haste and found both Mary and Joseph; and the baby was lying in the manger. ¹⁷After seeing it, they revealed the news which had been spoken to them about this child. ¹⁸All those who heard what the shepherds were saying were amazed, ¹⁹but Mary kept all these sayings, pondering them in her heart. ²⁰The shepherds returned, glorifying and praising God for all the things which they had heard and seen, just as it was told them.

²¹When the eight days were fulfilled and the time came for the circumcision of the child, he was named Jesus, the name given by the angel before he was conceived in the womb.

²²And when the days of their purification according to the law of Moses were fulfilled, Joseph and Mary brought him up to Jerusalem, to present him to the Lord. ²³(For it is written in the law of the Lord, "Every male who opens the womb shall be called holy to the Lord").[4] ²⁴[They also brought him] to offer a

---

[1] Compare Isaias (Isaiah) 7:14 LXX which also used the Greek word σημεῖον

[2] Or "swaddling clothes"

[3] CT reads "peace for those whom he favors/peace to those on whom his favor rests" (NJB/NAB)

[4] Exodus 13:2,12

sacrifice according to what is said in the law of the Lord, "A pair of turtledoves, or two young pigeons."[1]

[25] Behold, there was a man in Jerusalem whose name was Simeon. This man was righteous and devout, waiting for the consolation of Israel, and [the][2] Holy Spirit was upon him. [26] It had been revealed to him by the Holy Spirit that he would not see death before he had seen the Lord's anointed.[3] [27] He came in the Spirit into the temple. The parents brought in the child Jesus in order to do according to the custom of the law concerning him. [28] Then Simeon took Jesus in his arms and blessed God, saying,

[29] "Now you let your servant[4] depart in peace, Master, according to your word, [30] for my eyes have seen your salvation,[5] [31] which you have prepared before the face of all peoples; [32] a light to enlighten the Gentiles,[6] and the glory of your people Israel."

[33] Joseph[7] and his mother were wondering at the things which were spoken concerning him. [34] Simeon blessed them and said to Mary, his mother:

Behold, this child is set for the falling and the rising of many in Israel, and as a sign which is spoken against. [35] Yes, a sword will pierce through your own soul, so that the thoughts of many hearts may be revealed.

[36] There was a certain Anna, a prophetess, the daughter of Phanuel, of the tribe of Asher (she was of a great age, having lived with a husband seven years from her virginity,[8] [37] and she

---

[1] Leviticus 12:8

[2] The Greek actually uses the indefinite

[3] Or "Christ" (Greek) and "Messiah" (Hebrew) both mean "Anointed One"

[4] Actually "bondservant" ("servant" is kept here for poetic purposes but is not otherwise consistent with the EOB translation standard).

[5] Compare Tobit 11:9,14

[6] Or "a light of revelation to the nations"

[7] CT reads "his father" instead of "Joseph"

[8] This is the literal translation—it seems that Anna was married for seven years. NJB reads "Her days of girlhood over, she had been married for seven years"

had been a widow for about eighty-four years), who did not depart from the temple, offering divine service with fastings and petitions night and day. ³⁸Coming up at that very hour, she gave thanks to the Lord and spoke of Jesus[1] to all those who were looking for redemption in Jerusalem.

³⁹When Joseph and Mary[2] had accomplished all things that were according to the law of the Lord, they returned into Galilee, to their own city, Nazareth. ⁴⁰The child was growing, and was becoming strong in spirit, being filled with wisdom, and the grace of God was upon him. ⁴¹His parents went every year to Jerusalem for the feast of the Passover.

⁴²When Jesus[3] was twelve years old, they went up to Jerusalem according to the custom of the feast. ⁴³When they had fulfilled the days, as they were returning, the boy Jesus stayed behind in Jerusalem. Joseph and his mother did not notice[4] it. ⁴⁴Supposing him to be in the company, they went a day's journey and began to look for him among their relatives and acquaintances. ⁴⁵When they did not find him, they returned to Jerusalem, looking for him. ⁴⁶After three days, they found him in the temple, sitting among the teachers, both listening to them and asking them questions. ⁴⁷All who heard him were amazed by his understanding and answers. ⁴⁸When his parents[5] saw him, they were astonished, and his mother said to him, "Son, why have you treated us this way? Behold, your father and I were anxiously looking for you."

⁴⁹He said to them, "Why were you looking for me? Did you not know that I must be in my Father's house?" ⁵⁰But they did not understand what he said to them. ⁵¹After this, he went down with them, and came to Nazareth. He was obedient[6] to them, and his mother kept all these sayings in her heart. ⁵²And Jesus

---

[1] Greek "him"

[2] Greek "they"

[3] Greek "he"

[4] Or "know"

[5] Greek "they"

[6] Or "subject"

increased in wisdom and stature, as well as in favor with God and men.

i) Luke 21:1

¹⁶You will be handed over even by parents, relatives, friends, and brothers. Some of you will be put to death.[1]

j) John 2:12

¹²After this, he went down to Capernaum, he, and his mother, his brothers, and his disciples; and they did not stay there [more than] a few days.

k) John 7:1-10

After these things, Jesus went about in Galilee; he did not wish to travel around in Judea because the Jews were seeking to kill him. ²Now the feast of the Jews, the Feast of Tabernacles,[2] was at hand. ³So his brothers said to him, "Depart from here and go into Judea, so that your disciples may also see your works which you are accomplishing. ⁴Certainly, no one who seeks to be known openly does anything in secret! If you do these things, reveal yourself to the world!" ⁵For even his brothers did not believe in him.

⁶Jesus therefore said to them, "My time has not yet come, but your time is always ready. ⁷The world cannot hate you, but it hates me, because I bear witness concerning it, that its works are evil. ⁸You go up to the feast. I am not yet[3] going up to this feast, because my time is not yet fulfilled."

⁹Having said these things to them, he remained in Galilee. ¹⁰However, when his brothers had gone up to the feast, then he also went up, not publicly, but as it were, in private.[4]

---

[1] Acts 12:1-2
[2] Or "Tents/Booths"
[3] CT omits "yet"
[4] Or "in secret"

l) John 19:25-27

[25]But there were standing by the cross of Jesus his mother, and his mother's sister[1] (Mary [the wife][2] of Clopas), and Mary Magdalene. [26]When Jesus saw his mother and the disciple whom he loved standing there, he said to his mother, "Woman, behold your son!" [27]Then he said to the disciple, "Behold, your mother!" And from that hour, the disciple took her to his own home.

m) Acts 1:14

[14]With one accord, all these were continuing steadfastly in prayer and supplication[3], together with certain women, including Mary the mother of Jesus and his brothers.

n) 1 Corinthians 7:36-38

[36]Nevertheless, if any man thinks that he is behaving inappropriately toward his virgin, if she has past the flower of her age, and if it is required, let him do what he wills.[4] He does not sin; let them marry. [37]As for the one who stands steadfast in his heart, (having no necessity, but having control over his own will to keep his virginity): he does well. [38]And so, he who marries [his betrothed virgin[5]] does well, but he who does not does better.

o) 1 Corinthians 9:5

[5] Do we not have the right to be accompanied by a wife, as the other apostles and the brothers of the Lord and Cephas?

---

[1] In this verse, perhaps "sister-in-law" (Clopas may have been Joseph's brother or a close relative).

[2] The expression 'Mary of Clopas' in the Greek text is ambiguous as to whether Mary was the daughter or wife of Clopas, but exegesis has commonly favored the reading "wife of Clopas" (as reflected in above translation).

[3] CT omits "and supplication"

[4] Or "desires"

[5] Greek "her"

p) Galatians 1:19

[19]However, I did not see any of the other apostles,[1] except James, 'the Lord's brother.'

---

[1] It is unclear if 'apostles' is a reference to the Twelve, or to the Seventy, or to an even wider group. Here, James is included among the apostles and may be either James of Alphaeus (of the Twelve) or James of Jerusalem (if they are to be distinguished according to Orthodox tradition).

HOW IMPORTANT AN ISSUE?

1) DOGMA, DOCTRINE OR OPINION?

Does it really matter whether Joseph and Mary had sexual intercourse and children (after the birth of Jesus)? Does it really matter that the Last Adam should have had half-siblings from the same womb? "Blood brothers" is a commonly-used expression, and yet, sharing the same blood as Jesus, whose blood was the instrument of redemption, is not without theological implications.

On the one hand, it is tempting to answer "no" to the above question, because the sacred texts are clearly not concerned with providing details about Jesus' family and upbringing. Only Matthew and Luke have an account of Jesus' birth, and those two accounts are notoriously difficult to harmonize. Luke gives us a passing glimpse at Jesus when 12 years old, but that is all.

Worse, we are not privy to the details of the Lord's apparitions between the Resurrection and Ascension, and hardly have a trace of the ministries of the Twelve Apostles after 50 AD. Neither does the New Testament contain any instructions or information on how the sacred rites ('mysteries' or 'sacraments') are supposed to be performed. This could and perhaps should lead us to the topic of 'Sola Scriptura,' but it suffices here to be aware that the New Testament assumes the existence of the Church and is content to contain what is materially sufficient regarding the Gospel of Jesus Christ.

In order words, there are indeed things that are hardly discussed in the Scriptures what we still consider of great importance, notably the form and administration of the sacraments. As St Basil of Caesarea famously wrote:

> Of the beliefs and practices whether generally accepted or publicly enjoined which are preserved in the Church some we possess derived from written teaching; others we have received delivered to us in a mystery by the tradition of the apostles; and both of

these in relation to true religion have the same force. And these no one will dispute, no one, at any rate, who is even moderately versed in the institutions of the Church. Indeed, if we were to attempt to reject such customs as have no written authority, on the ground that the importance they possess is small, we should unintentionally injure the Gospel in its very vitals…[1]

We may wonder, then if affirming or denying the ever-virginity of Mary has to do with "the Gospel in its very vitals."

On this particular topic of the perpetual virginity and its relative importance, we shall see that we have three positions (Epiphanian, Hieronymian, Helvidian) that are basically aligned with the three historical "branches" of Christianity (Orthodoxy, Catholicism, Protestantism), respectively.

St Basil, a major teaching authority for the Orthodox tradition, is an important voice because of a homily ascribed to him, in which he makes two important statements:

> [The opinion that Mary bore several children after Christ] … is not against the faith; for virginity was imposed on Mary as a necessity only up to the time that she served as an instrument for the Incarnation. On the other hand, her subsequent virginity was not essential to the mystery of the Incarnation.[2]
>
> The friends of Christ do not tolerate hearing that the Theotokos ever ceased to be a virgin…

Clearly, there is a bit of tension between the two paragraphs, which provide a reflection of the Eastern Orthodox position to this very day. On the one hand, what is dogmatically essential to the Gospel

---

[1] Basil of Caesarea, *On the Holy Spirit*, 66

[2] Basil of Caesarea, *Homilia in sanctam Christi generationem*, PG 31:1468. Some of these ancient texts are sometimes of questionable authenticity and in some cases clearly spurious. Here, the probability that this homily ascribed to St Basil be spurious is very low, which is why this source is often cited without this issue being raised.

of Jesus Christ is that Jesus Christ was born of a virgin. This can be affirmed while bearing in mind the obvious but still noticeable fact that only 2 of 4 gospels actually teach the virginal birth. St Paul is content to teach that Jesus was "born of a woman" (Gal 4:4). Not surprisingly, there are those who have argued that Christianity would be just fine without the virgin birth.

A strange percentage (to illustrate the use and misuse of statistics) might be that out of the 27 books of the New Testament, only 2 (7.4%) bear witness to the virgin birth, considered here as a dogmatic essential. If we keep this peculiar fact in mind, we can understand why St Basil (along with the Orthodox Church) can also express indignation at the thought that some would question the every-virginity of the Theotokos, precisely because Mary being "theotokos" seems to imply exclusive motherhood.

One may say then, **from an Orthodox viewpoint**, that Mary's perpetual virginity is unquestionably 'the accepted conviction of the Church' but not strictly speaking a dogma of the Orthodox faith. To be technical, it does not even fall in the category called *theologoumenon*, but rather on the outer fringe of tolerable orthodoxy.

From a Roman Catholic perspective, the doctrine of the perpetual virginity of Mary is *de fide*, and can be considered as dogma of the faith, in particular in view of its inclusion in the dogmatic proclamation on the Assumption of Mary by Pope Pius XII:

> [By] the authority of our Lord Jesus Christ, of the Blessed Apostles Peter and Paul, and by our own authority, we pronounce, declare, and define it to be a divinely revealed dogma:
>
> that the Immaculate Mother of God, the ever Virgin Mary, having completed the course of her earthly life, was assumed body and soul into heavenly glory.
>
> 45. Hence if anyone, which God forbid, should dare willfully to deny or to call into doubt that which we have defined, let him

know that he has fallen away completely from the divine and Catholic Faith.[1]

We shall reserve our discussion of the generally-accepted Roman Catholic position (the Hieronymian view, that the "brothers and sisters" are in fact cousin) for the next chapter. It should be, noted, however, that the Roman Catholic Church affirms the dogma that Mary is ever-virgin but not a particular version (Hieronymian or Epiphanian) of this dogma. Also, it should be noted that many modern Roman Catholic scholars in good standing with Rome have nevertheless, in their scholarly work, argued in favor of Helvidian-Protestant view. This in no way affects the official teaching of the Roman Catholic magisterium, but it should be mentioned that scholarly perspectives do not always align with official teachings.

From a modern Protestant (and "Evangelical") perspective, we could first observe that few denominations have a well-defined 'dogma-making process.' What we can notice, however, is that during the nineteenth century, Protestant scholars departed from the position of the early Reformers, which was one of acceptance of the historic belief in the perpetual virginity of Mary. Indeed, it should be noted that the three "founding fathers" of reformed Christianity were unequivocal on the matter:

> **Zwingli:** "I firmly believe that Mary, according to the words of the gospel as a pure Virgin brought forth for us the Son of God and in childbirth and after childbirth forever remained a pure, intact Virgin."[2]
>
> **Luther:** "He, Christ, our Savior, was the real and natural fruit of Mary's virginal womb . . . This was without the cooperation of a man, and she remained a virgin after that."[3]

---

[1] Pope Pius XII, *Munificentissimus Deus*, 1950
[2] Ulrich Zwingli, *Corpus Reformatorum v. 1*, p. 424
[3] Martin Luther, *Sermons on John*, Chapters 1-4, 1537-1539

> **Calvin:** "There have been certain folk who have wished to suggest from this passage [Matt 1:25] that the Virgin Mary had other children than the Son of God, and that Joseph had then dwelt with her later; but what folly this is! For the gospel writer did not wish to record what happened afterwards; he simply wished to make clear Joseph's obedience and to show also that Joseph had been well and truly assured that it was God who had sent His angel to Mary. He had therefore never dwelt with her nor had he shared her company... And besides this, Our Lord Jesus Christ is called the first-born. This is not because there was a second or a third, but because the gospel writer is paying regard to precedence. Scripture speaks thus of naming the first-born whether or not there was any question of the second."[1]

Calvin used strong language on this matter ("folly") and he is certainly not the only one to have felt that changing course on this view was no mere preference or opinion. In the late 4th century, St Epiphanius of Salamis in Cyprus had predictably stronger language:

> There are many other things which the fathers did not venture to say in times gone by. And in a word, woe to our troubled generation with its salvation in peril, swamped on every side by the wicked second sowings of the devil's sick fancies and heretical reasonings! (5) How dare they < so degrade* > the undefiled Virgin who was privileged to become the Son's habitation, and was chosen for this from all the myriads of Israel, so that something deemed worthy to be a vessel and dwelling place is to become a mere sign of child-bearing? For I have heard from someone that certain persons are venturing to say that she had marital relations after the Savior's birth. And I am not surprised. The ignorance of people who do not know the sacred scriptures well and have not consulted histories, always turns them to one thing after another, and distracts anyone who wants to track down something about the truth out of his own head...

---

[1] John Calvin, *Sermon on Matthew*

This kind of language is simply unknown to many modern-day Christians who think that they have found the plain Gospel and a 'non-denominational' Church. Indeed, the contrast with modern-day Evangelical Christianity is rather compelling, inasmuch as one would be hard-pressed to find a single denominational source or mainstream pastor who does not, as a matter of fact, teaches that Mary and Joseph did engage in marital intercourse and consequently have children of their own after Jesus. The already-cited except from Mark Driscoll's 2014 sermon series is very typical of what is perceived, at least in the United States, as contemporary 'mere Christianity.'

In their reasonably open-minded *Roman Catholics and Evangelicals: Agreements and Differences*, Geisler and MacKenzie predictably conclude:

> In view of all this biblical evidence, there seems to be no real scriptural basis for the Catholic belief in Mary's perpetual virginity.[1]

It will be our task to carefully assess the various argument put forward in this two thousand year long debate.

---

[1] Norman Geisler and Ralph McKenzie, *Roman Catholics and Evangelicals: Agreements and Differences*, Chapter 15

2) A DIFFERENT GOSPEL?

Oddly enough, it seems that those who are most opposed to Mary's perpetual virginity – these would be for instance Protestant apologists willing to debate this topic or write about it – are also those who are the most convinced that 'Rome preaches a different gospel.' James White (Alpha and Omega Ministries) is a good example of this association between the Protestant/Helvidian view (which insists that Joseph and Mary must have had other children) and the strong Protestant rejection of Catholicism (and perhaps Orthodoxy) as invalid forms of Christianity. White (who debated Catholic apologist Gerry Matatics[1] on the doctrine of the perpetual virginity) is also the author of *Mary -- Another Redeemer?* and *The Roman Catholic Controversy* in which he denies that the Roman Catholic Church possess the saving gospel (while recognizing that individual Catholics may be saved in spite of being member of the Roman Catholic Church). Eric Svendsen (of *heos hou* doctoral fame – see below), also debated Matatics on the same topic and published his thesis in book form under the title *Who Is My Mother? The Role and Status of the Mother of Jesus.* Interestingly, he also published *Upon This Slippery Rock: Countering Roman Catholic Claims to Authority* which illustrates (in my view at least) the correlation between one's rejection of a foundational Marian belief (her perpetual virginity) and one's perception that the gospel is perverted by those who hold this view of the Lord's mother. Last but not least, Robert Zins (whom I debated on this topic in January 2015) is perhaps the most radically opposed to 'all-things-Catholic.' He is the founder of "A Christian Witness to Roman Catholicism" and

---

[1] Gerry Matatics eventually left mainstream Roman Catholicism and became a sedevantist.

never refers to Catholicism as "Christianity" but rather as "the Roman Catholic religion."[1]

It seems clear that for these defenders of the multiple maternity of Mary (for lack of a better expression), anything that might exalt the Lord's mother beyond the role of redeemed sinner who served as surrogate mother but then moved on to other things is suspect of altering the gospel. Svendsen questions:

> Yet, where in the ongoing life of the church do we find any similar mention of Mary's fiat in her earthly ministry; or any ongoing mediation in her supposed heavenly ministry-both of **which are absolutely central to the Roman Catholic gospel?**[2]

Perhaps the reverse could be said, that those who affirm so comfortably that Mary had other children after Jesus have failed to grasp some fundamental aspect of the Gospel: that lacking the illumination of the Holy Spirit, they cannot even look beneath the surface of the text ("brothers" "until" "firstborn") and end up inventing new and ultimately destructive ideas.

---

[1] I should mention that Robert Zins was remarkably cordial both during and after the debate.

[2] Svendsen, 214 (bold mine)

3) ST JAMES IS POPULAR...

Even before Dan Brown had authored his best-selling *Da Vinci Code*, it was no secret that magazine issues featuring a controversial article about Jesus (or Mary) sell amazingly well. There is always a ready audience for 'suppressed' and 'forbidden' truths about early Christianity, how St Paul got it all wrong, and how St James was eventually shoved to the side for representing the older, authentic and Jewish Christianity. Not to mention the nefarious role of the "sociopath" emperor Constantine who was the dark power behind the transformation of Christianity into a mind-numbing, Jesus-worshiping religion.[1]

A good example of this book-writing and book-selling approach is the 2010 book by Lutheran pastor Jeffrey Bütz entitled *The Brother of Jesus and the Lost Teachings of Christianity*.

In spite of this commercially appealing title, Bütz is actually quite reasonable in his overall perspective written from a Western-Lutheran perspective. However, two points should be noted. One, he quickly settles on the Helvidian view (Luther's opinion notwithstanding), having spent very little time giving serious consideration to the traditional position. Second, Bütz seems unaware that Orthodox Christians have always held St James in great honor, to the point that Greek-speaking Orthodox Christians often refer to him as "adelphotheos" (The Brother of God),[2] an exalted title if there ever was one. In fact, Orthodox Christians are never uncomfortable with the title "Brother of the Lord" because it

---

[1] Kurt Eichenwald, *The Bible: So Misunderstood It's a Sin* (Newsweek December 2014 issue)

[2] More properly perhaps, "the brother of the one who is God (by nature)" which is theologically correct since there is a single person of the incarnate Word who is indeed "theos" (John 1:1)

is James' distinct honor and memorial to be so-called. The Divine Liturgy ascribed to him continues to be served on his feast day, and its use has become more widespread in recent years. Unlike Western Christians who were embarrassed with this 'brother who really is a cousin' (Hieronymian view) or this half-brother who wrote what Luther called "an epistle of straw," Orthodox Christians have certainly never disowned or rejected this towering figure of the Mother Church of Jerusalem.

A somewhat older and much more controversial treatment of James was offered by maverick (and Jewish) scholar Robert Eisenman in his 1998 opus *James the Brother of Jesus: The Key to Unlocking the Secrets of Early Christianity and the Dead Sea Scrolls*. Eisenman published in 2012 an updated and more popular book on the same topic (and similar viewpoints) under the title *James the Brother of Jesus and the Dead Sea Scrolls I: The Historical James, Paul the Enemy, and Jesus' Brothers as Apostles*. Eisenman is certainly a scholarly mind, but he presses two hypotheses to the extreme, which is why his views have not been adopted by anyone else: (1) that Paul is James' arch-enemy (2) that the Dead Sea Scrolls are the key to fully understand the teachings and importance of James in the early Church.

Eisenman does provide citations and references to primary sources (Eusebius, etc.) but his interpretation of these various sources is highly controversial to say the least. Orthodox Christians already know and agree that 'to recover James is to recover Jesus' as Eisenman contends. But Orthodox Christians are already steeped in the tradition of James which is ascetical, liturgical, temple-oriented, and fully Christian.

Just James: The Brother of Jesus in History and Tradition by John Painter is also a noteworthy treatment of the subject from a scholarly and reasonably restrained perspective. Painter is rather dismissive of the Hieronymian view (that the *adelphoi* were cousins) but shows more consideration for the Epiphanian view.

Last but not least to be mentioned here is the 2009 publication *The Brother of Jesus* by Hershel and Witherington. It is both a defense of the authenticity of a limestone burial box with the inscription "James, son of Joseph, brother of Jesus" which set the world of biblical archaeology on fire for a short while. As of this writing, the consensus seems to be that the burial box is not authentic, which makes this particular part of the book less than current. Running in parallel is a discussion of James by Ben Witherington who is a respected mainstream Protestant professor and scholar. However, this portion of the book disappoints, and his engagement with the Epiphanian view is less than satisfactory.

Suffice it to say that James called "the Brother of Jesus" is indeed an important and fascinating figure. In exploring the issue of the ever-virginity of Mary (whose second-born son he is often believed to be by Evangelicals), we shall also have an occasion to provide an Orthodox perspective on this first bishop of the first Church.

THREE POSITIONS

1) INTRODUCTION

In this section, we will carefully examine the 3 positions put forward to explain why the New Testament refers to some people as "brother" or "brothers / brothers and sisters" of Jesus, noting at the outset that none of them is ever referred to as son(s) or daughter(s) of Mary.

I will present (with an effort towards impartiality) the arguments used to defend these positions, and consider the history of each position.

The three views are listed in alphabetical order according to their traditional names, names which are now entrenched but somewhat disputable. And it so happens that this alphabetical listing makes sense from another perspective. The **Epiphanian** view is not only the first alphabetically but also in terms of ancient origin and prevalence. The **Helvidian** view technically comes before the **Hieronymian** view in the sense that St Jerome specifically wrote his tract as a rebuttal of Helvidius.

Admittedly, it is an effort to remember the names (and spelling) of these three positions, which is why it is also possible to refer to them as the Orthodox view, the modern Protestant view, and the preferred Roman Catholic view respectively. After all, the Epiphanian view was certainly not invented or even first explained by St Epiphanius of Salamis at the close of the 4th century, since it can be traced to second century sources.

2) THE EPIPHANIAN VIEW

a) Proposal

The so-called Epiphanian view is named after St Epiphanius, the bishop of Salamis in Cyprus, who died in the year 403. In his *magnum opus* entitled *Against Heresies* (also known as the *Panarion*), the great bishop refutes the new view (which he calls new) that Mary had marital intercourse with Joseph and therefore other children after Jesus. In doing so, Epiphanius affirms and takes for granted the position that now bears his name, namely that:

- Mary remained ever-virgin
- Joseph was a widower when he took Mary as wife
- James is a son of Joseph, and the older "adoptive brother" of Jesus.

Let us read straight from Epiphanius:

> I have heard from someone that certain persons are venturing to say that Mary had marital relations after the Savior's birth. And I am not surprised! The ignorance of those who do not know the sacred scriptures well and have not consulted histories always turns them to one thing after another, and distracts anyone who wants to track down something about the truth out of his own head.

> To begin with, when the Virgin was entrusted to Joseph (lots having compelled her to take this step) she was not entrusted to him for marriage, since he was a widower. He was called her husband because of the Law, but it plainly follows from the Jewish tradition that the Virgin was not entrusted to him for matrimony...

> For how could such an old man, who had lost his first wife so many years before, take a virgin for a wife? Joseph was the brother of Cleopas but the son of Jacob surnamed Panther; both of these brothers were the sons of the man surnamed Panther.

> Joseph took his first wife from the tribe of Judah and she bore him six children in all, four boys and two girls, as the Gospels according to Mark and John have made clear. His firstborn son was James, whose surname was Oblias, or "wall," and who was also surnamed "The Just" and was a nazirite, or "holy man." He was the first to receive the episcopal throne, the first to whom the Lord entrusted his throne on earth.[1]

Epiphanius is very interested in the relative ages of Joseph, James and Jesus, although the ages he proposes seem extreme (and hard to believe) for us today. He writes:

> Joseph begot James when he was somewhere around forty years old. After him he had a son named Joses—then Simeon after him, then Judah, and two daughters, one named Mary and one, Salome; and his wife died. And many years later, as a widower of over eighty, he took Mary.

Epiphanius goes on to provide some biblical evidence for this position, yet all the while taking for granted the background story contained in the second-century text known as the *Protevangelium of James* (which however he does not cite by name). For the sake of convenience, this text is included in the Appendix.

Interestingly, Epiphanius, a fierce critique of Origen (who also accepted the account of the *Protevangelium of James*), is here in agreement with his theological nemesis.

Another point that should be noted and admitted regarding Epiphanius is his passionate defense of sexual continence. He is among those who argued that presbyters should be perpetually continent; and he called James a life-long virgin in spite of 1 Corinthians 9:5:

---

[1] Epiphanius of Salamis, *Panarion*, Book III, (page 620 in the Williams edition)

Have we no right to take about with us a sister-wife, like the rest of the Apostles, and the brothers of the Lord, and Cephas?[1]

Last but not least, it may be important to examine Epiphanius' sources, because unlike Eusebius who would always document his sources, the bishop of Salamis does not do so. In particular, we will have to wonder if Epiphanius followed the more ancient author Hegesippus, as this has been suggested.

Since the Orthodox view is named after Epiphanius, we should note here that he was very conservative theologian and hierarch. For instance, he strongly objected to Christians shaving their beard or growing long hair. He may have been against the use of icons and was cited as such by the iconoclasts during the great controversy. This point is somewhat controversial[2] and should be considered a less-than-settled issue, but this would not have been entirely out of character from someone like Epiphanius who was a 'radical conservative.' If anything, this supports the assessment that our Cypriot father was not an innovator in any sense, and that would include the received teaching on the ever-virginity of Mary.

This being said, we shall define the Epiphanian view (in an academic sense) as follows:

The so-called "brothers and sisters" of Jesus, notably James, are mostly children of Joseph by a previous marriage (and some may be other kinds of relatives as well). Strictly speaking, this view does not necessarily entail that Mary remained a virgin.

---

[1] But James is not mentioned by name, and some many argue that "sister-wife" might refer to a married relationship without marital intercourse, precisely on the model of Joseph and Mary.

[2] See Steven Bigham and Nicholas Ozoline, *Epiphanius of Salamis, Doctor of Iconoclasm? Deconstruction of a Myth*

On this last point, Richard Bauckham writes the following clarification, which is actually quite surprising:

> My own historical argument for the Epiphanian view of the brothers and sisters of Jesus should not be taken to be an argument for the perpetual virginity of Mary, for which I think there is no good historical evidence. In the absence of such evidence, I find it more natural to assume that, if the Epiphanian view is correct, Mary and Joseph had normal marital relations after the birth of Jesus but produced no children.[1]

Obviously, Epiphanius would not have appreciated that his name would be associated with any position that would allow Mary to be anything but ever-virgin. So we should more precisely articulate the Orthodox-Epiphanian view as follows:

> **The so-called "brothers and sisters" of Jesus, notably James, are mostly children of Joseph by a previous marriage (and some may be other kinds of relatives as well). Also, it affirms the perpetual virginity of Mary.**

This proposal can also be expressed as a narrative which is closely aligned with the *Protevangelium of James*, along these lines:

> **Around the year 2BC, a young woman named Mary (being about 15-16 years old) is entrusted to be married to a widower named Joseph, of the tribe of David. (Let us propose here that Joseph was 50-60 years old at the time and had several grown children). The reason for this situation is that she has been raised in the temple and had made a vow of virginity, yet needed to be entrusted to a betrothed for the rest of her life. At the time of her betrothal to Joseph, Gabriel announced to Mary that she would have a son, at which point she wonder how this**

---

[1] Richard Bauckham, *The brothers and sisters of Jesus: An Epiphanian response to John P. Meier*

could happen in view of her vow to remain a virgin. To this, the angel answered that this pregnancy would not involve sexual intercourse, and Joseph was then directed to accept Mary as wife.

During Mary's pregnancy, she becomes Joseph's wife but they do not (as would otherwise be expected) consummate the marriage. After the birth of Christ, we have the challenge of harmonizing the accounts of Matthew and Luke, but we do see Joseph and Mary in Jerusalem, then temporarily in Egypt, then back in Nazareth. Joseph, Mary and Jesus are mentioned as a family unit when Jesus is 12 years old, and we can suggest that Joseph died at an old and blessed age, around the year 25 AD. This would be 25-30 years after his betrothal to Mary, and dying at about 75 years old, which is quite short of the 110 years recorded for Joseph the Patriarch, but quite plausible.[1] Mary, a widow, would have been adopted in Joseph's clan, which would have included Clopas and his own family (cousins, uncles and aunts). At the time when Jesus was crucified, James would have been around 55-60 years old, a suitable age to become the chief-elder of the Church in Jerusalem. He would have been an old man, possibly 85 years old or more,[2] when martyred in Jerusalem in 62 AD.

We now move on to the arguments, biblical and historical, that support the above-stated position.

---

[1] The *Story of Joseph the Carpenter* (4th century) narrates that Joseph was 111 years old when he died.
[2] Epiphanius states that James was 96 when he died (*Panarion*, Book III, *De fide*; 13.4; page 626 in the excellent Brill/Williams edition)

b) Arguments

Here we, we must distinguish between (1) positive arguments in favor of Mary's perpetual virginity, which are common with the Hieronymian view (these are marked with a * after the heading); (2) positive arguments that are uniquely in favor of the Epiphanian view; and (3) counter-arguments that are actually rebuttals of the other two views.

It should also be noted that some arguments may not be fully documented in this section if they are to be developed in the historical study.

The arguments are as follows:

i. Son of Mary*

It is a certain fact that no one is called "son of Mary" except Jesus himself, notably in Mark 6:3, which reads:

> Is not this the carpenter, the son of Mary and brother of James and Joses and Judas and Simon, and are not his sisters here with us? And they took offense at him.

Now, Mark's version of the events at Nazareth is somewhat different than what is found in Matthew:

> Is not this the carpenter's son? Is not His mother called Mary, and His brothers, James and Joseph/Joses[1] and Simon and Judas? (Mat 13:55)

The Gospel of John contains a similar statement, perhaps expressed in a different context:

> They said, "Is not this Jesus, the son of Joseph, whose father and mother we know? How does he now say, 'I have come down from heaven'?" (Joh 6:42)

---

[1] There is a variant in the manuscripts, so it is hard to be certain as to the original reading of this verse.

Mark, who is always more 'raw' and 'authentic' in his transmission of Peter's memories, specifically noted that the locals knew Jesus as "the son of Mary." In English, we might even say: "*the* son of Mary." Richard Bauckham[1] offers this explanation, worth citing in full:

> The fact that in Mark's account of Jesus' visit to Nazareth, the people of Nazareth call him "son of Mary" (Mark 6:3) rather than "son of Joseph" (cf. Matt 13:55: Luke 4:22; John 6:42) has never been satisfactorily explained. Suppositions that it was Jewish custom to use a metronymic to refer either to the son of a widow, or (b) to an illegitimate son have been shown to have no convincing support from Jewish parallels. In a recent article Ilan has shown that there is some evidence from Josephus and rabbinic tradition that (c) "a man would be called after his mother when she possessed superior lineage." She suggests that Mark, unlike Matthew and Luke, knew nothing of Joseph's Davidic lineage, and could, therefore, consider Mary the more important parent. In fact, it is probable that Mark believed in Jesus' Davidic descent (Mark 10:48:11:10), which was the widespread belief of the early church (Acts 2:30:13:23:15:16; Rom 1:3; 2 Tim 2:8; Heb 7:14; Rev 5:5: 22:16; Did. 10:6), and he would have needed good reason not to assume that this descent was through Joseph. Even if Mark did not think Jesus was descended from David, we are still at a loss to know why he should have thought Mary the genealogically more distinguished parent. Another possibility, (d) that Mark refers to the virginal conception, is unlikely. None of the gospels represent the virginal conception as a matter of public knowledge, and so, even supposing Mark knew the tradition of the virginal conception, it is unlikely that he meant to refer to the virginal conception when he put the designation "son of Mary" on the lips of the people of Nazareth.

---

[1] Opus cit. (1996)

Finally, McArthur and Meier, having rightly rejected other proposed solutions, except (c), which they did not know, propose (e) that the phrase is not a formal designation but an "informal description" occasioned by the context. Wishing to point out that Jesus was an ordinary member of their own community, the Nazarenes naturally think of him as the son of his still living parent, who is presumably there in the synagogue as they speak. This is the best explanation that has so far been offered, but it is not quite convincing. If Jesus were normally known as "the son of Joseph," as Jewish custom seems to require, one would expect the Nazarenes to make their point by first calling him this, and then going on to refer to those relatives who were there with them: his mother, brothers, and sisters.

It is surprising that another possible explanation seems not to have been suggested: that in Nazareth Jesus would have been known as "the son of Mary" because this distinguished him from the children of Joseph by his first wife. This usage can easily be paralleled from the OT. Women only occasionally occur in biblical genealogies, but in a large majority of the cases where they do, their function in the genealogy is that of distinguishing a man's sons by one wife (from his sons by another wife) (e.g., Gen 4:19-22; 22:20-24; 36:)0-14; 46:10: Exod 6:15; I Chr 2:2-4,18-19,21,24,25-26,46,48-49; 3:1-9). This concern to distinguish the sons of different mothers means that sons of men who have children by more than one wife can be designated by their metronymic, instead of the usual patronymic. Thus Hur, who was the son of Caleb by one of his wives (1 Chr 2: 18-19) is known as "Hur the firstborn of Ephrath" (1 Chr 2:50; 4:4). Similarly, David's son Adonijah is known as "Adonijah the son of Haggith" (1 Kgs 1:5,11; 2:13; cf. 2 Sam 3:4; I Chr 3:2), distinguished from sons of David by other wives (2 Sam 3:2-5; 1 Chr 3:1-9). In rabbinic literature, not only Adonijah but also other sons of David are referred to by their metronymics (b. B. Bat. 109b; b. Ketub. 62b). Similarly, the sons of Jacob by his two wives and two concubines are sometimes designated by their metronymics (Philo Fug. 73; Joseph and Aseneth 22:11; 26:6; 27:6-7; 28: 1,9). It is possible that this is also the explanation of the most famous use of metronymics in the OT: the brothers Joab, Asahel, and Abishai are always called "the son(s) of Zeruiah," their mother (1 Sam 26:6 and twenty-three times in the OT; also Josephus Ant. 7.1.3,6 section 11,45; 7.3.2 section 65; 7.9.1 section 265; b. Qidd. 49b; b. Sanh. 95a; only Josephus Ant. 7.1.3 section 11, perhaps following 1 Chr 4:14, names their father). This usage cannot be intended just to highlight their relationship to David, who was Zeruiah's half brother, since Amasa, son of Zeruiah's sister Abigail, is known by his patronymic (2 Sam 17:25; 1 Kgs 2:5,32; cf. 1 Chr 2:16-17). But it is possible that Zeruiah's husband had sons by another wife and that her sons are distinguished by reference to her. (A less likely possibility is that the sons of Zeruiah had the same mother but different fathers and that they used the metronymic to indicate their relationship to each other.)

It is easy to suppose that, whereas outside Nazareth Jesus would have to be identified as "the son of Joseph," in Nazareth, where the family was known, the children of Joseph's two wives would be distinguished by their metronymics. Jesus would be called "the son of Mary" precisely because James, Joses, Judas, and Simon were not sons of Mary. This understanding of Mark 6:3 does not, of course, depend on the improbable assumption that Mark preserves an accurate historical report of what the people of Nazareth said. It simply assumes that Mark attempts to portray with verisimilitude what they would have said, just as he represents them as calling Jesus "the carpenter" because this is what people in his home village, though not elsewhere, would be likely to call him.

To summarize, it can certainly be argued that Jesus being called "son of Mary" in Mark 6:3 is significant, and most satisfactorily explained within the framework of the Epiphanian view.

As a negative argument, Mark 6:3 shifts the burden of proof onto those who would defend the Helvidian view, namely to explain why no one is called "son of Mary" except for Jesus himself. This would also mean that a high level of positive evidence would be needed to overthrow the traditionally received view.

ii. Second and third century authorities

Orthodox Christians can safely affirm (perhaps to a surprised and unprepared audience) that the Epiphanian view is the most ancient and most widely attested view on the identity of the brothers and sisters of Jesus, and on the lifelong virginity of Mary. Indeed, the Epiphanian view comes very close to what St Vincent of Lerins once described as "catholic" in his famous text:

> Moreover, in the Catholic Church itself, all possible care must be taken, that we hold that faith which has been believed everywhere, always, by all. For that is truly and in the strictest sense Catholic, which, as the name itself and the reason of the thing declare, comprehends all universally. This rule we shall observe if we follow universality, antiquity, consent. We shall follow universality if we confess that one faith to be true, which the whole Church throughout the world confesses; antiquity, if we in no wise depart from those interpretations which it is manifest were notoriously held by our holy ancestors and fathers; consent, in like manner, if in antiquity itself we adhere to the consentient definitions and determinations of all, or at the least of almost all priests and doctors.[1]

The historical record is as follows: between Pentecost and the first proclamation of the canon of the New Testament by St Athanasius of Alexandria in 367, no one with pastoral office in the Church is on the record as holding to another view.[2] Some of the authorities that support the Epiphanian view are:

- *The Protevangelium of James*

---

[1] St Vincent of Lerins, *Commonitory*, II
[2] This excludes Tertullian and the cut-off date is before Helvidius.

- Clement of Alexandria
- Origen of Alexandria
- Eusebius of Caesarea
- Hilary of Poitiers.

Basil of Caesarea and his brother Gregory of Nyssa certainly believed in the perpetual virginity of Mary, and (as we shall see) offer indirect support to the Epiphanian view.

In addition, I shall argue that indirect support is provided by:

- Justin Martyr
- Irenaeus of Lyons
- Gregory of Neo-Caesarea (the Wonderworker)

During these critical centuries, only Tertullian, the first Latin ecclesiastical writer (in North Africa) was almost certainly teaching that Mary had other children.

Justin Martyr and Irenaeus are sometimes listed as being, with Tertullian, among those who taught that Mary had other children, but this is highly controversial. In the historical section, we will discuss these two cases and conclude quite the reverse.

In summary, just as we find increasing convergence among the churches and Fathers leading to the proclamation of the canon in 367 AD, we likewise see convergence on the issue of Mary's virginity leading to a similar level of convergence at about the same time.

iii. The meaning of *adelphoi*

A major part of the controversy regarding the ever-virginity of Mary and the identity of the brothers and sisters of Jesus is precisely that, that if those people (of which 4 names are given) are called "brothers" and "sisters," it follows that they must be Jesus' maternal (or "uterine") siblings.

This is worth repeating. Although "not ... until" (Mat 1:25) and "firstborn son" are the other two factors leading many Christians to accept the Helvidian/Evangelical view, it does seem that taking "brother(s)" at face value is what makes so many people think that "of course, Joseph and Mary had children of their own after Jesus."

A good example of this situation was illustrated during a public debate on this topic, when the Protestant apologist asked "Did Peter's mother in law have a daughter?" The point was that words carry meaning, and that just as "mother-in-law" has specific meaning from which we can deduce the existence of a daughter, likewise "brother(s)/sister(s)" allows one to conclusively affirm that Mary had these other children with Joseph. Another Protestant apologist put it this way:

> You were able to logically deduce that the mother-in-law of Peter had a daughter without showing us from Scripture she had a daughter. And the Bible never mentions she had a daughter. Most probably that the title mother-in-law gave you the idea she had a daughter and that's enough evidence.
>
> You see we believe that Jesus had uterine brothers and sisters (Matthew 13:55). But in order for us to convince Roman Catholics that these are really his uterine brothers and sisters, you require us to present from the Bible that these are Mary's children and not simply being called brothers and sisters of Christ. Why is that?[1]

Yes, why is that?

The reason, quite plainly, is that *adelphoi* (brothers - to use the plural) is not at all like *pentheran* (mother-in-law) which has a very narrow semantic range. Unless we take the time to understand

---

[1] From a discussion posted on the website http://forum.thebereans.net/showthread.php?3287-Does-Peter-s-Mother-in-Law-have-a-Daughter

adelphoi from a linguistic and cultural perspective, we will end up believing that the earth is flat and that the sun rotates around the earth because 'it just seems that way.' This imagery from astronomy and physics is not out of place, as I have had the privilege to teach formal courses on relativity and quantum physics over the course of several years. To conclude that Mary had many children simply on the basis of our reading of *adelphoi* is indeed like holding to a geocentric view based on immediate impressions.

So what is the actual range of meanings of *adelphos/adelphoi* and how can we tell? And does such a study actually support the Epiphanian view?

Our immediate 'field of study' should be the corpus of the Bible, by which we mean the Hebrew text, parts in Aramaic, as well as the Septuagint (being the translation of the Old Testament into Greek used by the early Christians) and the New Testament. In addition, we should also explore the meaning of these words in contemporary literature.

The first thing to state and fully comprehend is that Hebrew, Aramaic, and LXX Greek use *adelphos/adelphoi* to mean various kinds of close family connections. Another way to express this is negative, by stating that the Old Testament culture does not have specific terms for cousins.[1] There are close relatives (parents; brothers in the broad sense and including uncles, nephews and cousins) and more distant relatives for which the Greek will have the useful word *sungenis*.[2]

To be precise, *adelphos/adelphoi*, can mean several things:

---

[1] But a word for uncle/aunt did exist (Lev 10:4; Num 34:11; Exo 6:20; Lev 20:20), with the possibility to refer to "my uncle's son." In fact, this makes the use of *adelphos* to refer to a nephew or uncle in the OT/LXX all the more interesting.
[2] Still used in modern Greek

(1) **Strict biological sibling(s)** (same father and same mother). In Matthew 10:2 for example, we can assume that Peter and Andrew, as well as James and John were strict *adelphoi*. Actually, it seems that the Gospel of John deemed it necessary to qualify the relationship between Peter and Andrew as τὸν ἀδελφὸν τὸν ἴδιον precisely to make it clear that these are in fact blood brothers. But this is certainly not the sense we Christians can accept for the brothers of Jesus because we understand the context and the scope of meaning of word *adelphoi*.

(2) **Half-sibling(s)**, with either the same father or the same mother. For instance, Sara could call her husband Abraham *adelphos* because he was in fact a half-brother (same biological father).[1] In the Luke 3:1, Philip is called Herod's "brother" but they were really half-brothers. So there are two possible meanings here: maternal (or uterine) half-brothers and paternal half-brothers.

The above information is already significant: when modern Evangelical Protestants argue that we should take the most literal and obvious reading that the 4 individuals referred to as "brothers/sisters" of Jesus are really just that, brothers and sisters in the modern English sense, they don't mean strict siblings with the same two biological parents as the word is used for Peter and Andrew for example. And they don't mean siblings in the sense of Genesis 20. **They mean half-siblings with the same mother ("uterine") but not the same father, which they say is a particular meaning informed by the context.** It should be noted, however, that this sense of *adelphoi* is not obvious, and actually quite rare. Let us be specific on what that means: according to the

---

[1] Gen 20:5

research published by Edgar Alan Nutt,[1] *adelphos* appears about 1,025 times in the Septuagint. The basic meaning of full-siblinghood prevails in about 520 instances, but in about 120 instances, the status of half-siblinghood is identified, **the common parent always is the father.**

Let us now discuss the other possible meanings of *adelphos/adelphoi*:

(3) **Adoptive or foster brother(s)/sister(s)**, which is not quite the same but related to the modern idea of step-siblings.

(4) **Uncle or nephew**, with the general meaning of close relatives (for instance possibly "sister-in-law" as in John 19:25).

(5) **Spiritual brother/family member**, as in people united by spiritual bonds or even friendship.[2]

In the New Testament, *adelphos/adelphoi* is used 343 times, of which the majority is meaning (5), which is the familiar opening of the public reading of the epistle in the Church (and also the opening greeting of the presbyter's sermon in many Orthodox traditions). "Brothers/sisters" most often means spiritual brothers and sisters, as in the Lord's statement:

> And stretching out his hand toward his disciples, he said, "Here are my mother and my brothers! For whoever does the will of my Father in heaven is my brother, and sister, and mother." (Mat 12:49-50)

But there is something even more important to notice here: this meaning of *adelphoi* (the most common in the New Testament) is actually the same as (3) above (adoptive brothers and sisters). We can call those of the Church *adelphoi* precisely because the entire

---

[1] By Edgar Alan Nutt, *Jesus the Virgin-Born*, 150-151

[2] We could perhaps add (6) and (7) as "one who shares a common ethnic heritage" (Acts 22:13) and "neighbor" (Mat. 7:3-5).

message of the New Testament is that, as adoptive sons and daughters of God the Father, we shall also inherit with Christ who is the co-eternal and only-begotten Son by nature. This theological theme is so important to really grasp the concept of *adelphos/adelphoi* that we must cite the relevant passages and let them sink in:

> All those who are led by the Spirit of God are children of God. Truly, you did not receive a spirit of slavery to fall back into fear, but you have received a spirit of adoption. When we cry, "Abba! Father!", it is that very Spirit bearing witness with our spirit that we are children of God. If [we are] children, then [we are] heirs, heirs of God and joint heirs with Christ; if, in fact, we suffer with him so that we may also be glorified with him. (Rom 8:14-17)

> But when the fullness of time had come, God sent his Son, born of a woman, born under the law, in order to redeem those who were under the law, so that we might receive adoption as children. And because you are children, God has sent the Spirit of his Son into our hearts, crying, "Abba! Father!" So, you are no longer a slave but a child, and if a child then also an heir, through God. (Gal 4:4-7)

> He destined us for adoption as his children through Jesus Christ, according to the good pleasure of his will… In Christ we have also obtained an inheritance, having been destined according to the purpose of him who accomplishes all things according to his counsel and will… (Eph 1:5, 11)

Equally relevant are these two:

> At this time Moses was born, and he was beautiful before God. For three months he was brought up in his father's house; and when he was abandoned, Pharaoh's daughter adopted him and brought him up as her own son. (Act 7:20-21)

> It was fitting that God, for whom and through whom all things exist, in bringing many children to glory, should make the pioneer of their salvation perfect through sufferings. For the one who sanctifies and those who are sanctified all have one Father. For this reason Jesus is not ashamed to call them brothers and sisters, saying, "I will proclaim your name to my

brothers and sisters, in the midst of the congregation I will praise you." (Heb 2:10-12)

The first conclusion of this survey is that the most common use of *adelphos/adelphoi* is in fact in the sense of adoptive siblings, because there is no practical difference between full siblings and adoptive siblings.

So let us now see how the Gospel of Matthew – the first book in the New Testament - uses that very term *adelphos/adelphoi*.

The first time, in Matthew 1:2, it means half-brother sharing the same father Jacob, with two different mothers Leah and Rachel. That was common in Biblical times. And it is interesting. Is it basically the meaning understood by the early Christians and ancient Churches to this very day for Jesus and his *adelphoi*: same father Joseph (biological or adoptive sense) but with different mothers. Mary has an only son, and would mourn her only son when a sword would pierce her soul. So we can argue that Matthew 1:2 sets the meaning for us.

In view of our discussion on the meaning of adoption, this is very important to understand: **Joseph was the adoptive father of Jesus, not what we could call 'a step-father.'** This is what Richard Bauckham explains to refute the common misunderstanding that the Epiphanian view requires *adelphoi* to mean step-brothers:

> But Matthew and Luke do not in fact portray Joseph as related to Jesus in the way that a stepfather would be. Since Jesus had no biological father, the relationship is strictly unique, but it is much more like an adoptive relationship than like a step-relationship… Therefore, if Joseph had children by a previous marriage, Jesus' relation to them would have much more reality than the relation of a step-sibling would. He would be their adoptive brother.[1]

---

[1] Opus cit.

We now move on to Matthew 1:11, the second instance of *adelphoi* in the New Testament. Here, the Jamieson-Fausset-Brown Bible Commentary[1] explains that *adelphoi* means "uncles" as in 2 Chronicles 36:10.

> The "brethren" of Jechonias here evidently mean his uncles—the chief of whom, Mattaniah or Zedekiah, who came to the throne (2Ki 24:17), is, in 2Ch 36:10, as well as here, called "his brother."[2]

At the outset, we can immediately see that Greek-Matthew[3] is going to be heavily influenced by the Septuagint (LXX), and this is going to be true for the 3 words we must consider as relevant to this discussion: (1) *adelphos/adelphoi*; (2) *heos | heos hou*; and (3) *protoktokos*.

In summary, we can say that in a family sense, *adelphoi* means very close relatives, especially relatives sharing the same household, the same roof. Beyond that, there is a wider circle, still denoting various types of relatives or family member, in Greek *sungenis*.

Because the meaning of *adelphoi* is so important in our perception of who the brothers/sisters of Jesus were, we need to be guided by both the Scriptural and common use of the terms, and not quickly assume things. In particular, once we understand that Jesus is the adoptive son of Joseph in the full legal sense, we also understand that the siblings are not just step-siblings (a modern reality), but rather true *adelphoi*.

From an Epiphanian perspective then, the use of the word *adelphoi* to refer to the adoptive siblings of Jesus makes perfect sense. This is

---

[1] Not recent (originally published in 1871) but valuable nonetheless

[2] Accessed at http://www.ccel.org/ccel/jamieson/jfb.xi.i.ii.html

[3] I say "Greek Matthew" because we only have Matthew in Greek, in spite of Eusebius' informed assurance that there also was (probably originally) an Aramaic/Hebrew version of Matthew.

exactly the word you would have expected the inspired authors to use to refer to Joseph's children by a previous marriage, as well as other 'members of the Joseph family clan.'

iv. The purpose of Matthew 1*

What is the purpose of Matthew 1? Clearly, the author wants to show that Jesus is the fulfillment of the hopes and promises of the Old Testament types and prophecies. Jesus is shown as the new Moses and the new David and son of David:

> An account of the genealogy of Jesus the Messiah, the son of David, the son of Abraham. (Mat 1:1)

Matthew has this driving agenda in his first chapter:

- Joseph has nothing to do with Jesus' biological conception and birth
- Yet, Jesus is the adoptive son of Joseph and therefore in the line of David.[1]

In addition, we can assert that:

- Matthew is not interested in what happens after the immediate birth of Jesus as far as sexual relations between Joseph and Mary are concerned
- Jesus does not need to be Joseph's legal firstborn[2] to be a true heir of the throne of David.[3]

---

[1] Matthew does not mention that Mary is also of the line of David, which is theme featured in second century sources.

[2] In fact, Jesus is called Mary's legal *prototokos*, not Joseph's, both in Matthew 1: 24 and Luke 2:7

[3] This is discussed below among the Helvidian arguments. See 1Chr 3:1-6.

This is very important to understand the relationship between Joseph (and his children) with Jesus (as adoptive son) and also with Mary, as we see unfold in the rest of the New Testament.

v. A different look at Matthew 1:18, 20 and 24-25

Mathew 1:18-24 is a key passage in the debate over the idea that Mary and Joseph eventually engaged (or not) in conjugal relations. It reads (bold added on key points):

> [18]Now the birth of Jesus Christ happened like this: after his mother Mary was promised in marriage to Joseph but **before they came together**, she was found pregnant by the Holy Spirit. [19]Joseph, her betrothed,[1] who was a righteous man did not want to make her a public spectacle and so intended to put her away[2] quietly.[3] [20]But as he was thinking about these things, behold, an angel of the Lord appeared to him in a dream, saying, "Joseph, son of David, do not be afraid **to take Mary your wife home**, for what is conceived in her is by the Holy Spirit. [21]She will give birth to a son and you shall give him the name Jesus because he will be the one to save his people from their sins."

> [22]Now all this happened so that what had been spoken by the Lord through the prophet might be fulfilled:

> [23]Behold, the virgin shall be with child and bring forth a son. They shall call his name Emmanuel; which means, 'with us [is] God.'[4]

> [24]Joseph arose from his sleep and did as the angel of the Lord had commanded him: **he took his wife to [live with] him,**

---

[1] Or "husband"

[2] Some translations have "to divorce her" or "to dismiss her"

[3] Or "secretly/in private"

[4] Isaias (Isaiah) 7:14. NT agrees with LXX against MT ("virgin" instead of "young woman").

²⁵and **had no relations with her before[1] she had brought forth her firstborn[2] son**; and he named him Jesus.

In 1:18, the message is clear: Mary (who is then betrothed to Joseph) is found to be pregnant even though there has been no sexual intercourse. She is still a virgin, and the rest of the chapter shows that she will remain a virgin (at least) until the birth of the conceived child Jesus. The emphasis is two-fold: no human sexual relations can be associated with the conception of this child, in fact not only before the conception proper but even (and this is unusual) during the nine months of pregnancy.

This point is often overlooked. Virtually all married couples engage in sexual relations during the course of the pregnancy. Matthew makes it clear that this is not the case. His focus is on the time between the conception and the birth: no human sexual intercourse is involved, and the prophecy (Isaiah 7:14 LXX) is fulfilled: not only is it a virgin who did conceive, but it is also a virgin who has given birth!

In verse 20, the angel does not say 'do not be afraid to take your wife in the sense of marital intercourse' but rather 'do not be afraid to accept/receive Mary as your wife, yet with the understanding that there is to be no sexual relationship.' This marriage between Joseph and Mary does not affect Mary's statement to the angel in Luke 1:34: "I do not know man" which in plain language means "I do not engage in sexual intercourse."

Matthew 1:25 is the logical ending of Matthew 1:18: there was no sexual intercourse before the conception, and there was none before the actual birth of Jesus, after which there may or may not have

---

[1] EOB footnote has been removed to avoid untimely discussion of this verse.

[2] This expression indicates a legal status, not that other siblings are implied. Other ancient manuscripts (א, B) omit "firstborn" which seems to have been added in Matthew to harmonize with Luke 2:7.

been change. What happens after that is not Matthew's concern or point of interest in chapter 1, as we can deduct from the ending of the NOT/UNTIL temporal clause.

The end point of the emphatic "NOT" is not in fact a point at which sexual intercourse would be possible (that would be several weeks after the birth, most obviously after the rite of purification). Rather, the end point is the birth itself, which the obvious implication that no, there was no change of behavior right after that point because sexual intercourse is not possible right after birth anyways, as everyone knows. To be medically specific here, intercourse is not permitted by modern OB/GYN doctors until after 6 weeks of delivery.

Not surprisingly then, the Jamieson-Fausset-Brown Bible Commentary explains:

> And knew her not till she had brought forth her first-born son: and he called his name JESUS—The word "till" does not necessarily imply that they lived on a different footing afterwards (as will be evident from the use of the same word in 1Sa 15:35; 2Sa 6:23; Mt 12:20).

This is not a modern commentary, but recent scholarly commentaries agree that Matthew 1:25 cannot be pressed to infer anything conclusive about a change of behavior after the event.

Another point to notice in Matthew 1:25 is the tense used by Matthew. Here, I would agree with Roman Catholic scholar John McHugh that the tense is in favor of Matthew's intent to focus on the past, not the future:

> Those who see in this phrase a hint that the marriage was later consummated overlook a most significant fact: the verb used for 'know' stands in the imperfect tense, not in the aorist (*eyivwokev*), and therefore lays the stress on the duration of the period throughout which Joseph and Mary abstained from intercourse. The meaning is that Joseph had no carnal knowledge of Mary during the period which preceded the birth of her son. This

> interpretation suits the context perfectly, for the whole of Mt. 1:18-25 is concerned with the virginal conception of Jesus and its consequences for paternity. If the author had wished to imply after the birth of Jesus, Joseph and Mary consummated their marriage, it is more likely that he would have used there the Aorist (*eyvw*). His choice of the imperfect implies rather that he did not exclude the possibility that Joseph and Mary lived a life of virginity after the birth of the Lord.[1]

We will revisit the entire argument surrounding this NOT/UNTIL construction when discussing the arguments used in favor of the Helvidian view.

vi. The age of Joseph

It is almost certain that Joseph was dead by the time Jesus was baptized. Some have read John 6:42 to indicate that Joseph was still alive:

> They were saying, "Is not this Jesus, the son of Joseph, whose father and mother we know? How can he now say, 'I have come down from heaven'?" (Joh 6:42)

However, this is extremely unlikely when we consider the totality of the New Testament record. It seems that Joseph had in fact died several years before, and that the locals knew who the Lord's parents were, and they still remembered Joseph the head of the household. Indeed, it would be a truly bizarre state of affairs if Joseph, a righteous man chosen by God for such a providential purpose, would not be mentioned in the Gospels if he was still alive, lest we be led to speculate that he did not believe in his adoptive son's messiahship.

---

[1] John McHugh, *The Mother of Jesus in the New Testament*, 204

It is therefore reasonable to conclude that Joseph may have died between 22 and 29 AD, which means 24 to 31 years after the birth of Jesus.

In spite of Protestant denials that any signs exist that Joseph would have been an older man when betrothing Mary, we can easily explore the implications of both theories.

In the Helvidian/Evangelical Protestant view, the reader assumes that Joseph and Mary are both young people getting married for the first time and surprised (if not inconvenienced) by the angelic annunciation. This scenario has Joseph being around 25 years old and dying before turning 60 years old. This should strike anyone with a Biblical mindset as less than stellar for someone living under the same roof as the Lord of Glory. After all, the Old Testament defined satisfactory life expectancy as follows:

> The days of our life are seventy years, or perhaps eighty, if we are strong... (Psa 90:10)

If we compare the fate of Joseph with that of Joseph the Patriarch and King David, the contrast would be alarming:

> And Joseph died, being one hundred ten years old; he was embalmed and placed in a coffin in Egypt. (Gen 50:26)

> David was thirty years old when he began to reign, and he reigned forty years. (2Sa 5:4). King David was old and advanced in years... (1Ki 1:1)

Not surprisingly, the apocryphal *History of Joseph the Carpenter* has Joseph dying at the blessed age of 111, one year more than his namesake and 'fellow-dreamer.' Theologically speaking, this is certainly more believable than Joseph dying at 55 or even 60 years old, in the blessed presence of Mary (compared to Ark) and the One who could heal the sick with a mere word.

To be conservative, let us consider Joseph dying at 78 years old in the year 28. This means that he would have been about 48 years old in 2 BC when he took Mary as wife. This is very consistent with the Epiphanian view.

vii. The age of James

If the relative age of Joseph and Jesus needs to be considered to assess the credibility of the three views, the age difference between James (Jesus' most prominent "brother") and our blessed Lord should also be investigated.

Again, the Helvidian/Evangelical Protestant view yields a very unlikely scenario. If one wants to treat James as "Jesus' kid brother," the best situation would be for James to be 2 years younger than Jesus. Even this close spacing is unlikely in view of Matthew's account of the sojourn in Egypt. Be that as it may, the end result is that James would have hardly been 30 years old, when he was chosen to be the chief-presbyter of the mother Church of Jerusalem. This is, to put it mildly, rather improbable. In order to command authority over the council of presbyters and apostles, James would have had to be 50 or 60 years old.

The *Apostolic Constitutions*,[1] interestingly, requires that a bishop should be at least 50 years old.[2] This is important because James was seen as the prototype of the episcopacy, having been consecrated by the Apostles themselves.

We also know that James was martyred in 62 AD, but only Epiphanius gives his age: 96 years old. This is rather difficult to believe, although one should note that even Josephus was amazed as the lifespan of the so-called Essenes. But even if James was 75 years old (which is consistent with the respect and admiration ascribed to

---

[1] The probable date is 341-381 but reflecting ancient if not primitive practices ascribed to the Apostles

[2] *Apostolic Constitutions*, Book II, Chapter 1

him), **this would make him older than Jesus, and therefore not a uterine brother.**

In fact, this relative age scenario is also consistent with two ancient streams of tradition worth mentioning here.

> (1) In the early apocryphal text known as *Infancy Gospel of Thomas*. Scholars agree that this is a very ancient text, most probably written during the second century. In this text (which is full of miraculous stories), James is presented as a son of Joseph who is older than Jesus, so that a 10 to 15 year age difference seems consistent with the above.[1]

> (2) Many ancient icons[2] of the flight into Egypt feature not only Joseph, Mary and Jesus but also James as a teenager or young man. Again, this is consistent with the Epiphanian view.

---

[1] "Then, Joseph sent his son James to tie up wood and bring it into his house, but the child Jesus also followed him. And while James was collecting the bushes, a viper bit his hand. And as he lay on the ground dying, Jesus approached and blew on the bite. And immediately, his anguish ceased and the animal broke apart and at once James was healthy." (*Infancy Gospel of Thomas*, Chapter 16)

[2] An important example is a 12th century icon from St Catherine's Monastery on Mount Sinai, which incidentally is on the path of the journey into Egypt.

viii. James and "James the Less"*

At this point, it seems useful to deal with the confusion that may exist on account of the common use of such names as "James" and "John." That these names are common today is still the case, but one may safely say that "James (Jacob)" was an extraordinarily common first names. The same can be said of Mary and Simon for instance. This makes our identification task quite difficult, as we shall see.

There are several individuals named James in the New Testament that need to be discussed to help clarify the Epiphanian view. This is important because the *adelphoi* of the Lord are listed as "James, and Joses, and Judas, and Simon" (Mar 6:3).

In the New Testament, the first "James" is John's brother, one of the Twelve, who was the first-martyred apostle.

The second "James" is another apostle among the Twelve, who is called "[son] of Alphaeus" (Luk 6:14).

In the same list of apostles, there is a certain "Judas [son] of James" who is not to be confused with Judas Iscariot. We do not know who this James is, and it does not seem necessary to assign a 'number' to him.

The third "James" is the one called "brother of the Lord" (Gal 1:19) and who is generally identified as the author of the Epistle of James. He is also generally identified as the James mentioned in Mark 6:3 among the four named *adelphoi*.

New Testament Greek does not make things easy for us because, for example, "Mary of James" (Luk 24:10) could mean "Mary [mother] of James" or perhaps "Mary [wife/daughter] of James." In the case of Mark 15:40, all modern translations interpret the verse as follows:

> There were women there, who stood watching from far off; among them were Mary Magdalen, and Mary the mother of James the Less[1] and of Joseph, and Salome. (Mar 15:40)

Who is this "James the Less" described, it seems, as the uterine brother of one named "Joses/Joseph?" **On the one hand, it is tempting to conclude that "James the Less and Joses" are simply the same two people mentioned in Mark 6:3. If so, who is their mother Mary?** Helvidians can here simply suggest say that this Mary is no other than the Mother of Jesus.[2]

Sadly, for the already confused reader, the plot thickens here, because we need to engage in some serious detective work to identify the women at the cross. The texts to consider (and hopefully reconcile) are:

> Many women were also there, looking on from a distance; they had followed Jesus from Galilee and had provided for him. Among them were Mary Magdalene, and Mary the mother of James and Joseph, and the mother of the sons of Zebedee. (Mat 27:55-56) Mary Magdalene and the other Mary were there, sitting opposite the tomb… (Mat 27:61)

---

[1] "τοῦ μικροῦ" means "the small / the less / the younger" which the French translates well by rendering the expression as "Jacques le Petit"

[2] Even Gregory of Nyssa, an Epiphanian, still suggested that Mary the mother of Jesus could have been called mother of James and Joses in the sense of having adopted them. As we shall see, this is a very unlikely option.

> There were also women looking on from a distance; among them were Mary Magdalene, and Mary the mother of James the younger and of Joses, and Salome. These used to follow him and provided for him when he was in Galilee; and there were many other women who had come up with him to Jerusalem… Mary Magdalene and Mary the mother of Joses saw where the body was laid. When the Sabbath was over, Mary Magdalene, and Mary the mother of James, and Salome bought spices, so that they might go and anoint him. (Mar 15:40-41; 16:1)
>
> Now it was Mary Magdalene, Joanna, Mary the mother of James, and the other women with them who told this to the apostles. (Luk 24:10)
>
> And that is what the soldiers did. Meanwhile, standing near the cross of Jesus were his mother, and his mother's sister, Mary the wife of Clopas, and Mary Magdalene. (Joh 19:25)

Clearly, Mary Magdalene and Mary the mother of Jesus were there, although Mary (the mother of Jesus, only mentioned by John) seems to have been with John and perhaps considered separately from the other women who followed Jesus.

There is another Mary who is called "the other Mary" and "[the mother] of James (the less) and Joses." This Mary seems to have been the wife (or daughter) of a certain Clopas, who was Joseph's brother according to Hegesippus.

In fact, John 19 is a difficult text, because it could refer to 3 or 4 women. The most likely option is that 4 women are considered:[1] (1) Mary the mother of Jesus, (2) Mary's sister (name unknown but not "Mary," possibly also a close relative), (3) Mary the wife of Clopas, and (4) Mary Magdalene.

Another option (less likely) is that John describes 3 women: (1) Mary the mother of Jesus, (2) Mary's sister (or relative / sister-in-law) who was Mary the wife of Clopas and the mother of James and

---

[1] The traditional icon of the crucifixion shows four women.

Joses, and (3) Mary Magdalene. For this option to work, "sister" must be understood as meaning 'relative' or 'sister-in-law' because it is almost impossible to imagine two full-sisters bearing the same name.

Either way, we see that there was a woman named Mary, also called "the other Mary" and therefore who was not the mother of Jesus. She was the wife (or daughter) of Clopas and the mother of two individuals known to many early Christians: James (the Less) and a certain Joses/Joseph. If Clopas was indeed Joseph's brother (as we have no reason to disbelieve), it results that these two men were in fact the Lord's cousins, **not** his uterine brothers.

The additional mystery here is that this Mary ("the other Mary") is called: (1) "mother of James and Joseph/Joses" in Matthew 27:56; (2) "mother of James the Less and of Joses" in Mark 15:40; (3) mother of Joseph/Joses" in Mark 15:47; "mother of James" in Mar 16:1; and (4) "mother of James" in Luke 24:10.

This presents a problem because it is unlikely that the famous James "the brother of the Lord" would have been referred to as "the Less" or that Mary would be called "mother of Joses (only)" in Mark 15:47. For this reason, the Epiphanian view is that James the Less (brother of Joses) should be distinguished from James "the brother of the Lord."

However, if "James the Less and Joses" are indeed the sons of Clopas and "the other Mary", they would be Jesus' cousins by adoption through Joseph and may qualify as *adelphoi* in the Old Testament biblical sense. If Joseph had died before his brother Clopas, the cousins would have been coopted in the uncle's household, which would better justify the use of *adelphoi*.

This extraordinary journey through the complexity of the New Testament record regarding James and Mary of Clopas has also allowed us to discover the Hieronymian view (that James and Joses were in fact cousins of Jesus). We will discuss further aspects of the

Hieronymian view in our next chapter, but it should be noted here that **the Epiphanian view sees James the Less as different from James the Lord's brother**. This, in my opinion, could be treated as the weakest link in the Epiphanian framework, because it is an attractive proposal to identify the James and Joses of Mark 6:3 with the James and Joses/Joseph of Mark 15:40.

ix. Mary's vow of virginity*

A significant argument to be considered in favor of Mary's perpetual virginity is the interpretation of Luke 1:34 as indicating that Mary had taken a vow of virginity. It is useful to consider this entire passage to assess the strength of this argument.

In the story, Mary is a virgin engaged to marry Joseph. It is quite clear that the actual marriage (Joseph taking Mary into his house and in the case of a normal marriage engaging in marital intercourse) is not very far away in time. At this time, an angel appears and announces that she will (shall) have a son. This seems reasonable enough, since she is weeks, perhaps months away from entering into married life (as many understand). However, Mary's reaction, in the form of a question, is rather strange: "How can this be, since I have no relations with [a] man?"

It can certainly be argued that Mary simply expressed surprise at the timing, as in: "What? Now? But I am still a betrothed virgin!" This is the interpretation offered by modern Protestant apologists. It is indeed plausible, but less than fully satisfactory.

Another approach is to conclude, from the text, that Mary had taken a vow of virginity, and this approach is nothing new. We have already documented that even after being taken into Joseph's house as wife (being pregnant), Mary and Joseph did not engage in sexual intercourse, which is fully established before the birth of Jesus. If vow there was, as indicated by the reaction, it was respected.

This is how St Gregory of Nyssa (+394) understood the text:

> What is Mary's response? Listen to the voice of the pure Virgin. The angel brings the glad tidings of childbearing, but she is concerned with virginity and holds that her integrity should come before the angelic message. She does not refuse to believe the angel; neither does she move away from her convictions. She says: I have given up any contact with man. "How will this happen to me, since I do not know man?"
>
> Mary's own words confirm certain apocryphal traditions. For if Joseph had taken her to be his wife, for the purpose of having children, why would she have wondered at the announcement of maternity, since she herself would have accepted becoming a mother according to the law of nature? But just as it was necessary to guard the body consecrated to God as an untouched and holy offering, for this same reason, she states, even if you are an angel come down from heaven and even if this phenomenon is beyond man's abilities, yet it is impossible for me to know man. How shall I become a mother without [knowing] man? For even though I consider Joseph to be my husband, still, I do not know man.[1]

One Roman Catholic commentator uses an interesting analogy to share his reading of the text:

> To my mind, Mary's question (and the ensuing dialogue) lacks historical plausibility unless you presuppose a vow of virginity. Imagine that you are building a rocket ship. It is very near completion, and just then an angel appears to you. He tells you that you will go to the moon, that you're going to build a castle and alien armies are going to join you in a crusade against your enemies. You will overcome them in victory and reign supreme over your enemies forever. At this point in the dialogue, the absolute last question you would ask is, "How will I get to the moon?"

---

[1] Gregory of Nyssa, PG 46, 1140 C-1141; as cited in Gambero, 157

The only person who is going to ask such a question is a person who is not in the midst of building a rocket. It is just the same in Mary's case. She is betrothed to Joseph. The angel says that she will conceive. If she has not resolved to remain a virgin, then she would naturally assume that the conception will take place after having intercourse with her soon-to-be husband. The angel didn't mention anything miraculous in connection with the conception. For her to ask about the nature of the conception after hearing what the angel said reveals that she has no laid-plans of pursuing natural relations with her future husband.

In the scenario with the rocket ship, the person building the rocket asks how he will get to the moon. If the angel had responded by saying that he will be magically teleported, I hope you see how this conversation would appear entirely staged. A false dialogue fabricated by someone in the know who simply wants to convey some truth by a made-up conversation. To my mind, the same would be true in Mary's case if she intended to have sex with her future husband and had asked the question she did.[1]

Admittedly, the Old Testament does not explicitly mention such vows of perpetual virginity, but it is useful to remember that there is an entire chapter in the book of Numbers (30) dedicated to vows taken by women, including young women.

We will also have to discuss (below) the idea (or perhaps "ideal") of 'betrothal without consummation,' which may well be the best explanation of 1 Corinthians 7:28 and inspired by the example of Mary and Joseph.

---

[1] Pete Holder, forum posting accessed at http://forums.catholic.com/showthread.php?p=6234943

x. Mary as the Ark*

There are several reasons to view not only Jesus himself but also his mother as the antitype or fulfillment of the Ark of the Covenant, a most holy and sacred object if there ever was one. To touch the Ark meant instant death, and the Old Testament gives us not only the stern warning (Num 4:5-15) but also an account of a man dying for doing just that (2Sa 6:6-7).

It may be useful to keep in mind that the Ark was both a container and a throne. It contained three significant items: Aaron's staff (sign of the high priesthood), the manna (associated in the New Testament with the Eucharist) and the tablets of the covenant (Heb 9:4).

The Ark itself was "overshadowed" with angelic wings and with the cloud of glory of God's presence.

The account found in the Gospel of Luke seems to interweave a sense of parallelism between Mary and the Ark, not overly so but with several significant hints:

In Luke 1:35, we read:

> The Holy Spirit will come upon you and the power of the Most High will overshadow (ἐπισκιάσει) you. (Luk 1:35)

This first use of "overshadow" in the New Testament echoes the LXX description of the presence of God settling upon the tent, which itself was the tabernacle of the Ark:

> Then the cloud covered the tent of meeting, and the glory of the Lord filled the tabernacle. Moses was not able to enter the tent of meeting because the cloud overshadowed (ἐπεσκίαζεν) it and the glory of the Lord filled the tabernacle." (Ex 40:34-35)

In St Luke's account of Mary's visit to Elizabeth, we can detect several other elements that connect Mary's three-month stay with the Ark's transport to the house of Obed-Edom where it also remained for three months:

> And the ark of the LORD remained in the house of Obededom the Gittite three months; and the LORD blessed Obededom and all his household. (2Sa 6:11)

> Mary stayed with Elizabeth for about three months and then returned home. (Luk 1:56)

Another similarity in the two accounts is the reaction of both David and Elizabeth when put in the presence of the Ark:

> David was afraid of the LORD that day; he said, "How can the ark of the LORD come into my care? (2Sa 6:9)

> And why has this happened to me, that the mother of my Lord comes to me? (Luk 1:43)

We should be careful not to overly press these similarities, in part because the underlying Greek terms are not identical, even though the general meaning is very close. In some cases ("David arose and travelled" in 2 Samuel 6:2 // "In those days Mary arose and went" in Luke 1:56), the Greek verbs are the same but the characters unrelated. In the case of the symmetry between David's leaping and dancing being echoed by John's leaping in the womb, the verbs differ and the connection between David and John the Baptist is tenuous.

We may do well to remember the inspired proverb:

> It is the glory of God to conceal things, but the glory of kings is to search things out. (Pro 25:2)

As far as concealing and revealing is concerned, the Ark is a good example. It was concealed by God (through Jeremiah), before the destruction of Jerusalem and the first Temple, with a very relevant prophecy attached to it:

> It was also in the same document that the prophet [Jeremiah], having received an oracle, ordered that the tent and the ark should follow with him, and that he went out to the mountain where Moses had gone up and had seen the inheritance of God. Jeremiah came and found a cave-dwelling, and he brought there the tent and the ark and the altar of incense; then he sealed up the entrance. Some of those who followed him came

> up intending to mark the way, but could not find it. When Jeremiah learned of it, he rebuked them and declared: "The place shall remain unknown until God gathers his people together again and shows his mercy. **Then the Lord will disclose these things, and the glory of the Lord and the cloud will appear, as they were shown in the case of Moses**, and as Solomon asked that the place should be specially consecrated." (2Ma 2:4-8)

It is impossible to miss the importance of this text, especially in light of Luke 1 (the "overshadow" connection with Exodus 40) and Revelation 12-13:

> Then God's temple in heaven was opened, and the ark of his covenant was seen within his temple; and there were flashes of lightning, rumblings, peals of thunder, an earthquake, and heavy hail. A great portent appeared in heaven: a woman clothed with the sun, with the moon under her feet, and on her head a crown of twelve stars. She was pregnant and was crying out in birth pangs, in the agony of giving birth. Then another portent appeared in heaven: a great red dragon, with seven heads and ten horns, and seven diadems on his heads. His tail swept down a third of the stars of heaven and threw them to the earth. Then the dragon stood before the woman who was about to bear a child, so that he might devour her child as soon as it was born. And she gave birth to a son, a male child, who is to rule all the nations with a rod of iron. (Rev 12:19-13:5)

It is precisely when the mercy of God is proclaimed (Luk 1:50, 54, 58, 72, 78) that the Ark is indeed revealed, both in its historical manifestation (Mary giving birth to Jesus and pursued by Herod) as well as it its even greater and ultimate spiritual fulfillment (Holy Wisdom/Church giving birth to the spiritual *adelphoi* under persecution).

St Gregory of Neocaesarea (+270) may have been the first ancient authority to discuss this typology in his *Homily on the Annunciation*:

> Let us chant the melody that has been taught us by the inspired harp of David, and say: "Arise O Lord to Thy resting place; Thou and the ark of Thy holiness" (Psa 132:8).[1] In this regard, he said, "For the holy Virgin is in truth an ark, wrought with gold both within and without (Exo 25:10-11, 37:1-2), that has received the whole treasury of the sanctuary."[2]

A text ascribed to the great St Athanasius of Alexandria (+373) but of questionable authenticity, likewise:

> O noble Virgin, truly you are greater than any other greatness! Who is your equal in greatness, O dwelling place of God the Word? To whom among all creatures shall I compare you, O Virgin? You are greater than them all O Covenant, clothed with purity instead of gold! You are the Ark in which is found the golden vessel containing the true manna, that is, the flesh in which divinity resides.[3]

Once a Christian becomes, spiritually speaking, "an Israelite in whom there is no deceit" (Joh 1:47), the understanding that Mary fulfills in human history the mystery of the Ark of the Covenant is nothing short of overwhelming. How, indeed, if this typology is valid, could the righteous Joseph have reached out to the overshadowed virgin and not perish? We can then also understand and appreciate the strong language of those who defended Mary's perpetual virginity and considered "folly" the modern view.

xi. Mary as the Gate facing East*

Anyone able to contemplate the wonder of Mary walking the earth with the Lord of Glory ("who sustains all things by the happening

---

[1] Amazingly, this *prokeimenon* verse is still sung in Orthodox services on several of the Feasts of the Theotokos

[2] *Homily I on the Annunciation*

[3] *Homily of the Papyrus of Turin*

of his power" according to Hebrews 1:3) in her womb would have had to exclaim with the Patriarch Jacob:

> "Surely the LORD is in this place-- and I did not realize it!" And he was afraid, and said, "How fearful is this place! It is none other than the house of God and this is the gate of heaven." (Gen 28:19)

To understand the importance of this "gate of heaven" and its relationship with the Ark/Mary, we must review the following texts and see how (with bold added) they connect:

> The man named his wife **Eve**, because she was **the mother of all living**. And the LORD God made garments of skins for the man and for his wife, and clothed them. Then the LORD God said, "See, the man has become like one of us, knowing good and evil; and now, he might reach out his hand and take also from the tree of life, and eat, and live forever"-- therefore the LORD God sent him forth from the garden of Eden, to till the ground from which he was taken. He drove out the man; and **at the east of the garden of Eden he placed the cherubim, and a sword flaming and turning to guard the way to the tree of life.** (Gen 3:20-24)

We can now connect the cherubim and the Ark:

> You shall make two cherubim of gold; you shall make them of hammered work, at the two ends of the mercy seat. Make one cherub at the one end, and one cherub at the other; of one piece with the mercy seat you shall make the cherubim at its two ends. The cherubim shall spread out their wings above, overshadowing (συσκιάζοντες) the mercy seat (ἱλαστηρίου[1]) with their wings. They shall face one to another; the faces of the cherubim shall be turned toward the mercy seat. You shall put the mercy seat on the top of the ark; and in the ark you shall put the covenant that I shall give you. **There I will meet with you**, and from above the mercy seat, from between **the two**

---

[1] "Means by which sins are forgiven and mercy is revealed" (Rom 3:25)

> **cherubim that are on the ark of the covenant**... (Exo 25:19-22)

The cherubim can now be related to the East Gate or Gate of Heaven:

> The **cherubim lifted up their wings** and rose up from the earth in my sight as they went out with the wheels beside them. They **stopped at the entrance of the east gate** of the house of the LORD; and **the glory of the God of Israel was above them**... The spirit lifted me up and brought me to the east gate of the house of the LORD, which faces east... (Eze 10:19-11:1)

The cherubim/ark are now clearly associated with an event taking place at the East Gate. The vision culminates with these words:

> Then he brought me back to the outer gate of the sanctuary, which faces east; and it was shut. The LORD said to me: This gate shall remain shut; it shall not be opened, and no one shall enter by it; for the LORD, the God of Israel, has entered by it; therefore it shall remain shut. Only the prince, because he is a prince, may sit in it to eat food before the LORD; he shall enter by way of the vestibule of the gate, and shall go out by the same way. Then he brought me by way of the north gate to the front of the temple; and I looked, and behold, the glory of the LORD filled the temple of the LORD; and I fell upon my face. (Eze 44:1-4)

Again, it takes the mind of a spiritual Israelite and the spiritual experience of the Church to grasp these texts, the way the Lord himself (as Orthodox Christians believe) would have understood them. Both Ambrose of Milan and Augustine of Hippo offer the same mystical interpretation of the text:

> Who is this gate (Eze 44:1-4), if not Mary? Is it not closed because she is a virgin? Mary is the gate through which Christ entered this world, when He was brought forth in the virginal

birth and the manner of His birth did not break the seals of virginity.[1]

Ezekiel is much more related to Christ than many Christians realize. To study this theme is beyond the scope of this book, but we should be able to see that the Eve-Mother of the Living / Ark – Cherubim / East Gate imagery is consistent with the Church's conviction that the Mother of the true Living One would be the fulfillment of the Ark, the end of the curse and the inception of the New Creation, and would therefore have to remain inviolate.

xii. Mary as the New Eve*

In our previous section, we connected Genesis 3 with a chain of texts that culminate in Mary's act of divine wisdom through obedience and humility: "Behold, the handmaid of the Lord; be it unto me according to thy word" (Luk 1:38).

In doing so, Mary becomes the mother of the true Living One, Jesus Christ, the one with "the power of an indestructible life" (Heb 7:16). Here, we must remember that Eve was called "Eve" (in the LXX Greek "Zoe" which means "life") because she was supposed to be "the mother of all living" (Gen 3:20). But it wasn't so: all of Eve's children and descendants would die because sin had entered the world through her disobedience. Her name/title was actually tragic, because she became the 'mother of all the dying,' until a woman would come whose seed would conquer death and fulfill the prophecy:

> I will put enmity between you [the serpent] and the woman, and between your offspring/seed and hers; he will strike your head, and you will strike his heel." (Gen 3:15)

---

[1] Ambrose of Milan, *The Consecration of a Virgin and the Perpetual Virginity of Mary*, 8:5

> Now the promises were spoken to Abraham and to his seed. He does not say, "And to seeds," as referring to many, but rather to one, "And to your seed," that is, Christ. (Gal 3:16)

The seed is singular because the woman whose seed overcomes has a son who is truly *monogenes* – one of a kind, one who is first-born (πρωτότοκον, Luk 2:7), only-born and unique (μονογενὴς, Joh 1:18).

Mary's obedience is the end of the curse, and this realization that Mary can be understood as the New Eve is found in two very important early Christian authors: Justin (+165) and Irenaeus (+202, text written in 180):

> Now, Eve, who was a virgin and undefiled, having conceived the word of the serpent, brought forth disobedience and death. But the Virgin Mary received faith and joy, when the angel Gabriel announced the good tidings to her that the Spirit of the Lord would come upon her, and the power of the Highest would overshadow her.[1]

> In accordance with this design, Mary the Virgin is found obedient, saying: "Behold the handmaid of the Lord; be it unto me according to your word" (Luke 1:38). But Eve was disobedient; for she did not obey when as yet she was a virgin. And even as she, having indeed a husband, Adam, but being nevertheless as yet a virgin (for in Paradise they were both naked, and were not ashamed... having been created a short time previously, had no understanding of the procreation of children: for it was necessary that they should first come to adult age, and then multiply from that time onward), having become disobedient, was made the cause of death, both to herself and to the entire human race; so also did Mary, having a man betrothed [to her], and being nevertheless a virgin, by yielding obedience, become the cause of salvation, both to herself and the whole

---

[1] Justin Martyr, *Dialogue with Trypho*, 100

> human race... Wherefore also Luke, commencing the genealogy with the Lord, carried it back to Adam, indicating that it was He who regenerated them into the Gospel of life, and not they Him. And thus also it was that the knot of Eve's disobedience was loosed by the obedience of Mary. For what the virgin Eve had bound fast through unbelief, this did the virgin Mary set free through faith.[1]

In another important work called the *Demonstration of the Apostolic Preaching* (a short catechism of essentials), Irenaeus explains:

> Adam had to be recapitulated in Christ, so that death might be swallowed up in immortality, and Eve [had to be recapitulated] in Mary, so that the Virgin, having become another virgin's advocate, might destroy and abolish one virgin's disobedience by the obedience of another virgin.[2]

Both Justin and Irenaeus are uniquely important in their testimony, not only because they are so early, but also on account their personal histories.

What does it matter if Mary is indeed "the New Eve," as far the idea of perpetual virginity is concerned? Are not Justin and Irenaeus among those who taught that Mary did in fact have other children? We shall see in our review of the ancient authorities that such is not the case, and here, we can see why Mary as New Eve implies the singularity of the birth of Jesus and therefore Mary's perpetual virginity. Why? Because it would be unthinkable, after becoming the mother of the living one (Jesus) and the 'end of Eve' to then move on to have many other children with Joseph, none of which would have been intrinsically living, but rather who may well have been dying ones.

---

[1] Irenaeus of Lyons, *Against Heresies*, Book III, Chapter 22
[2] Irenaeus of Lyons, *Proof of the Apostolic Preaching*, 33, (Sources Chrétiennes 62 [Paris], 83-86), also cited in Gambero, 54.

If after her disobedience Eve "knew" a man/Adam and thus gave birth to a dying and sinful offspring, the New Eve Mary did no such thing and never gave birth to a dying and sinful offspring.

Last but not least here, mother and unborn child have a critical blood interface. Even though there is no mixing or exchange of blood, there is a close biological and physiological connection. Because the blood of Christ is of such great importance biblically and one may even say cosmically, this unique blood-relationship between mother and son would have to remain just that, unique.[1]

xiii. Joseph as antitype of Joseph and David*

Nothing in God's providence happens by accident, and we can see that Joseph of Egypt is spiritually related to the other Joseph of Egypt, by their name, association with Egypt, and by receiving messages from heaven through dreams. Joseph, it should be remembered, was a man of great sexual self-control, having resisted the advances of Potiphar's wife (Gen 39:12).

Joseph and David are also physically and spiritually related, because Jesus is not only called "Son of David" but also "Son of Joseph." And if King David is often remembered for his weakness with Bath-Sheba in his younger days, his sexual continence in old age tends to be overlooked:

> Now King David was old and advanced in years; and although they covered him with clothes, he could not get warm. Therefore his servants said to him, "Let a young maiden be sought for my lord the king, and let her wait upon the king, and be his nurse; let her lie in your bosom, that my lord the king may be warm." So they sought for a beautiful maiden throughout all the territory of Israel, and found Abishag the Shunammite, and brought her to the king. The maiden was very

---

[1] As previously mentioned, ascribing "blood brothers/sisters" to Jesus also raises theological issues.

beautiful; and she became the king's nurse and ministered to him; but the king knew her not (1Ki 1:1-4)

Not only that, but David understood that in special cases, he may have been legally allowed to engage in sexual intercourse but still decided not to do so:

> David came to his house at Jerusalem; and the king took the ten concubines whom he had left to care for the house, and put them in a house under guard, and provided for them, but did not go in to them. So they were shut up until the day of their death, living as if in widowhood. (2Sa 20:3)

With this background in mind, it is certainly not difficult to understand that Joseph, described a righteous man, would have been entrusted with the care of the Virgin Mary.

And this is as good place as any to remember that Joseph was needed to be a provider, protector and legal father. It was not only Mary who was chosen "at the fullness of time" but also the greatly honored and blessed St Joseph. As the saying goes, the apple does not fall far from the tree, and we can see how James' great holiness speaks highly of Joseph the Righteous.

xiv. The entrusting at the cross*

In the account of the crucifixion found in the Gospel of St John, a remarkable scene is recorded:

> But there were standing by the cross of Jesus his mother, and his mother's sister, Mary [the wife] of Clopas, and Mary Magdalene. When Jesus saw his mother and the disciple whom he loved standing there, he said to his mother, "Woman, behold your son!" Then he said to the disciple, "Behold, your mother!" And from that hour, the disciple took her to his own home. After this Jesus, knowing that all was now finished, said (to fulfil the scripture), "I thirst." A bowl full of vinegar stood there; so they put a sponge full of the vinegar on hyssop and held it to his mouth. When Jesus had received the vinegar, he said, "It is finished"; and he bowed his head and gave up his spirit. (John 19:25-28)

What is remarkable is that the entrusting at the cross is essentially the last act performed by our Lord before it could be said that 'all is finished' and before he gave up his spirit and died.

The question needs to be asked: why would Jesus entrust his widowed mother to John if she had several other younger children, as some claim? Under Jewish law, these other alleged uterine children, notably James and Joses (Mar 6:3) would have been responsible for their mother's care. In fact, the loss of one out of six children would have been a tragedy but not one requiring this special provision on the part of the crucified Lord. A tract ascribed to St Athanasius, whom the entire Christian world trusts to have properly proclaimed the contents of the New Testament in 367, offers a most rational comment:

> If Mary would have had another son, the Savior would not have neglected her nor would he have confided his mother to another person, indeed she had not become the mother of another. Mary, moreover, would not have abandoned her own sons to live with another, for she fully realized a mother never abandons her spouse nor her children. And since she continued to remain a virgin even after the birth of the Lord, he gave her as mother to the disciple, even though she was not his mother; he confided her to John because of his great purity of conscience and because of her intact virginity.[1]

Here, we should not postpone our discussion of the Helvidian/Protestant counter-argument, which is that (1) this may have been a temporary measure, and (2) this entrusting to John is best explained by the fact that Mary's other children were (at the time) not believers, based on John 7:

---

[1] Athanasius, *De virginitate*, in Buby, *Mary of Galilee*, III, 104. This passage may or may not be from Athanasius, but it is certainly very ancient and worth considering regardless of its assured authorship.

> So his brothers (ἀδελφοὶ) said to him, "Leave here and go to Judea, so that your disciples may see the works you are doing. For no man works in secret if he seeks to be known openly. If you do these things, show yourself to the world." For even his brothers did not believe in him. (Joh 7:2-5)

This approach has several grave problems:

(1) It assumes that *adelphoi* means uterine brothers, which as we have seen is far from settled.

(2) It assumes that <u>all</u> his *adelphoi* disbelieved, which again is far from settled.[1]

(3) It assumes that if Mary's alleged sons were not (or not yet) believers, this would overturn Jewish custom regarding the care of one's mother.

(4) It seems to imply that Jesus did not know that his *adelphoi* would in fact turn out to be believers within days or weeks of the crucifixion. For on the day of Pentecost, we read:

> All these with one accord devoted themselves to prayer, together with the women and Mary the mother of Jesus, and with his brothers (ἀδελφοῖς). In those days Peter stood up among the brethren (ἀδελφῶν) (the company of persons was in all about a hundred and twenty)… (Act 1:14-15)

In particular, we know that James called "the brother of the Lord" was chosen to be the chief-presbyter of the Church in Jerusalem, which one reason among many why Richard Bauckham argues successfully that several of the *adelphoi* were in fact disciples of Jesus.

All in all, John 19 is a difficult scene to explain away if one wants to maintain that the last thing Jesus did before dying was to offend his brothers and sisters by transferring the care of Mary to John.

---

[1] Richard Bauckham has conclusively argued (*Jude*) that such is not the case. Indeed, James the Lord's brother is remembered as one of the 70 disciples in the Orthodox tradition.

xv. A widow mourning an only son*

Orthodox and Roman Catholic Christians are fully convinced that Mary not only lost her firstborn son on the great day of our redemption at Calvary (which is tragic enough), but indeed her **only** son.

Without diminishing the loss of a child among many, we can perceive in the depth of our being the magnitude of the "piercing of the soul" that takes place at the foot of the cross. There, Mary, a widow, beheld the cruel torturing and killing of her one and only child, her beloved Jesus. It is only then that we can fully grasp Simeon's prophecy:

> And his father and his mother marveled at what was said about him; and Simeon blessed them and said to Mary his mother, "Behold, this child is set for the fall and rising of many in Israel, and for a sign (σημεῖον) that is spoken against, and a sword will pierce through your own soul also, so that thoughts out of many hearts may be revealed." (Luk 2:33-35)

Here, it can be said that our Helvidian brethren do not seem aware that they are, if one may say so, 'robbing' Mary of this tremendous piercing of the soul in the loss of her only child. Indeed, Simeon's prophecy indicates a mysterious purpose, "that the thoughts of many hearts may be revealed," and this is linked both to the sign-child (with reference to sign/σημεῖον in Isaiah 7:11-14) and to the piercing of Mary's soul. The two are inseparable, just as the Lord and the Ark of his holiness were inseparable (Num 10:35; Psa 132:8).

Not only that, but the very prophecy of the piercing of the Messiah is in itself incredibly revealing:

> I will pour out on the house of David and on the inhabitants of Jerusalem, the Spirit of grace and of supplication, so that they will look on Me whom they have pierced; and they will mourn for Him, as one mourns for **an only son**, and they will weep bitterly over Him like the bitter weeping over **a firstborn**. (Zac 12:10)

This prophecy is fulfilled at the cross, and the bitter weeping over a firstborn who is also the only son is experienced by the mother of the Lord at this moment of the piercing of her son, and this is also why the last act of our Lord is to entrust his mother to the care of John. This is the biblical idea of extreme sorrow:

> O daughter of my people, Dress in sackcloth and roll about in ashes! Make mourning as for an only son, most bitter lamentation… (Jer 6:26)

> I will turn your religious feasts into mourning and all your singing into weeping. I will make all of you wear sackcloth and shave your heads. I will make that time like mourning for an only son and the end of it like a bitter day. (Amo 8:10)

We can now understand what happened in the city of Nain:

> Soon afterward he went to a city called Nain, and his disciples and a great crowd went with him. As he drew near to the gate of the city, behold, a man who had died was being carried out, the only son of his mother, and she was a widow; and a large crowd from the city was with her. And when the Lord saw her, he had compassion on her and said to her, "Do not weep." And he came and touched the bier, and the bearers stood still. And he said, "Young man, I say to you, arise." And the dead man sat up, and began to speak. And he gave him to his mother. (Luk 7:12-15)

In this instance, Jesus takes it upon himself to intervene, because of his compassion for the mourning mother, and now we can also understand, because this is exactly what his own mother would experience as Simeon had foretold. We can see here the explanatory power of the theory being considered, namely that Mary had only one child: Jesus. As an academic theologian or researcher might say:

> Explanatory scope refers to how many things a theory explains. A theory has more explanatory scope than another if it explains more things.

As we have seen, the Helvidian theory does not explain Simeon's prophecy, the entrusting at the cross, nor Jesus' unexpected super-miracle (a resurrection) in Luke 7. By contrast, the traditional position (either Epiphanian or Hieronymian) certainly does.

xvi. Four virgins*

It is fair to say that modern-day Evangelical Protestantism (often presented as "non-denominational") is less than sympathetic towards asceticism, mortification, abstinence and the idea of a vow of life-long virginity.

In the scene of the entrusting at the cross, what we see from a traditional perspective is a virgin (Jesus[1]), the son of a virgin mother who is still a virgin at the foot of the cross (Mary), entrusting his mother to a disciple who is and would remain a life-long virgin (John). The Lord's own forerunner (John the Baptist) was himself a virgin. Biblically, we can state that virginity is gift and sign of the age to come and of the risen life:

> But Jesus answered them, "You are wrong, because you know neither the scriptures nor the power of God. For in the resurrection they neither marry nor are given in marriage, but are like angels in heaven. (Mat 22:29-30)

St John leaves no doubt on this point:

> And they sing a new song before the throne and before the four living creatures and before the elders. No one could learn that song except the hundred and forty-four thousand who had been redeemed from the earth. These are the ones who were not defiled with women, as **they are virgins** (παρθένοι). These are the ones who follow the Lamb wherever He goes. These were redeemed from among men, being first-fruits to God and to the Lamb. (Rev 14:4)

---

[1] The ever-virginity of Jesus is generally taken for granted, although this is also from silence, inference and tradition.

For some reason (perhaps not unrelated to this very discussion), the NIV and other modern translation are not eager to use "virgin(s)" here, even though the Greek word *parthenoi* means just that:

> NIV Revelation 14:4 These are those who did not defile themselves with women, for they kept themselves **pure**. They follow the Lamb wherever he goes. They were purchased from among men and offered as firstfruits to God and the Lamb.

> RSV Revelation 14:4 It is these who have not defiled themselves with women, for they are **chaste**; it is these who follow the Lamb wherever he goes; these have been redeemed from mankind as first fruits for God and the Lamb.

Be that as it may, an underlying perception among Helvidians is that (1) Joseph was a young man caught by surprise by this almost unfortunate development (2) it would have been 'horrible' for Joseph and Mary to be deprived of that 'supreme earthly satisfaction.' However, we have seen that both of these points are not required by the text and lack explanatory power.

The great misperception here is that many people believe (wrongly) that the theory of the perpetual virginity of Mary was invented to conform to the growing asceticism of the second and third-century Christianity. Svendsen (citing the Roman Catholic scholar John Meier) offers a good example of this mindset:

> As Meier (1992:15-16) also points out: "To be honest, the so-called 'Epiphanian solution,' ... strikes one from the start as arbitrary and gratuitous .... It may well be that we are dealing with a solution thought up after the fact to support the emerging idea of Mary's perpetual virginity." Certainly there seems to be no other motivation to adopt this view than to uphold Mary's perpetual virginity while at the same time avoiding the charge of contradicting the NT evidence that Jesus had siblings.[1]

---

[1] Svendsen, 57

However, the reverse seems to be true: it is precisely because Mary was ever-virgin (like Jesus as well as John the Baptist, John the Evangelist and possibly James the Lord's brother) that Christians held virginity is such high esteem. As St Athanasius' predecessor (Alexander of Alexandria, +326) is said to have written:

> You have as an example the conduct of Mary, who is a type and image of the life that is proper to heaven (i.e. without intercourse).[1]

xvii. Betrothal without consummation*

There is one interesting passage in the New Testament that may well bear witnesses to a practice of being betrothed yet without consummating the union, on the model of Joseph and Mary. The full text (RSV) deserves careful attention:

> Now concerning the unmarried, I have no command of the Lord, but I give my opinion as one who by the Lord's mercy is trustworthy. I think that in view of the present distress it is well for a person to remain as he is. Are you bound to a wife? Do not seek to be free. Are you free from a wife? Do not seek marriage. But if you marry, you do not sin, and if a girl marries she does not sin. Yet those who marry will have worldly troubles, and I would spare you that. I mean, brethren, the appointed time has grown very short; from now on, let those who have wives live as though they had none, and those who mourn as though they were not mourning, and those who rejoice as though they were not rejoicing, and those who buy as though they had no goods, and those who deal with the world as though they had no dealings with it. For the form of this world is passing away. I want you to be free from anxieties. The unmarried man is anxious about the affairs of the Lord, how to please the Lord; but the married man is anxious about worldly affairs, how to please his wife, and his interests are

---

[1] Cited in O'Caroll, *Theotokos*, 178. The primary source is hard to track down and seems to be from the Gnomai of the Council of Nicea.

divided. And the unmarried woman or girl is anxious about the affairs of the Lord, how to be holy in body and spirit; but the married woman is anxious about worldly affairs, how to please her husband. I say this for your own benefit, not to lay any restraint upon you, but to promote good order and to secure your undivided devotion to the Lord.

If anyone thinks that he is not behaving properly toward his betrothed, if his passions are strong, and it has to be, let him do as he wishes: let them marry -- it is no sin. But whoever is firmly established in his heart, being under no necessity but having his desire under control, and has determined this in his heart, to keep her as his betrothed, he will do well. So that he who marries his betrothed does well; and he who refrains from marriage will do better.

A wife is bound to her husband as long as he lives. If the husband dies, she is free to be married to whom she wishes, only in the Lord. But in my judgment she is happier if she remains as she is. And I think that I have the Spirit of God. (1Co 7:25-40)

Verses 36-38 are of particular interest. NIV reads:

If anyone thinks he is acting improperly toward the virgin he is engaged to, and if she is getting along in years and he feels he ought to marry, he should do as he wants. He is not sinning. They should get married.

What is all that about? It seems very reasonable to read this passage as referring to couples who had a betrothed-virgin relationship (on the model of Joseph and Marry, since he was called "betrothed" even after their marriage).[1] This practice may well have been well-intentioned and inspired by this exceptional union of Joseph and Mary, and the Apostle was giving wise advice: this type of spiritual

---

[1] Others (such as some of the the apostles) may have lived in such betrothed/marital unions without marital intercourse. In 1Co 9:5 (RSV), St Paul asks: "Do we not have the right to be accompanied by a wife (ἀδελφὴν γυναῖκα), as the other apostles and the brothers of the Lord and Cephas?" The Greek expression "sister-wife" is interesting and may serve to qualify the nature of the relationship.

union was not for everyone; consummating the betrothal would not have been a sin.

xviii. Where are the other children?

Only the Gospel of Luke provides a glimpse of Jesus' life between his birth (with the flight to Egypt) and the beginning of his ministry when he was about 30 years old. In this well-known passage, a 12-year old Jesus stays behind in the Temple and causes much alarm to his parents:

> The child grew and became strong, filled with wisdom; and the favor of God was upon him. Now his parents went to Jerusalem every year at the feast of the Passover. And when he was twelve years old, they went up according to custom. When the feast was ended, as they were returning, the boy Jesus stayed behind in Jerusalem. His parents did not realize it, but supposing him to be in the company they went [ahead] a day's journey, and they sought him among their relatives (συγγενεῦσιν) and acquaintances. As they did not find him, they returned to Jerusalem, looking for him. After three days, they found him in the temple, sitting among the teachers, listening to them and asking them questions. And all who heard him were amazed at his understanding and his answers. When [his parents] saw him, they were astonished; and his mother said to him, "Son, why have you treated us so? Behold, your father and I have been looking for you anxiously." And he replied to them, "How is it that you sought me? Did you not know that I must be in my Father's house?" And they did not understand the saying which he spoke to them. And he went down with them and came to Nazareth, and was obedient to them; and his mother kept all these things in her heart. And Jesus increased in wisdom and in stature, and in favor with God and man. (Luk 2:40-52)

Admittedly, this is an argument from silence, but the impression given here is not that there were many other children in the family. Joseph, Mary and Jesus are portrayed as family unit, without reference to any *adelphoi* at that time.

c) Criticism and rebuttal

We have concluded our overview of more than 15 lines of evidence supporting the view that Mary was ever-virgin, and we have done so in the context of defending the Epiphanian view which has the claim to be the most ancient and the most widely accepted by the fourth century.

The majority of these arguments can also be used (probably by our Roman Catholic friends) to support St Jerome's interpretation of the same biblical data.

Having presented these points from a positive point of view, we may well ask ourselves if these are indeed strong arguments or if powerful rebuttals have been offered. Some of them have already been discussed (for instance the issue of the entrusting at the cross on account of unbelieving *adelphoi*) and others will be introduced in the positive presentation of the Helvidian view.

Argument (i) for instance (as developed by Richard Bauckham and exploring the implications of the metronymic) is interesting but not compelling on its own. There is a cumulative effect that takes places and which presents us with **a theory having maximal explanatory power** as well as the least amount of difficulties explaining the totality of the data at hand. Regarding argument (i), no counter-arguments have been offered, and John Meier (who did reply to the rest of the arguments) simply states in a footnote that "Bauckham's exegesis of key Synoptic passages dealing with the mother and brothers of Jesus--Matt 12:46-50; 13:55; and Mark 6:3 (Bauckham, "Brothers," 694-95, 698-700)—is highly unlikely."[1]

Regarding (ii – Second and third century authorities), Meier is among those who consider the apocryphal texts supporting the

---

[1] John Meier, *On retrojecting later questions from later texts: a reply to Richard Bauckham*, 511

Epiphanian view as historically worthless and unable to provide reliable information on Jesus' family. I beg to disagree and will engage in a comprehensive evaluation of the *Protevangelium of James (PJ)* in our historical section. From an Orthodox perspective, PJ, being the main text under consideration, presents a perfectly credible storyline. That Joseph was an older man has been shown to be consistent with the overall biblical record. That Mary would have been raised as virgin in the temple is certainly not an 'a-historical possibility,' because we know that virgins could be raised in the temple, as indicated by 2 Maccabees 3:19-20. According to Jewish tradition:

> The veil of the Temple was a palm-length in width. It was woven with seventy-two smooth stitches each made of twenty-four threads. The length was of forty cubits and the width of twenty cubits. Eighty-two virgins wove it. Two veils were made each year and three hundred priests were needed to carry it to the pool.[1]

When the *Protevangelium of James* presents Mary as born of an older couple, raised in the temple, and commissioned to weave the curtain for the Temple, this is (after due investigation) completely consistent with the biblical and Jewish data. Not only that, but this is tremendously significant from a theological perspective. The curtain was the boundary between the holy and the holy of holies in the Temple, being a symbol of space/time and matter. When the high priest exited the holy of holy, he wore vestments made from the same material as the curtain, which served to foreshadow the necessary incarnation of the LORD whose name the high priest bore on the turban. The gospel of St Matthew makes the connection between the body of the Lord and the curtain abundantly clear:

---

[1] *Mishna Shekalim*, chapter 8, 5-6

> Then Jesus cried again with a loud voice and breathed his last. At that moment the curtain of the temple was torn in two, from top to bottom. (Mat 27:50-51)

The Orthodox icon of the Annunciation to the Theotokos[1] makes perfect historical and theological sense: even as Mary the virgin is weaving the curtain-symbol of the high priest's incarnation, she accepts the angelic message and begins weaving the Lord's body in her sacred womb:

> For it is impossible for the blood of bulls and goats to take away sins. Consequently, when Christ came into the world, he said, "Sacrifices and offerings you have not desired, but a body you have prepared for me." (Heb 10:4-5)

---

[1] The virgin is shown holding a spindle and a curtain is seen in the background.

When we analyze the various elements found in these second century witnesses, a pattern of underlying historicity and theological consistency emerges. Ignatius of Antioch (+110) may well have alluded to the birth-giving in a cave,[1] an account found in full in the *Protevangelium*, a text often traced back to Antioch.[2] In a book written to a die-hard skeptic (Celsus), Origen confirms the historicity of this important detail:

> With respect to the birth of Jesus in Bethlehem, if any one desires, after the prophecy of Micah and after the history recorded in the Gospels by the disciples of Jesus, to have additional evidence from other sources, let him know that, in conformity

---

[1] *To the Ephesians*, 19
[2] Justin Martyr and the *Infancy Gospel of Matthew* likewise

with the narrative in the Gospel regarding His birth, there is shown at Bethlehem the cave where He was born, and the manger in the cave where He was wrapped in swaddling-clothes. And this sight is greatly talked of in surrounding places, even among the enemies of the faith, it being said that in this cave was born that Jesus who is worshipped and reverenced by the Christians.[1]

To disregard the historical value of these second-century witnesses as many argue should be done, is problematic indeed.

Regarding (iii.), Eric Svendsen takes Richard Bauckham to task on the meaning of *adelphoi* in the case of the Joseph-Jesus-*adelphoi* relationship. He writes:

> Second, while Bauckham is certainly right about his insistence that we take into account the usage of *adelphoi* outside the NT, he has offered no instance in which this word is unambiguously used of a stepbrother in any literature.[2]

However, Svendsen (and to an extent Meier) have missed the main point: Jesus was adopted by Joseph and truly became his son. Hence, he could truly be called brother (as in 'adoptive brother') rather than a step-brother in relationship to James for example. The reader will have to judge if our discussion of *adelphoi* and adoption is not more compelling than Svendsen's arguments.

Regarding (v.), there is a strong affirmation on the part of some Evangelical-Protestant apologists that the Greek construction of Matthew 1:25 (not/until) must imply reversal of the previous course of action. We shall discuss this particular argument when presenting the Helvidian view.

---

[1] Origen, *Against Celsus*, 51
[2] Svendsen, 56

Inasmuch as arguments (vi.) and (vii.) are rarely put forward, no rebuttal seems to exist, except that one could argue[1] that a young James, age 31 or so, could still have been selected as chief-presbyter since Jesus himself was less than 40 years old. This is possible, but in my view much less probable and acceptable than the Epiphanian view that James was in fact older than Jesus. Indeed, it does not seem that Helvidians pay close attention to the relative age of Joseph. Svendsen writes:

> As it is, neither Matthew nor Luke, in their respective infancy narratives, gives us any hint that this is a subsequent marriage for Joseph (which is what this view requires) (Meier, 1992:16). It seems best, therefore, to abandon the Epiphanian view from further consideration.[2]

Certainly, the infancy narratives do not directly inform us on the age of Joseph, but we have seen that a well-rounded reflection on the implication of his death before AD 29 or 30 makes an older Joseph a lot more reasonable than a 25-year old stricken by death before reaching 60. It is also easy to overlook the implications of Joseph being called "righteous" (δίκαιος). A young man can be righteous, but the first instance of a righteous man in the Scripture refers to an older man with children (Noah in Genesis 9:6). There is an overall pattern that needs to be considered, or as our Protestant friends correctly say, *Tota Scriptura*.

d) Recent proponents

As far as the credentials of proponents is concerned, it is not useless to remind those considering the various positions that the Epiphanian view can boast the majority of the 'big names' in

---

[1] As Robert Zins did in our debate
[2] Svendsen, 57

Church history, notably Clement of Alexandria, Origen, Eusebius, Hilary of Poitiers, and Basil the Great.

Obviously (or not so obviously), every single Orthodox theologian takes the Epiphanian view for granted, as this is part and parcel of the liturgical life of the Church, for instance in the Feast of the Entrance of the Theotokos into the Temple.

In more recent times, the great nineteenth century scholar J. B. Lightfoot (Anglican bishop of Durham, +1889) offered a still relevant defense of the Epiphanian view in his *Dissertations on the Apostolic Age*.

Finally, we have already mentioned the interesting case of the British scholar Richard Bauckham (born 1946) who has offered an excellent defense of the Epiphanian view in his authoritative *Jude and the Relatives of Jesus in the Early Church*, yet (surprisingly) without endorsing the tradition belief in Mary's perpetual virginity.

3) THE HELVIDIAN VIEW

a) Proposal

The Helvidian view is named after a certain Helvidius, the author of a work written before 383 in which he argued against the common belief in the perpetual virginity of Mary. He maintained that the existence of the "brothers and sisters" of Jesus established that Mary had normal marital relations with Joseph and thereby additional children after the miraculous conception and birth of Jesus. Helvidius also cited the writings of Tertullian and Victorinus to support this interpretation and avoid the accusation of novelty.

In reply, St Jerome wrote a still-important treatise known as *Against Helvidius (The Perpetual Virginity of Blessed Mary)*, in which he sets forth his interpretation known as the Hieronymian view, namely that the *adelphoi* were cousins rather than half-brothers or Joseph's children by a previous marriage.

The Helvidian (not Hieronymian) proposal is rather simple:

> **Some time after Jesus was born, Joseph, being a healthy young man who had married a young woman, began engaging in marital intercourse with Mary, from which at least 6 children (some named in Mark 6:3) were born.**

b) Key arguments

The Helvidian view typically rests on 3 keys arguments: the (perceived) plain meaning of *adelphoi* in the New Testament; the implications of the NOT/UNTIL language found in Matthew 1:25; and the similar implications of Jesus being called "firstborn" in Luke 2:5. In addition, Helvidians contend that the Gospel accounts presenting the relationship between Jesus and his mother and *adelphoi* is best explained by their theory. From an historical perspective, some support is brought forward from Tertullian as well as, in some presentations, Justin and Irenaeus.

Let us now explore these arguments in further detail.

i. Matthew 1:18

Matthew 1:18 is a straightforward text:

> When his mother Mary had been engaged to Joseph, but before (πρὶν) they lived together (συνελθεῖν), she was found to be with child from the Holy Spirit (RSV).

Helvidians argue that the "before they had marital relations" clause (which may well be implied[1] by the verb expressing "coming together") also implies the idea of not/before but yes/after, that is the implication of reversal.

Certainly, the language of Matthew 1:18 does not exclude the possibility of reversal, but our discussion of the overall intent of Matthew chapter 1 has shown that Matthew's point is to establish that Jesus' conception cannot in anyway be ascribed to what happened before and during the betrothal.

ii. Matthew 1:20

Matthew 1:20 is also a straightforward text:

> But just when he had resolved to do this, an angel of the Lord appeared to him in a dream and said, "Joseph, son of David, **do not be afraid to take Mary as your wife**, for the child conceived in her is from the Holy Spirit.

This text is not used as an argument in itself, except to state that Joseph (who had considered terminating the betrothal) is instructed to proceed as planned. He is told to espouse Mary in the sense of taking her into his house as legal wife, which is crucial for God's

---

[1] Here, I would agree with Svendsen against McHugh that συνελθεῖν should be understood as implying 'living together in phase two of the betrothal which is marriage with marital relations.' Otherwise, Matthew's entire point here (to affirm the virginal conception) would be defeated. (Cf. Svendsen, 22-23)

dispensation to work out. Jesus needs Joseph as an adoptive father, provider and teacher of righteousness. Also, Mary's unusual pregnancy will become socially accepted as she too needs a provider and father for the divine child. We have seen that even though Joseph espouses Mary and takes her as wife (we may assume into his house), he does not engage in sexual intercourse with her during the pregnancy. We have noted that this is actually rather unusual, but necessary so that Isaiah 7:14 may properly be fulfilled.

This text is not usually pressed to imply anything regarding the nature of Joseph's marital intercourse with Mary after the birth (and flight to Egypt).

iii. Matthew 1:24-25 and *heos hou*

Matthew 1:24-25 may well be the most important text in this entire discussion over the perpetual virginity of Mary. A typical translation reads:

> When Joseph awoke from sleep, he did as the angel of the Lord had instructed him; he took [Mary] as his wife but had no marital relations with her until she had borne a son, and he named him Jesus. (Mat 1:24-25)

Certainly, this text (especially in English) can be read to imply that the angel's instruction to Joseph to take Mary as his wife (into his home, but also not to have intercourse with her) only applied until the birth of the child, and that afterwards Joseph could (and did) have conjugal intercourse with Mary. It is not new that even in Greek, "until/ ἕως οὗ" **seems to imply reversal** and therefore can be used as an argument against the idea of Mary's perpetual virginity. St John Chrysostom (+407) discusses this very point with his Greek-speaking audience:

> [Matthew] here used the word "until," not that you should suspect that afterwards [Joseph] did know her, but to inform you that before the birth, the Virgin was wholly untouched by man. But why then, it may be said, has he used the word "until?" Because it is usual in Scripture often to do this, and to use this

expression without reference to limited times. Here, likewise, it uses the word "until," to make certain what was before the birth, but as to what follows, it leaves you to make the inference. Thus, what it was necessary for you to learn, this He Himself has said; that the Virgin was untouched by man until the birth; but that which both was seen to be a consequence of the former statement, and was acknowledged, this in its turn he leaves for you to perceive; namely, that not even after this, she having so become a mother and having been counted worthy of a new sort of travail and a child-bearing so strange, could that righteous man ever have endured to know her.

This discussion by Chrysostom is relevant in view of the argument put forth by Svendsen in his doctoral thesis, which is that *heos hou* as used in the Gospel of St Matthew, actually does imply reversal.

Svendsen's argument is as follows: considering a window of about 200 years before and after the putative date of writing of the Gospel of Matthew, *heos hou* (as distinguished from *heos*) is always used when temporal reversal is implied. Now, Svendsen recognizes that before and after this somewhat arbitrary window, *heos hou* can be used when no reversal of the main clause is implied. But he does argue that during that particular window of time, *heos hou* must have implied certain reversal:

> As for the NT, there are no instances in which *heos hou*, when it means "until," denotes the action of the main clause continuing after the action of the subordinate clause, in spite of Sungenis' three proposed examples above.[1]

His discussion on *heos hou* thus concludes:

> Matthew had intended for us to see in his birth narrative evidence for the perpetual virginity of Mary, we might have expected him

---

[1] From an email communication by Eric Svendsen replying to Robert Sungenis' claims that *heos hou* may imply non-reversal in the NT.

to use a phrase that would more readily lend itself to this idea **(nearly half of the NT occurrences of ἕως; without a particle have this connotation, as do 75% of the occurrences of ἕως α'ν)**. In light of the lack of general attestation for this usage of ἕως οὗ during Matthew's time, we should perhaps look elsewhere for support of Mary's perpetual virginity.[1]

Svendsen's research is very useful and seems to provide, at first glance, the strongest linguistic argument in favor of the Helvidian position.

However tempting it may be to assess Svendsen's theory here and now, it is better to postpone this particular discussion so as to address it fully in a dedicated section.

For now, it suffices to state that Greek scholars on both sides agree on the following points:

(1) *Heos* and *heos hou* are essential interchangeable, including in the Gospel of Matthew, as was perceived by native speakers of the language such as Origen and Eusebius. And as Svendsen indicates, *heos* (by itself) in completely neutral as far as reversal is concerned.

(2) Matthew favors the *heos hou* construction and seems to have used it in Matthew 1:25 precisely because it matches the NOT clause as well as the verbal end point ("had given birth").

(3) Both the LXX and contemporary Greek literature do have instances of the *heos/heos hou* clause not implying reversal of the main clause.

In fact, we have already noticed that Matthew 1:25 is written with a specific emphasis and purpose:

---

[1] Svendsen, 40 (bold added).

- The emphasis is on the NOT (οὐκ) because Isaiah 7:14 would be fulfilled and Joseph overcame his awe/fear to take in Mary as wife yet in abstinence, remaining in fact "betrothed" (Luke 2:5).
- The choice of the tense ("was not knowing her" is an imperfect rather than the aorist) confirms the focus on the time **before** birth.
- The end point chosen by Matthew (the birth) is not itself a natural point of reversal.

As one Protestant commentator puts it fairly well, "The plain reading would appear to be that Joseph and Mary consummated their marriage, commencing normal sexual activity after the birth of Jesus."[1] This is an apt description of what many readers are tempted to hastily conclude on the basis of Matthew 1:25, so that we may indeed say that 'the initial and surface-level reading would appear to be that Joseph and Mary consummated their marriage.'

Matthew 1:25 (and we shall see Luke 2:7) are two instances where the reader might reach the wrong conclusion on the basis of lack of knowledge of the Biblical usage of the Greek as well as lack of reference to the totality of the Scriptural data. However, the same can be said of a number of Christian doctrines. For instance, John 17:3 is read by some to teach that only the Father is God, and therefore deny the Trinity. Hebrews 10:26 can easily be understood to mean that Christians who commit a grave sin cannot be restored. 1 Peter 3:21 can be used to teach that we are saved by the rite of baptism, and Romans 3 ("no one is righteous") is often wrongly interpreted as a bleak exposition of total depravity. In fact, every Christian could probably find more than 10 verses that are easily, on the basis of surface-level reading, misunderstood. The Apostle

---

[1] Accessed at http://www.blogspy.com/contend/bookBecomingOrthodox.html

Peter could write, regarding the letters of the Apostle Paul, that "there are some things in them hard to understand, which the ignorant and unstable twist to their own destruction, as they do the other scriptures" (2Pe 3:6).

Matthew 1:25 is one of those texts, which is why the interpretation of the ancient Greek-speaking fathers is all the more indispensable to set the record straight.

iv. "First-born son" (Luke 2:7)

Luke 2:7 is sometimes cited to imply that if Jesus is called Mary's "first-born" (*prototokos*) son and not "only son" (*monogenes* or sometimes *agapetos*), surely, it is because there would one day be a second-born, third-born etc. Again, we sense the influence of our own modern culture, language and assumptions in this argument, because when English-speaking parents introduce a son or daughter as "this is my firstborn," there is little doubt that other children are assumed.

However, this is not the point of Jesus being called "first-born," as Luke himself is careful to explain in the same chapter:

> And while they were there, the time came for her to be delivered. And **she gave birth to her first-born son** and wrapped him in swaddling cloths, and laid him in a manger, because there was no place for them in the inn. (Luk 2:6-7)... And at the end of eight days, when he was circumcised, he was called Jesus, the name given by the angel before he was conceived in the womb. And when the time came for their purification according to the law of Moses, they brought him up to Jerusalem to present him to the Lord (as it is written in the law of the Lord, "**Every male that opens the womb** shall be called holy to the Lord") and to offer a sacrifice according to what is said in the law of the Lord, "a pair of turtledoves, or two young pigeons." (Luk 2-22-24)

Luke makes it clear (by citing Exodus 13:2 LXX) that the new-born child Jesus has the legal and spiritual status of first-born/one who opens the womb, and therefore "belongs to the LORD." This is what the passages about opening the womb and therefore being *prototokos* is all about. The (apocryphal) *Apocalypse of Ezra*[1] makes the point quite well:

> But we thy people, whom thou hast called thy **first-born, only begotten**, zealous for thee, and most dear, have been given into their hands. If the world has indeed been created for us, why do we not possess our world as an inheritance? How long will this be so?" (3Es 6:58-59)

Clearly, "first-born" (as in heir) and "only-begotten" (only son) are compatible and in special cases they are in fact joined: Jesus is the *prototokos* **and** *monogenes* (only-begotten), not only of God the Father but also of Mary, the daughter of Israel mourning at the cross:

> And I will pour out on the house of David and the inhabitants of Jerusalem a spirit of grace and supplication. They will look on me, the one they have pierced, and they will mourn for him as one mourns for an only child, and grieve bitterly for him as one grieves for a first-born son. (Zec 12:10)

Luke 2:7 is like Matthew 1:25, an argument indeed, but one based on a very superficial reading of the text colored by a modern (as in non-biblical) frame of mind.

v. "Your brothers and sisters" (Mark 3:32)

The fact that the Bible calls certain people "brothers and sisters" of Jesus conveys a certain immediate perception in the modern reader's mind, just as we have seen for "first-born" and "until."

If Jesus has "brothers and sisters," many think that they *must be* his mother's other children which he had with Joseph. This particular reading of "brothers and sisters" in the English language is actually

---

[1] This is text is placed in the Appendix of the Old Slavonic and Georgian bibles as 3 Esdras, and is often called 2 or 4 Esdras.

qualified and influenced by the context (Mary's virginal conception of Jesus, Joseph's adoptive fatherhood, perceived semantic range of *adelphoi*).

But things are not that simple, certainly not in Semitic Greek (yes, there is such a thing), even in our own context. My own experience of modern-society, with the ongoing unravelling of family ties and high-levels of out-of-wedlock births is that someone mentioning a "brother" or "sister" may very well be referring to a half or step sibling.

At a more sophisticated level, the Helvidian argument is that in the New Testament, *adelphoi* (when not used of spiritual relations), means just that – people sharing the same biological parents – and so the meaning should be plain and abundantly clear.

For instance, John Meier (Roman Catholic and Helvidian proponent) states (bold added):

> In the NT *adelphos*, when not used merely figuratively or metaphorically but rather to designate some sort of physical or legal relationship, **means only full or half-brother, and nothing else**. Outside our disputed case, **it never means step-brother (the solution of Epiphanius), cousin (the solution of Jerome), or nephew**. When one considers that *adelphos* (in either the literal or metaphorical sense) is used a total of 343 times in the NT, the consistency of this "literal" usage is amazing. To ignore the strikingly consistent usage of the NT in this regard . . . and to appeal instead to the usage of koine Greek in various Jewish and pagan texts cannot help but look like special pleading.

Coming from Meier who is a respected scholar, this argument alone would seem to be the only-needed nail to close the coffin of the Epiphanian and Hieronymian views.

So, is Meier's assessment false or based on a serious misunderstanding? In short, yes, Meier's statement reveals a grave misunderstanding, and our initial discussion of the meaning of *adelphoi* (Argument iii) should have prepared the reader to read

Meier's statement critically. Richard Bauckham (no less an eminent scholar than Meier) provides several rebuttals which we can examine one by one before adding our own:

> This is in more than one respect an odd argument. We may notice at once that the total number of occurrences of adelphoi, in the NT (in both literal and metaphorical senses) is quite irrelevant to the consistency of the literal usage. Meier omits to tell us that, of the 343 occurrences of adelphoi, 268 are in a metaphorical sense, and only 75 refer to literal family relationships (14 of these to the brothers of Jesus). But this is a relatively minor flaw in the argument.[1]

This is something that must be emphasized. In the New Testament (which we can use as our first but not only source of linguistic data), *adelphoi* is most often used "figuratively or metaphorically" to mean 'spiritual relatives' or better 'adoptive siblings' (through spiritual adoption). This **adoptive sense**, being the most prevalent, is in fact the Epiphanian view ascribes to the *adelphoi* of Jesus: they are the adoptive brothers and sisters through Joseph and Joseph's 'clan.' In the 61 cases where *adelphoi* refers to literal family relationships (excluding the *adelphoi* of Jesus), there is a range of meaning, including half-brothers as well as (possibly) uncles[2] and sister-in-law.[3] In these New Testament instances, the meaning of "step-siblings" is not found, which Meier believes is disqualifying for the Epiphanian view. Likewise the meaning of "cousin" does not seem to be found in these 61 instances, which leads Meier to also reject the Hieronymian view.

Bauckham counters on several fronts:

---

[1] Opus cit.

[2] Meier may not be aware that *adelphoi* may well mean kinsmen in Matthew 1:11. This is not entirely certain but it is very probable. See for instance John Nolland, *Jechoniah and His Brothers (Matthew 1:11)*, Bulletin for Biblical Research 7 (1997): 169-178

[3] John 19:25

> To realize how extraordinary Meier's argument is, we need only to notice the effect it would have if it were applied consistently to NT vocabulary. There are many Greek words which in the NT usually have one meaning but occasionally have another. Meier's principle would mean that this rare meaning, however well attested outside the NT, should not be allowed within the NT because the general usage of the NT (its amazing consistency) would exclude it. For example, τράπεζαν occurs 15 times in the NT, normally with the meaning "table." Just once, in Luke 19:23, it means "bank," according to all translators and exegetes, but Meier's principle would have to disallow this. To take another example, τέλη occurs 41 times in the NT, always with the meaning "end," except on three occasions when it means "tax" (Matt 17:25; Rom 13:7). This ratio of common meanings to rare ones (38 to 3) is much more unfavorable to the rare meaning than is the ratio of *adelphos*... It is probably unnecessary to labor the point that Meier's argument contradicts what nearly all translators and exegetes assume: that the range of use from which the meaning of a word in the NT must be chosen is the range of use in the language, not the range of use in the NT.

Bauckham's closing comment on this point is very important for anyone engaged in biblical studies:

> When Meier himself argues that *adelphos* in Mark 6:17 must mean "half brother" rather than "full brother," there is nothing in the context of this verse in Mark, or indeed in the rest of the NT. which enables him to know this. He has to assume that information be has from Josephus was common knowledge to Mark and his readers. The case is parallel to that of the brothers of Jesus. Defenders of the Epiphanian view do not claim that the information that the brothers of Jesus were sons of Joseph by a previous marriage can be deduced from the immediate context of references to them in the NT. It is sufficient to claim that their actual relationship to Jesus can be deduced from other evidence.

Because Jesus is simply called "son of Joseph," yet without implication (owing to the totality of the information provided) that there was blood relationship there, it is extremely important to be very precise. Bauckham explains this very well:

> Meier might have come to different conclusions had he extended his study of *adelphos* to other words for family relationships. When Luke calls Joseph and Mary the "parents" of Jesus (2:41,43) and has Mary refer to Joseph as Jesus' "father" (2:48), Meier must presume that these terms designate Joseph Jesus' stepfather, yet the use of these terms for literal family relationships elsewhere in the NT provides no example of a meaning other than biological parenthood. The point is that **the Epiphanian view postulates Jesus' standing in the same kind of relationship to his brothers and sisters as he did to Joseph.** If Luke can call Joseph Jesus' parent or father without implying blood relationship, then it is arbitrary to insist that reference to Jesus' brothers and sisters must imply blood relationship.[1]

In the end, Meier's argument regarding the meaning of *adelphoi* in the New Testament (expressed with great assurance and convincing power) is surprisingly weak because based on false assumptions and a faulty scope of data.

However, the reader will probably agree with Meier (and others) that ascribing the meaning of cousin to *adelphoi* (without supplemental circumstances to explain the qualification) is much more difficult, which is the greatest weakness of the Hieronymian view still to be discussed.

vi. Not the heir!

In their interesting book entitled *Roman Catholics and Evangelicals*, Geisler and MacKenzie display what can only be described as the usual dismissiveness of Protestants towards the Epiphanian view. Noting that a Roman Catholic scholar had mentioned the

---

[1] Ibid. Bold added.

possibility that the *adelphoi* were Joseph's biological children, they comment:

> Even Ott calls implausible the suggestion that these "brothers" and "sisters" of Jesus were Joseph's children from another marriage. If this were so then Joseph's oldest son would have been heir to David's throne and not Jesus, but the Bible affirms that Jesus was the heir (Matt. 1:1)[1]

Ben Witherington likewise:

> The Epiphanian view labors under the difficulty that if Joseph previously had other sons, Jesus could not legally be his firstborn or first in line for the Davidic throne, and it also depends on dubious and weak church traditions.[2]

Their argument is straightforward: unless Jesus was Joseph's first-born, he could not have been the lawful heir to the throne of David. Therefore, Jesus must have been the first-born and Joseph could not possibly have had other sons prior to his engagement and marriage to Mary.

The first thing to notice, from the perspective of sound engagement with the Scriptures, is that **Jesus is not called Joseph's first-born**. In Matthew 1:25, some manuscripts read:

> And knew her not till she had brought forth **her firstborn son**: and he called his name JESUS. (KJV)

However, most scholars agree that the original text of Matthew did not contain "first-born" but consider it most likely that it was inserted to better correspond with Luke 2:7 which reads:

---

[1] Norman L. Geisler, Ralph E. MacKenzie, *Roman Catholics and Evangelicals: Agreements and Differences*, Chapter 15 (no page number in this edition, locator is footnote 13)

[2] Ben Witherington, *The Gospel of Mark: A Socio-rhetorical Commentary*, 194

> And she gave birth to **her first-born son** and wrapped him in swaddling cloths, and laid him in a manger, because there was no place for them in the inn. (Luk 2:7)

Interestingly, Jesus is not called **Joseph's** "first-born son" (or "their first-born"), even though the very first use of "first-born" in the Bible shows that this could have been done:

> Canaan became the father of Sidon his first-born, and Heth. (Gen 10:15)

Regarding the issue of Jesus being heir to the throne of David, as son of David (noting that Joseph himself is called "Son of David"), it is quite clear that **Jesus is compared to Solomon**, as in "behold, something greater than Solomon is here" (Mat 12:42). It seems unlikely that Geisler and MacKenzie were unaware that Solomon was not David's first-born (2Sa 3:2), but they may have failed to perceive how relevant this is to their argument! As a matter of fact, David's first-born son was Amnon (who was killed during his father's lifetime), but eventually all of David's surviving sons pledged allegiance to King Solomon (1Ch 29:24).

This argument turns out to be quite an embarrassment for the Helvidian side and squarely in favor of the Epiphanian view: Jesus is called Mary's first-born, not Joseph's, and Jesus' status as the true Solomon is echoed by his own placement in Joseph's line of succession. Not only that, but even as the older "brothers of the Lord" (notably James) eventually pledged allegiance to the Great Solomon and became 'princes of the spiritual Davidic Kingdom,' likewise those of the house of Joseph and thus the Lord's *adelphoi* also acquired special status in the early Church, being known as the *desposynoi*.

vii. "Not even his brothers"

A less common argument, that may be associated with Tertullian's comments, is that the scenes involving Jesus and his closest relatives only make sense if these *adelphoi* are indeed uterine siblings. For instance:

> While he was still speaking to the people, behold, his mother and his brothers stood outside, asking to speak to him. But he replied to the man who told him, "Who is my mother, and who are my brothers?" And stretching out his hand toward his disciples, he said, "Here are my mother and my brothers! For whoever does the will of my Father in heaven is my brother, and sister, and mother." (Mar 12:46-50)
>
> NAU John 7:5 For not even His brothers were believing in Him.

There is no question that if these *adelphoi* were his uterine siblings, the statement would be very strong and makes perfect sense. If this people were only cousins, the same scene may seem more strained. If however, the *adelphoi* are Jesus' closest relatives (adoptive sibling and perhaps some cousins) with whom he had shared his early years, the statement remains powerful.

However, this cuts both ways: others have seen this scene as an argument *against* the Helvidian view, because younger relatives would not have treated a first-born brother in such a way, in the context of Jewish culture.

The only thing that we can conclude is that Jesus never saw the bonds of the flesh as constituting family in the true spiritual sense. In fact, human family bonds are portrayed as possibly inimical to discipleship. For Jesus and subsequently for the Christian Church, the true eternal and spiritual family is the Church, which one enters by a new birth and adoption by the Father. In this sense, the Epiphanian view provides a very good symmetry: Jesus' adoptive siblings (under the laws of a family according to the flesh and human rules) are not true siblings; the only true adoption is of the Spirit. This symmetry works well under the Helvidian model of course, but in the end this pericope does not amount to a solid argument either way.

viii. Mary as mother of Jesus, James and Joses

We have already discussed that a certain "Mary" was at the cross and identified as the mother of James and Joses/Joseph. It seems, from Jerome's argumentation against Helvidius, that the latter was arguing that Mary the mother of Jesus was the same person as Mary the mother of James and Joses, which would then prove that all three were indeed uterine brothers:

> But at this stage, I do not wish to argue for or against the supposition that Mary the wife of Clopas and Mary the mother of James and Joses were different women, provided it is clearly understood that Mary the mother of James and Joses was not the same person as the Lord's mother.[1]

It is unclear whether Svendsen ultimately makes the same argument as Helvidius, namely that there were 3 women at the cross: Mary Magdalene, Salome, and Mary the mother of Jesus (also called the mother of James and Joses).

The fact is that only John indicates that Mary the mother of Jesus was also present at the foot of the cross, with John himself. It is simply too unlikely to contend that the mother of Jesus could adequately and reasonably be referred to as "the mother of James (and/or Joses)." Admittedly, John 19:25 is a mysterious text because we cannot be certain if John is describing two or three women, and whether Mary of Clopas is the wife or daughter of Clopas. As a result, we cannot fully determine the nature of the relationship between Mary the mother of Jesus and this other Mary described as "the other Mary" and the "the mother of James (the Less) (and/or Joses)."

In my opinion, John 19:25 probably refers to four women: (1) Mary the mother of Jesus, (2) Mary's sister or close relative (exact

---

[1] Jerome, *Against Helvidius*

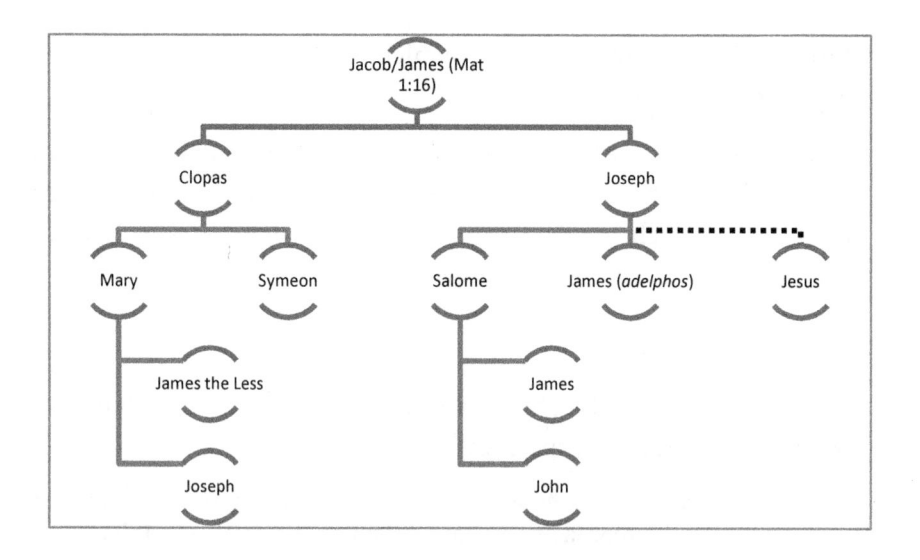

```
                    Jacob/James (Mat
                         1:16)

        Clopas                           Joseph

  Mary       Symeon            Salome    James (adelphos)    Jesus

       James the Less                James

           Joseph                    John
```

relationship unknown). She could possibly be Salome (the mother of the apostles James and John) and one wonders if this Salome could have been Joseph's daughter by his previous marriage as taught by Epiphanius, (3) Mary the daughter (or wife) of Clopas who was Joseph's younger brother, and the mother of James the Less and Joses/Joseph, and (4) Mary Magdalene.

Here, it should be frankly stated that the Orthodox/Epiphanian view really does not want to see Mary's sister as her actual sister, because Mary is normally seen as the only daughter of Joachim and Anna.[1] Maintaining this view requires *adelphe* to be used in the

---

[1] As in the *Protevangelium of James*. The account suggests that a certain Solome was his daughter (per Epiphanius) and that Joseph considered Mary, in a way, as his daughter ("Should I register her as my daughter?"). If we see only 3 women in the scene, this Mary of Clopas could be Mary's sister-in-law, which is a possible but less than usual meaning of *adelphe* (with reference to Bauckham's discussion of rare meanings, already cited). In late medieval times, the *Golden Legend* held that Anne was married three times first to Joachim, then to Clopas and finally to a man named Solomas and that each marriage produced one daughter: Mary, mother of Jesus, Mary of Clopas, and Mary Salomæ, respectively. The same account had the sister of St Anne as Sobe, presented as the mother of St Elizabeth.

broader Old Testament sense which is less plausible than the expected literal sense.

These family trees are not easy to recreate based on the totality of the Biblical record, if we also take into account credible ancient information, such as Hegesippus' claim that Clopas was Joseph's brother.[1]

ix. **Psalm 69:8**

Psalm 69 is a fairly long prayer (36 verses), of which several have Messianic applications, specifically:

> For zeal for your house has consumed me and the reproaches of those who reproach you have fallen on me. (verse 9; John 2:13-17)
>
> They gave me poison for food, and for my thirst they gave me sour wine to drink. (verse 21; cited in Matthew 27:34)

It may be argued that other verses may also have Messianic applications, but the main ones are the ones cited above. Verse 8 (if the entire Psalm is to read as spoken by Christ), is relevant to our discussion:

> I have become a stranger unto my brothers/brethren and an alien to my mother's children. (Psa 68:8)

Not surprisingly then, Psalm 69:8 has been used as argument, since if put in the mouth of Christ it would be an explicit reference to his mother's children.

---

[1] I couldn't help but reflect on the fact that in traditional Greek Orthodox families, at least one son is named after the grand-father. Applying this principle to Joseph and Clopas, we could imagine both of them having a son named James/Jacob, which would lead us to distinguish between James the Just ("the Lord's brother" and son of Joseph) and James the Less (Clopas' son or even grandson). It is certainly best not to be dogmatic on any of the above.

However, it is difficult to argue that Psalm 69 should be read this way, simply because too many verses in this Psalm cannot possibly be placed in the mouth of Jesus. The opening verses express the distress of one accused (possibly of stealing from verse 4) and feeling abandoned by God after a long time of crying. Verse 5 could not possibly apply to the Messiah, because the Psalmist exclaims:

> O God, you know my folly; the wrongs I have done are not hidden from you!

To ascribe folly and wrongdoing to Jesus is clearly out of the question. Verse 10 likewise has no echo in the New Testament, on the contrary:

> When I wept and humbled my soul with fasting, it became my reproach. When I made sackcloth my clothing, I became a jest to them. (Psa 69:10-11)

> For John the Baptist has come eating no bread and drinking no wine; and you say, `He has a demon.' The Son of man has come eating and drinking; and you say, 'Behold, a glutton and a drunkard, a friend of tax collectors and sinners!' Yet wisdom is justified by all her children. (Luk 7:33-35)

The Psalmist then launches into what is called an imprecatory[1] prayer:

> Let their eyes be darkened, so that they cannot see, and make their loins tremble continually. Pour out your indignation upon them, and let your burning anger overtake them. May their camp be a desolation, and let no one dwell in their tents. For they persecute him whom you have struck down, and they recount the pain of those you have wounded. Add to them punishment upon punishment! May they have no acquittal from you! Let them be blotted out of the book of the living; let them not be enrolled among the righteous. (Psa 69:23-28)

---

[1] Imprecatory psalms are those psalms that contain curses or prayers for the punishment of the psalmist's enemies. To imprecate means to invoke judgment, calamity, or curses, upon one's enemies.

Even if one considers the famous "Father, forgive them, for they do not know what they are doing" as an interpolation,[1] it remains that this entire part of the Psalm is at odds with the remembrance that the Lord had indeed uttered these words of mercy, not imprecation.

It is difficult, then, to apply all the specifics and verses of this Psalm to Jesus, including verse 8. Even if one would wish to do so, the figurative sense is still possible, albeit unlikely; the *adelphoi* who rejected the Messiah would be his fellow Jews, sons of Israel and of mother Rachel/Jerusalem.

x. Temporary abstinence

For many Helvidians, the idea that Joseph would have been coaxed into taking Mary as wife only to be ultimately deprived of marital intercourse is quite unthinkable. James White reminds his reader that marriage is a debt, and therefore that Joseph would have been defrauded if forced to live in a 'dreadful state of abstinence.' Geisler and MacKenzie likewise:

> There is nothing unnatural or unbiblical about Joseph having sex with Mary after Jesus was born. In fact it can be argued that it would have been unnatural and unbiblical for him not to do so, since Scripture considers sex to be an essential part of marriage (cf. Gen. 1:28 ; 1 Cor. 7:1–7 ; Heb. 13:4).[2]

The problem with this very human perspective is that it ignores the completely unique circumstances of this extraordinary family unit. Joseph is assumed to be a young man eager to finally engage in marital intercourse with the mother of his Lord, a picture which

---

[1] Luke 23:34 is a complex matter indeed. While recognizing the fact that several ancient authorities do not include this verse, it remains that the Lord's Prayer of mercy on the cross is attested by many important manuscripts as well as by several early fathers, notably Hippolytus and Irenaeus.

[2] Opus cit.

actually seems quite "unnatural and unbiblical" to both Orthodox and Catholic Christians, for reasons already discussed.

xi. Irenaeus, Tertullian, etc.

When Helvidius argued that the *adelphoi* of Jesus were no other than his uterine siblings, he was probably aware that his position would be perceived as new and highly controversial (this is the fourth century). He was therefore careful to seek support among the ancient writers that could be enrolled to confirm his view, in this case only Tertullian (+c. 225) and Victorinus of Pettau (+304).

Other defenders of the Helvidian view have also enlisted Hegesippus, Justin Martyr, and Irenaeus of Lyons (all second century) as (alleged) supporters.

Since we have a dedicated historical section to discuss the testimony of the ancient authors and fathers, let us simply say that only Tertullian can be firmly identified (yet not with absolute certainty) as a proponent of the Helvidian view.

If the argument from antiquity does exist for those who identify the *adelphoi* as uterine siblings, it is a very weak one indeed, and for this reason rarely pressed forward.

c) A detailed discussion of the *heos hou* thesis[1]

i. A new argument worth assessing

Some readers may be keenly interested in whether the use of *heos hou* in Matthew 1:25 actually implies the reversal of the main clause. For this reason, we now proceed with a very detailed discussion of Svendsen's thesis.

---

[1] This entire section is taken (with permission and minor modifications) from the excellent research done by John Pacheco of Catholic Legate. Accessed at: http://www.catholic-legate.com/articles/heoshou.html

Already, we have seen that native readers of the Greek language (e.g. Origen and Chrysostom) did not read the text in this way. However, Svendsen has put forth the **thesis of temporary linguistic obsolescence**, contending that during a window of about 200 years, *heos hou* acquired the exclusive usage of reversal (both in the New Testament and contemporary literature).

At the outset, it seems fair to point out that Svendsen's doctoral thesis did not result in any peer-reviewed articles or widespread (if any) adoption by other Greek scholars. However, since it has been cited by Helvidian apologists as being sound scholarship, an in-depth discussion is warranted.

There is little debate over the fact that the use of the Greek word *heos* does not necessarily mean that the action (or non-action in this particular case) in the main clause ceases or discontinues itself in the subordinate clause. Applying this principle to Matthew 1:25 means that this text does not necessarily convey a cessation or change in Mary's virginity after the birth of Christ. There are many references in the Bible which attest to this fact (as Chrysostom pointed out with his own selection of examples). One typical example of the action of the main clause being continued into the subordinate clause occurs in 2 Samuel 6:23: "Michal the daughter of Saul had no child until [*heos*] the day of her death." Obviously, Michal will remain childless after her death, just as Mary could remain virgin after Christ's birth. The New Testament also provides ample evidence against the Helvidian proposal, for instance:

> For this reason the Jews were persecuting Jesus, because He was doing these things on the Sabbath. But He answered them, 'My Father is working until [*heos*] now, and I Myself am working.'" (Joh 5:16-17).

The Father has obviously kept working since Jesus spoke those words.

But the *heos hou* argument proponents (notably Svendsen and White), while conceding that *heos* alone is not sufficient to prove that Mary lost her virginity, note that **Matthew 1:25 has *heos* accompanied by the particle *hou*.**

In his 1999 debate with Catholic Apologist Gerry Matatics on Mary's Perpetual Virginity, Svendsen makes his case thus:

> [Rarely] is it mentioned by these [Catholic] apologists that this is not the Greek phrase [*heos* alone] used in Matthew 1:25. In all of these passages cited by Catholic Apologists, the word *heos* alone is used, but in Matthew 1:25, the Greek construction *heos hou* is used. The phrase *heos hou* with its variant form *heos hotou* which grammarians treat as the same, occurs a total of 22 times in the New Testament. Four of these have the meaning 'while' noting contemporaneous (Mat 5:25, Mat 14:22, Mat 26:36, Luk 13:8) whereas the other 18 instances have the meaning 'until' and these are all instances where the action of the main clause is changed by the action of the subordinate clause, and requires the meaning up to a specified time but not after.[1]

In plain language, Svendsen contends that *heos* + *hou* has implications (reversal) that *heos* alone does not. His study only takes into account the use of *heos* + *hou* (as distinguished from heos alone), not the tense used with the construction.

ii. The Greek Particle *Hou*

Before addressing Svendsen's methodology and other relevant matters on this question, it would be beneficial first to provide a brief overview of the grammatical significance of *heos*. Insofar as the parts of speech are concerned, *heos* is generally a relative adverb while *hou* is a particle. In the construction of the phrase in question, however, "until" takes the character of a subordinate conjunction.

"Joseph kept her a virgin--until--she gave birth to a Son."

|Main Clause|----|conjunction|----|Subordinate Clause|

---

[1] The time locator is [00:12:54-00:13:44].

Our thesis, *contra* Svendsen, is that the pronoun *hou* really has no effect on the meaning of the couplet under discussion. (In fact, as we will soon discover, not only does *hou* not affect the meaning of *heos*, it does not even affect the meaning of synonyms for *heos* either.) English equivalents of *heos* hou might be translated as "until which," "until which time," or "until such time as." In fact, *heos hou* is simply a shorthand for the phrase *heos hou chronou en hoi* - literally: "until the time when."

iii. Lexical Evidence

As Sophocles in his *Greek Lexicon of the Roman Byzantine Periods* and Stephanus in his *Thesaurus Graecae Linguae* attest that from a grammatical point of view, there is no relevant difference between *heos* alone and *heos hou*. Both make no distinction between *heos* alone and *heos hou*, treating them as if they were equivalent in meaning. In addition to these older sources, we can turn to more contemporary references which also maintain there is no difference in meaning by adding the particle *hou* to *heos*. According to Burton's *Grammar*:

> In the New Testament *heos* is sometimes followed by *hou* or *otou*. *Heos* is then a preposition governing the genitive of the relative pronoun, but the phrase *heos hou* or *heos otou* is in effect a compound conjunction having the same force as the simple *heos*.[1]

No distinction or restriction in meaning is made between *heos* alone and *heos hou* in a number of other Biblical lexicons - all of which explicitly include *heos hou* in their explication of *heos*: Thayer's Greek-English Lexicon, Robinson's Greek-English Lexicon, Zorrell's Lexicon Graecum, Arndt & Bauer's Greek-English Lexicon, Liddell & Scott's Greek-English Lexicon, and Luow & Nida's Greek-English Lexicon. Neither is a distinction made in

---

[1] Burton's *Syntax of the Moods and Tenses*, 128-129

Muraoka's Greek-English Lexicon or Lampe's Patristic Greek Lexicon. Zerwick and Grosvenor also concur with this opinion:

> [*Heos hou*], until (the time when) but not excluding continuation of action beyond the time indicated; author only concerned here to indicate virginal conception.[1]

These authorities are quite emphatic: no cessation of the action in the main clause is demanded after *heos hou* is employed (although it may of course be possible or implied, based on the overall context). There is no distinction between *heos* and *heos hou* as they both signify the same meaning: "expressing the point in time up to which an action goes" (Liddell and Scott); "to denote the end of a period of time" (Arndt and Bauer); "marking the continuance of an action up to the time of another action" (Robinson's). In fact, Louw and Nida also make this observation as a footnote:

> *heos*, *axpi*, and *uexpi* frequently occur with a postposed marker of indefinite temporal reference: *hou*, occurring with all three markers, and *hotou* with heos.

In other words, *heos hou* is as likely to refer to Mary retaining her virginity, through an indefinite temporal reference, as *heos* alone does.

iv. Scholarly Commentaries

One of the most widely respected commentaries on Matthew's gospel is written by W.D. Davies and Dale Allison Jr. in the respected ICC (International Critical Commentary) series. In this work, the contributors say this regarding Matthew 1:25:

> This retrospective observation does not necessarily imply that there were marital relations later on, for *heos* (until) following a negative need not contain the idea of a limit which terminates the

---

[1] Zerwick and Grosvenor, *Grammatical Analysis*, 2

preceding action or state (cf. Gen. 49.10 Septuagint; Mt 10.23; Mk 9.1).[1]

While it is true that Davies and Allison go on to question the awkward construction of the verse if indeed Mary was perpetually a virgin, the fact that they mention solely *heos* instead of *heos hou* is indicative of the opinion of many that, grammatically, there is no such special exception for the latter as opposed to the former as regards to the continuation of the action in the main clause.

This view is further supported by a work which is frequently cited in Svendsen's book: *The Birth of the Messiah: A Commentary on the Infancy Narratives in the Gospels of Matthew and Luke*. In this work, Raymond Brown essentially concurs with the evidence adduced from all scholarly sources thus far:

> Leaving aside post-Reformation quarrels, we must seek to reconstruct Matthew's intention, first from the immediate context and then from the whole Gospel. How does "not know her until" fit into the immediate context? In English when something is negated until a particular time, occurrence after that time is usually assumed. However, in discussing the Greek *heos hou* after a negative, K. Beyer, *Semitishce Syntax im Neuen Testament* (Gottingen: Vandenhoeck, 1962), points out that **in Greek and Semitic such a negation often has no implication at all about what happened after the limit of the "until" was reached...The immediate context favors a lack of future implication here**, for Matthew is concerned only with stressing Mary's virginity before the child's birth, so that the Isaian prophecy will be fulfilled: it is as a virgin that Mary will give birth to her son. As for the marital situation after the birth of the child, in itself this verse gives us no information whatsoever. In my

---

[1] *International Critical Commentary*, Vol. 1, p. 219

judgment, the question of Mary's remaining a virgin for the rest of her life belongs to post-biblical theology [...][1]

In *Mary In the New Testament*, Brown (et. al.) further concede that it is only on the basis of other passages that one would be inclined to accept that Mary did not remain a virgin. They write:

> It is only when this verse is combined with Matthew's reference to Mary and the brothers of Jesus (12:46), along with the sisters (13:55-56), that a likelihood arises that (according to Matthew's understanding) Joseph did come to know Mary after Jesus' birth and that they begot children.[2]

However, these other references taken in the overall context of the question at hand are by no means conclusive either. The *adelphoi* of Jesus are not necessarily uterine brothers and sisters, but might refer to close relatives who grew up with Jesus under the same roof.

Indeed, Svendsen himself even concedes the scholarship arrayed against him:

> Protestants scholars who take this view include Robert Gundry, *Matthew: A Commentary from His Handbook on a Mixed Church Under Persecution*, 2d ed. (Grand Rapids: Eerdmans, 1994), 25, who says, "By itself *heos hou*, which belongs to Matthew's preferred diction (4,2) does not necessarily imply that Joseph and Mary entered into normal sexual relations after Jesus' birth"; Richard B. Gardner, *Matthew (Believers Church Bible Commentary*; Scottsdale, P.A.: Herald Press, 1991), 41,...states that "the language of the text leaves open the question of how Joseph and Mary related to each other after Jesus' birth..."[3]

---

[1] Raymond Brown, *Birth of the Messiah*, 132 (bold added)
[2] Raymond Brown, *Mary in the New Testament*, 86-87
[3] Opus cit.

Even John Meier corroborates the judgment that indeed, the text neither affirms nor denies Mary's perpetual virginity, stating his reply to Bauckham:

> Both authors admit that one cannot entirely exclude the possibility of either the Epiphanian solution or the Helvidian solution... I stressed in my article that absolute proof of the Helvidian view is impossible and that the Epiphanian view could be upheld with intellectual integrity...[1]

v. Survey of scholars

In addition to the findings of the standard lexicons and commentaries presented above, a random survey was conducted among both Roman Catholic and (mostly) Protestant academics and scholars in order to ascertain if there were any other considerations which may lend credence to the newly advanced *heos hou* argument. Not surprisingly, while some scholars maintained that the context or other biblical passages contribute to the belief that Mary did not remain a virgin, of the dozens of scholars contacted, not one scholar concurred with a necessary restriction on *heos hou* on a grammatical basis.

vi. Grammatical Conclusion

As an addition to *heos*, we would expect that the particle *hou* would have the same inconsequential effect on other prepositions or conjunctions. Indeed, this is exactly what happens when we consider the Greek preposition/conjunction *achri* which has the same common meaning in English as *heos* does. The addition of *hou* to *achri* does not change or restrict the fundamental meaning of *achri* at all, and therefore does not demand that the text imply a cessation from a grammatical basis alone.

---

[1] Meier (1997), Op. cit.

One surveyed commentator also questioned whether those advancing this new *heos hou* argument considered the relevance of *mechri hou* and *achri hou*, writing:

> Do these persons confine their research to *heos* and *heos hou/hotou*? Or do they also consider the comparable *achri* and *achri hou/hotou* (Luke 21:24, Acts 7:18, Acts 27:33, Romans 11:25, 1 Corinthians 11:26, 1 Corinthians 15:25, Galatians 3:19, Hebrews 3:13, Revelations 2:25) and *mechri* and *mechri hou/hotou* (Mark 13:30, Galatians 4:19). These are synonymous expressions with precisely comparable usage, so far as I can tell. And for what it's worth I'll cite below Louw & Nida's lexicon of the Greek NT by semantic domains.

The commentator went on to cite the relevant texts in Louw and Nida's lexicon which confirm his assessment.

The evidence amply demonstrates that there is no intrinsic quality to the particle *hou* which would cause a material shift in meaning to the preposition (or conjunction) immediately preceding it. The grammatical addition of the particle *hou* to *heos* has absolutely no bearing or impact in determining the temporal result of the action in the main clause.

vii. Svendsen's Methodology (Textual Issue)

Before addressing the methodology employed by Svendsen on this issue, it is worthwhile to quickly review the significance of textual issues. The textual witness to *heos hou* is not unanimous. *Hou* is not present in manuscript k, the most important witness to the African Old Latin (4th/5th century). As a result, several critical editions have placed *hou* in brackets, as does Nestle-Aland (1963).

Furthermore, the textual variants of *heos hou* found in the New Testament, namely, Matthew 18:30, Matthew 18:34, and Luke 12:50 are also suggestive. Matthew 18:30 has a textual variant with Codices Sinaiticus, Vaticanus, et al. having *heos*, while Codices Beza and Freer, and the Majority Text have *heos hou*. Matthew 18:34 also has a textual variant. Only Codex Vaticanus has *heos hou* while the others have *heos* alone. With respect to Luke 12:50, Codices Alexandrinus, Beza, Freer, and the Majority text have *heos hou* while Codices Sinaiticus and Vaticanus only have *heos*.

While it is always precarious to mix literary and textual criticisms, the above evidence suggests that both the New Testament writers and their copyists did not perceive a tangible difference between *heos* and *heos hou*. In the case of the copyists, the above evidence is insinuative that *heos hou* is used interchangeably with *heos* (verses 30 and 34).

viii. Statistical Analysis

The issue surrounding *heos hou* can be better appreciated after a survey of its usage in the Bible. *Heos hou* is used 19 times in the New Testament (Mt 1:25; 13:33; 14:22; 17:9; 18:30, 18:34, 26:36; Lk 12:50, 13:21; 15:8; 22:18; 24:49; Jn 13:38; Ac 21:26; 23:12; 23:14; 23:21; 25:21; 2 Pt 1:19). There are textual variants in Matthew 18:30, Matthew 18:34, and Luke 12:50. Svendsen tabulates the following statistics. *Heos hou* is used 85 times in the Septuagint while *heos hotou* is used 4 times in the NT (Mt 5:25; Lk 13:8; 22:16; Jn 9:18 with Luke 12:50 being a textual variant) and 14 times in the Septuagint. *Heos* an is used 20 times in the NT including Mt 2:13; 5:18; 5:26; 10:11, 23; 12:20; 16:28; 22:44; 23:39; 24:34 and 105 times in the Septuagint. Of the above references, according to Svendsen himself, *heos* "in all its forms occurs only 1,710 times in the LXX and the NT; 1,564 times in the LXX and 146 times in the NT." Although the preponderance of these instances terminate the action of the main verb, in a significant number of cases, *heos* and its associated conjunctions is clearly designed to continue the action of the main verb.

In his book, Svendsen tabulates 58 occurrences of *heos hou* in the Septuagint which carry a temporal meaning, 6 of these clearly denoting the contemporaneous while and 52 denoting either a continuation or cessation of the action in the main clause. Of these occurrences, Svendsen identifies only 5 occurrences which he identifies as clear examples of a continuation of the action in the main clause. Again, we should note that the issue of the tense, in spite of the unusual use of the indicative imperfect in Matthew 1:25, is not dealt with by Svendsen. Even with these tense-lacking statistics, the following observations can be made.

First, in submitting our survey to various scholars, not one of them excluded the Septuagint from consideration in determining the meaning of *heos hou*. In fact, all of them who offered a comment on the Septuagint affirmed that there are no grounds for dismissing it in assessing the grammatical range of *heos hou*. But even though Svendsen discusses the usage of the phrase in the Septuagint, he then dismisses its usage as being "semantically obsolete" for consideration in the New Testament, which is very problematic.

Second, as the results above indicate, the temporal-continuation meaning of *heos hou* equals 9.6% (5/52) of the relevant temporal population in the Septuagint or 8.6% (5/58) of the entire temporal population in the Septuagint (including the 6 instances of "while" identified by Svendsen). The low percentage found in the Septuagint (a larger body of text) already suggests a certain difficulty in terms of finding many instances of *heos hou* in the New Testament even before an examination is conducted.

If we were to extrapolate the percentage of occurrence from the Septuagint to the 15 occurrences of the relevant *heos hou* population in the New Testament, we would expect to find 1.44 instances (9.6% * 15) of *heos hou* where the action in the main clause continues. From a statistical point of view, even if no such instances were found in the New Testament, this would not be significant enough to draw a conclusion on Matthew 1:25. In fact, the only thing that one may conclude is that the usage is rare. And in relation to over relying on the mere use of such statistics, Svendsen's own mentor, D.A. Carson, in his book *Exegetical Fallacies*, cautions against exegetical judgments based on an statistically insufficient populations. Indeed, if we were to insist on such a deficient approach proposed by Svendsen, we would be allowed to conclude that the one instance (1.44 to be exact) projected to occur in the New Testament is Matthew 1:25. Moreover, this (Mat 1:25) is the only New Testament verse with the use of the imperfect tense with *heos hou*, which should reinforce our caution again statistical conclusions of any kind.

ix. Svendsen's New Testament Exegesis

As mentioned previously, there are 15 occurrences of *heos hou* in the New Testament relevant to this discussion. Because this phrase is used only rarely to indicate a continuation of the main clause in the Septuagint, it is not surprising to discover that most of these occurrences in the New Testament do not have such meaning. Svendsen maintains that none of the 15 pertinent occurrences of *heos hou* in the New Testament imply a continuation of the main clause. Instead, he insists that all of them have the meaning "until a specified time (but not after)."

Since there is no point in exploring those passages which do clearly indicate a cessation of the action in the main clause, the following discussion will focus only on those passages which may not support Svendsen's thesis.

Matthew 18:22-34 [Luke 12:58-59]

> Jesus said to him, "I do not say to you, up to seven times, but up to seventy times seven. For this reason the kingdom of heaven may be compared to a king who wished to settle accounts with his slaves. When he had begun to settle them, one who owed him ten thousand talents was brought to him. But since he did not have the means to repay, his lord commanded him to be sold, along with his wife and children and all that he had, and repayment to be made. So the slave fell to the ground and prostrated himself before him, saying, 'Have patience with me and I will repay you everything.' And the lord of that slave felt compassion and released him and forgave him

the debt. But that slave went out and found one of his fellow slaves who owed him a hundred denarii; and he seized him and began to choke him, saying, 'Pay back what you owe.' So his fellow slave fell to the ground and began to plead with him, saying, 'Have patience with me and I will repay you.' But he was unwilling and went and threw him in prison until he should pay back what was owed. So when his fellow slaves saw what had happened, they were deeply grieved and came and reported to their lord all that had happened. Then summoning him, his lord said to him, 'You wicked slave, I forgave you all that debt because you pleaded with me. Should you not also have had mercy on your fellow slave, in the same way that I had mercy on you?' And his lord, moved with anger, handed him over to the torturers <u>until</u> he should repay all that was owed him." (Matthew 18:22-34)

In the ancient Greco-Roman world, the punishment exacted on those who broke a law was often draconian and merciless. This is no less true for a creditor who was seeking to recover amounts owing from his debtor. A creditor could, for instance, demand slave labor from both the debtor and the members of the debtor's family. In fact, the law was so ruthless and exacting that the whole family could be sold into slavery to discharge debt. This was also true in the time of Christ when Israel was under the rule of the Roman Empire. Roman law, it was well known, provided for swift and severe punishment by imprisonment and torture against debtors who fell into default. The reason for the imprisonment was to coerce the victim to pay the debt anyway he could through hidden wealth, family assistance, or other unknown sources.

This is the context of Jesus teaching in Matthew 18. He wishes to draw on this harsh imagery to describe the utter foolishness of someone who, on the one hand, expects almost infinite mercy from his creditor but, on the other hand, he himself is unwilling to forgive one of his debtors 1/100th of the amount he himself was forgiven. Jesus' teaching therefore is a stern admonition to all who wish to follow Him: in order not to be judged and thrown into prison, His followers are to forgive unconditionally and totally.

Since everyone is under the debt of sin, no one can possibly repay back the debt owed to God for sin. So in this passage, as in others, Jesus places a condition on being forgiven by the Father: should one wish to be forgiven of sin, one must forgive one's brother from the heart. No forgiveness? No eternal inheritance.

For the Reformers, the context of this passage is speaking of judgment and eternal punishment. Since it is speaking in such a context for them, then the prison and torturers being referred to in verses 30 and 34 can only refer to hell. But if that is the case, there is a significant problem for Svendsen's thesis regarding *heos hou*. The action in the main clause of being thrown into prison and handing him over to the torturers cannot therefore cease since the punishment in the debtor's prison and the punishment that Our Lord cautions about is an eternal one.

A number of commentators have confirmed this view. John Calvin, for instance, says this about Matthew 18:34:

> "Delivered him to the tormentors, till he should pay all that he owed." The Papists are very ridiculous in endeavoring to light the fire of purgatory by the word 'till'; for it is certain that Christ here points out not temporal death, by which the judgment of God may be satisfied, but eternal death.[1]

A popular early eighteenth century Protestant commentary concurs with this view:

> He delivered him to the tormentors, till he should pay all that was due unto him. Though the wickedness was very great, his lord laid upon him no other punishment than the payment of his own debt. Those that will not come up to the terms of the gospel need be no more miserable than to be left open to the law, and to let that have its course against them. See how the punishment answers the sin; he that would not forgive shall not be forgiven;

---

[1] John Calvin, *Commentary on Matthew*

> He delivered him to the tormentors; the utmost he could do to his fellow servant was but to cast him into prison, but he was himself delivered to the tormentors. Note, The power of God's wrath to ruin us, goes far beyond the utmost extent of any creature's strength and wrath. The reproaches and terrors of his own conscience would be his tormentors, for that is a worm that dies not; devils, the executioners of God's wrath, that are sinners' tempters now, will be their tormentors forever.[1]

John Wesley also came to the same conclusion:

> His lord delivered him to the tormentors - Imprisonment is a much severer punishment in the eastern countries than in ours. State criminals, especially when condemned to it, are not only confined to a very mean and scanty allowance, but are frequently loaded with clogs or heavy yokes, so that they can neither lie nor sit at ease: and by frequent scourgings and sometimes rackings are brought to an untimely end. Till he should pay all that was due to him - That is, without all hope of release, for this he could never do. How observable is this whole account; as well as the great inference our Lord draws from it: The debtor was freely and fully forgiven; He wilfully and grievously offended; His pardon was retracted, the whole debt required, and the offender delivered to the tormentors for ever.[2]

The *People's New Testament*, a nineteenth century, commentary concurs:

> His lord . . . delivered him to the tormenters. This language is to be interpreted by customs that still prevail in the East, where torture is still used to compel debtors to confess where they have hidden treasures that they are suspected of having concealed. In both Greece and Rome torture was used on prisoners to compel confession, and until within a century or two it was still employed in Great Britain and Europe. "Till he should pay all." As,

---

[1] Matthew Henry, *Commentary on the Whole Bible (1721)*, Commentary on Matt 18:34
[2] John Wesley, *Notes on the Bible*, Commentary on Matthew 18:34

however, he never could pay, he was condemned to perpetual imprisonment.[1]

Consistent with Svendsen's own denominational leanings (Reformed Protestantism) and its founder (John Calvin), Matthew 18:34 is one instance in the New Testament where Protestant commentators have consistently maintained that the action before *heos hou* continues - if only to distance themselves sufficiently from the purgatorial flames.

Acts 25:20-21

> Being at a loss how to investigate such matters, I asked whether he was willing to go to Jerusalem and there stand trial on these matters. But when Paul appealed to be held in custody for the Emperor's decision, I ordered him to be kept in custody *until* I [might] send him to Caesar.' (Act 25:20-21)

This passage can suggest a cessation of the action in the main clause since the 'custody' that is being spoken of is Festus' direct "keeping" of Paul. Once Festus releases Paul to Caesar, Paul can no longer be said to be kept by Festus. However, this is not the only interpretation. The continuation of the main clause in this passage (being kept in custody) is terminated by the aorist subjunctive [I might send]. Since the infinitive *threisqai* (to be kept) is in the present tense, it is not unlike Matthew 1:25 in that the text does not demand that Paul be released from custody once he is sent to Rome. On the contrary, it refers only to Festus' command to restrain Paul while under Festus' jurisdiction. We would expect that Paul would remain "kept," that is, "in custody," for an indefinite period of time even after arriving in Rome.

This interpretation becomes even more persuasive when one considers that it was Paul who himself requested to be held for the Emperor's decision. Earlier in the passage, St. Paul asserts: "I am

---

[1] *The People's New Testament*, Commentary on Matthew 18:34

now standing before Caesar's court, where I ought to be tried" (Act 25:10). By this statement, Paul reminds Festus that he is a Roman citizen who is now standing before Caesar's court and consequently has a right to appeal to Caesar for adjudication of his case. The fact that he is now being kept in Caesar's court (Act 25:10) and awaiting the Emperor's decision (Act 25:21) implies that his corresponding custody is predicated on his appeal to the Emperor. As such, he is to be held in custody until his case is eventually tried and settled by the Emperor, after which he will be either acquitted or convicted. Hence, the custody which is spoken of in Acts 25:21 could conceivably continue after *heos hou*. At the very least, such an interpretation cannot be ruled out.

2 Peter 1:19

> So we have the prophetic word made more sure, to which you do well to pay attention as to a lamp shining in a dark place, until the day dawns and the morning star arises in your hearts. (2Pe 1:19)

Commenting on this passage, Svendsen proposes that this passage is:

> [A reference] to the parousia [the Second Coming], after which it will no longer be necessary to turn to the words of the prophets as a guide which navigates us through a dark place; Christ himself will supercede such need.[1]

While this is certainly a very possible interpretation of the passage, it is by no means the only one. In fact, there are cogent explanations which vindicate a continuance of the main clause. One commentator offered this view:

> [In] 2 Peter 1:19, oil lamps do not automatically go out at dawn, and some 'darkened' places need lamps even in the daytime. Of course this is being used as a simile for needing illumination (receiving knowledge) at night (during the present age) by a lamp

---

[1] Svendsen, 57

(the prophetic word = the bible) until the sun rises (the Messianic age) when we will be much more greatly illuminated. But that does not mean that the bible as we have it will become utterly superfluous! I am sure it will remain an important historical document to point back to for how we were dealt with.[1]

The issue here hinges on the references "day" and "morning star." If these references do indeed point to the second coming of Christ, then Svendsen's argument stands. On the other hand, if, as the above commentator suggests, the "day" and "star" refer to the inauguration of the Messianic age, then it is difficult to understand how a Protestant can maintain the view which Svendsen does. The coming of the Messianic age does not, in fact, exempt us from studying the Bible, the prophetic word of God. Hence, it is more likely that the action in the main clause does not cease but continues well into the Messianic age.

The point at hand which is simply this: there are varying interpretations to this passage which may cause one to view "attending to the prophetic word" beyond *heos hou*. Even in Calvin's day, he met with various interpretations of the passage:

> This passage is, indeed, attended with some more difficulty; for it may be asked, what is the day which Peter mentions? To some it seems to be the clear knowledge of Christ, when men fully acquiesce in the gospel; and the darkness they explain as existing, when they, as yet, hesitate in suspense, and the doctrine of the gospel is not received as indubitable; as though Peter praised those Jews who were searching for Christ in the Law and the Prophets, and were advancing, as by this preceding light towards Christ, the Sun of righteousness, as they were praised by Luke, who, having

---

[1] Dennis Hukel, Critical Consultant/Translator, Lockman Foundation

heard Paul preaching, searched the Scripture to know whether what he said was true.[1]

The translator of Calvin's work also provides us with yet another view of the dawn of the 'day-star' which he interprets as the Gospel itself, but more importantly, the view that is being advanced here once again supports the action in the main clause (attending to the prophetic word) continuing through *heos hou*.

x. *Heos hou* used between 100 BC-100 AD

In his thesis, Svendsen examines the construction *heos hou* [and *heos hotou*] in the literature outside of the New Testament between 100 B.C and 100 AD. Before addressing some of the evidence within or just outside of this period, there exist innumerable difficulties with Svendsen's methodology which should be addressed first.

Firstly, as already intimated, the Septuagint refutes an absolute and unequivocal understanding which excludes the possibility of continuance of the action in the main clause. As Svendsen himself points out, *heos hou* is used to indicate a temporal occurrence where the action of the main clause is continued through the subordinate clause (Cf. 2Ch 29:28; Psa 71:7; Psa 93:15; Psa 112:8; Psa 141:8). For instance, Psalm 112:8 reads:

> His heart is upheld, he will not fear, until he looks with satisfaction on his adversaries. (Psa 112:8)

Obviously his heart will be upheld and will continue not to fear after he looks with satisfaction on his adversaries.

Nevertheless, Svendsen suggests that relying on the Septuagint to allow *heos hou* to be understood as a continuance of the action after *heos hou* during the New Testament period is etymologically

---

[1] John Calvin, *Commentary on 2 Peter* [1:19]. (Translated and edited by John Owen, Thrusslington, 1855).

unsustainable, resulting in a kind of 'semantic obsolescence.' It is more cogent, Svendsen suggests, given the apparent wide gap of time between the writing of the Septuagint (i.e. during the reign of Ptolemy II Philadephus 283-264 BC) and the Gospel of Matthew (50 AD), to instead restrict the population under study to the 200 years surrounding the birth of Christ. Svendsen writes:

> [If] we can find corroborating evidence of this usage in the literature of the century just prior to the composition of Matthew's Gospel, then the prospect becomes stronger that Matthew may have understood this phrase in his gospel in the same way. Thirdly, if this usage for the phrase can also be found in the literature contemporaneous to Matthew's gospel (i.e. the first century A.D), then there can be little objection to seeing this same usage in the passage in question, and Mary's perpetual virginity becomes a strong exegetical option. While we do find support for this usage in the LXX there are nevertheless no clear examples of this usage for at least a century and a half before Matthew wrote his Gospel; nor up to half a century afterwards.[1]

However, many scholars and academics do not share Svendsen's concerns. A number of correspondents to our survey, for instance, objected to the fact that the Septuagint usage or the usage of the Greek fathers would be somehow subordinated in significance to the 200-year period surrounding the birth of Christ chosen by Svendsen.

Moreover, Svendsen appears to have used only the *The Thesaurus Linguae Graecae* database on CD-ROM to conduct his research, which, although housing virtually all ancient Greek texts from the 8th century BC to 600 A.D, does not take into account the epigraphic and papyrus data. Participating on the condition of anonymous contribution, one scholar put his reservations this way:

---

[1] Svendsen, 77

> I am familiar with the TLG CD-ROM disk E; the only problem with it is that it includes only literary texts, and I think it likely (a) that literary texts after 100 AD might well show the impact of the Atticist archaizing tendencies of reversion to 'purist' grammar of an earlier era; but the epigraphic evidence and especially the papyri...are much more likely to show evidence of variation from some 'normal' usage taught by schoolmasters. This is a well-known fact, so I would be wary of an argument based solely upon the literary texts included in the TLG database. As for inscriptions, they too ought to be checked, although I think any official inscriptions are more likely to reflect official grammatical usage.

Aside from the population of extant Greek texts, there is the question of equating New Testament Greek with non-New Testament Greek texts, otherwise known as 'Semitic interference.'

> Comparing the Greek of biblical texts with other contemporary texts can be like comparing 'apples and oranges', if the biblical text is: 1) translating a Semitic original; 2) written by someone used to thinking in a Semitic language; 3) imitating the usage of the Septuagint, which often displays a Semitized Greek. In such cases it is necessary to look at the meaning of the underlying Hebrew or Aramaic preposition...Some have alleged that the Greek of the infancy narratives of Matthew and Luke, for various reasons, is more subject to 'Semitic interference' than the NT in general. If this is the case, even comparing the usage of Matthew in the infancy narrative with that of, say the epistles of Paul, would be an 'apples and oranges' problem.[1]

One commentator noted the following regarding Svendsen's downplay of the Septuagint's influence on the New Testament:

> It would be as if a modern writer echoed Shakespeare and some critic discounted the possibility of a Shakespearean connection

---

[1] Patrick J. Madden, M.A., M.Div., Ph.D., Director, Greco Institute

because he [Shakespeare] was not 20th century. Matthew read the Septuagint and reflected its style.

Another participant in the scholarly survey not only echoed this observation, but introduced the Greek Fathers of the Church into the equation, as we have already done, noting:

> [since] this is their language, the same as the New Testament, with the same degree of comfort as we have with English and our various nuances of meaning for phrases, it would be negligent to skip over their interpretation of the virginity of Mary prior to the birth of Jesus and afterwards. The other factor with the New Testament Greek is the Semitic mind involved in most of its composition, and that colors much of the meaning implied in words.[1]

As it is, it is likely that parts of the Septuagint are, by Svendsen's own (and arbitrary) standard, not exempt from the relevant population he is considering. He is counting on the Septuagint being written well before 100 BC yet this is not at all established. There is much debate over when the different parts of the Septuagint were written spanning centuries i.e. 285-100 BC. Consequently, the closer the writing of the Septuagint is to the arbitrary year Svendsen has established for his search (i.e. 100 BC), the less he can dismiss the Septuagint's impact on his thesis.

Indeed, all lexicons consulted in this study referred to the Septuagint in discussing this issue. It is almost inconceivable how the Septuagint's influence cannot have a significant effect on the usage of Greek words and phrases in the New Testament.

Since there is no dispute regarding the fact that, as far as the Septuagint is concerned, *heos hou* can be understood as a continuation of the action in the main clause, we now turn our attention to the non-biblical texts to see if some other information

---

[1] Correspondence on file at Catholic Legate

can be introduced to challenge the proposition under discussion. Before doing so, however, it would be beneficial to recall a few facts collected thus far.

First, let us recall that the meaning of *heos hou* as a continuation of the action in the main clause is relatively rare in the Septuagint (just under 10%). Our earlier extrapolation yielded 1.44 projected occurrences in the New Testament. Even without finding an instance of *heos hou*, this factor by itself would make Svendsen's thesis itself statistically irrelevant. Yet, we discovered that we could find in the New Testament, excluding Matthew 1:25, one instance where the understanding of *heos hou* likely contradicts Svendsen's thesis (Mat 18:34), and two other passages where there is also such a possibility (Act 25:20-21, 2Pe 1:19).

As already discussed, Svendsen chose the period between 100 BC and 100 AD, which translates into 150 years before Matthew's gospel (~50 AD) and 50 years afterwards. We have already discussed the inherent bias of such a proposal, but for the sake of argument, let us keep Svendsen's model, but instead calibrate the gap somewhat more equitably. Instead of the period of 150 years before Matthew's gospel and 50 years after his Gospel, let us balance the equation and set the period as 100 years before and after Matthew's gospel. This would set the period of search between 50 BC and 150 AD.

If this range were selected as the range of significance to help form our conclusion, Svendsen's thesis would be contradicted by an interesting source in the period:

> And Aseneth was left alone with the seven virgins, and she continued to be weighed down and weep [*heos hou*] until the sun set. And she ate no bread and drank no water. And the night fell, and all (people) in the house slept, and she alone was awake and

continued to brood and to weep; and she often struck her breast with (her) hand and kept being filled with great fear and trembled (with) heavy trembling.[1]

Regarding the dating of this text, Burchard says that:

> Every competent scholar has since affirmed that Joseph and Aseneth is Jewish, with perhaps some Christian interpolations; none has put the book much after AD 200, and some have placed it as early as the second century BC As to the place of origin, the majority of scholars look to Egypt. [...] A book glorifying the mother of the proselytes ought to have been written before Greek-speaking Judaism ceased to make its impact on the ancient world and gave way to Christianity. On the other hand, Joseph and Aseneth presupposes at least some of the Septuagint, and probably all of it. It is hard to decode this into dates, but we are probably safe to say that the book was written between 100 BC and Hadrian's edict against circumcision, which has to do with the Second Jewish War of AD 132-135. If Joseph and Aseneth comes from Egypt, the Jewish revolt under Trajan (c. AD 115-117) is the latest possible date. It does appear to have originated in Egypt, since Aseneth, and not another woman such as Ruth or Rahab (Josh 2), is the heroine of the story.[2]

However, this instance is not included in Svendsen's research, and we find among his chosen texts additional evidence to challenge his thesis. Svendsen writes:

> All five instances of *heos hou* in the pseudepigraphical book The Apocalypse of Moses have this meaning....
>
> "But when I die, leave me alone and let no one touch me until the angel of the Lord shall say something about me; for God will not

---

[1] *Joseph and Aseneth*. (In Old Testament Pseudepigrapha, Vol. 2: Expansions of the "Old Testament" and Legends, Wisdom and Philosophical Literature, Prayers, Psalms, and Odes, Fragments of Lost Judeo-Hellenistic Works. Editor: James H.Charlesworth), 215
[2] Ibid.

forget me, but will seek his own vessel which he has formed. But rather rise to pray to God until I shall give back my spirit into the hands of the one who has given it (31:3-4)."

Here it seems reasonable to suppose that in both instances the action in the main clause would cease after the action in the subordinate clause, so that in both cases, the meaning is only 'until [but not after]'.[1]

In the first instance of "until," it is quite debatable indeed whether the action in the main clause ceases once "until" is reached. On the contrary, as the evidence will show, the action (i.e. "not touching him") actually continues into the subordinate clause. There is no hint at all to suggest that after the angel "says something about him," his audience would be allowed to touch him. In fact, the presumption should really be that no one should touch him ever again, because, in the next part of the sentence Adam says that God will "seek his own vessel" as if to suggest that his body is God's alone. Although he talks about his spirit in the next sentence, a vessel is normally associated with a body. If it is his body he is talking about, then the action in the main clause does continue.

And this is precisely the most cogent understanding if we were to keep reading for the next several chapters:

> But after all this, the archangel asked concerning the laying out of the remains. And God commanded that all the angels should assemble in His presence, each in his order, and all the angels assembled, some having censers in their hands, and others trumpets. And lo ! the 'Lord of Hosts' came on and four winds drew Him and cherubim mounted on the winds and the angels from heaven escorting Him and they came on the earth, where was the body of Adam. And they came to paradise and all the leaves of paradise were stirred so that all men begotten of Adam

---

[1] Svendsen, 69

slept from the fragrance save Seth alone, because he was born 'according to the appointment of God '. Then Adam's body lay there in paradise on the earth and Seth grieved exceedingly over him. (38:1-5)...Then God spake to the archangel(s) Michael, (Gabriel, Uriel, and Raphael): 'Go away to Paradise in the third heaven, and strew linen clothes and cover the body of Adam and bring oil of the 'oil of fragrance' and pour it over him. And they acted thus did the three great angels and they prepared him for burial. And God said: 'Let the body of Abel also be brought.' And they brought other linen clothes and prepared his (body) also. For he was unburied since the day when Cain his brother slew him; for wicked Cain took great pains to conceal (him) but could not, for the earth would not receive him for the body sprang up from the earth and a voice went out of the earth saying: 'I will not receive a companion body, till the earth which was taken and fashioned in me cometh to me.' At that time, the angels took it and placed it on a rock, till Adam his father was buried. And both were buried, according to the commandment of God, in the spot where God found the dust, and He caused the place to be dug for two. And God sent seven angels to paradise and they brought many fragrant spices **and placed them in the earth, and they took the two bodies and placed them in the spot which they had digged and builded**. (Apocalypse of Moses, 38:1-40:7)

As the bolded text above indicates, God sent his angels to recover Adam's body and to bury it. This means that, in the preceding chapter referred to by Svendsen, Adam did indeed expect his body to be retrieved by God, and instructed his followers therefore NOT to touch him - either before his death or after it. As such, the main action of "not touching" continues through the *heos hou*.

These two instances alone prove, rather convincingly, that Svendsen's arguments are, under fair scrutiny, highly problematic. Indeed, as we widen the search from 100 years from the referent point (whether the Birth of Christ or the writing Matthew's Gospel), Svendsen's thesis becomes more and more unsustainable as more instances of *heos hou* are found where the action in the main clause continues.

There are also examples of *heos hou* continuation slightly past Svendsen' arbitrary period of search which are relevant. For instance

1) In the third century AD (and perhaps in the late second century), Clement of Alexandria (+215) wrote:

> Accordingly, in fifteen years of Tiberius and fifteen years of Augustus; so were completed the thirty years till the time He [Jesus] suffered.[1]

Obviously the thirty years would remain completed after Jesus has died. The writer is not concerned with the temporal situation after the "until" has been reached. As such, the best expression in understanding this particular text is to substitute "till" with "before:" as in "so were completed the thirty years before Jesus suffered."

Clement, like the author of Matthew 1:25, is not concerned with the actions or non-actions of the main clause the once temporal point has been reached, in this case, Jesus' death, in Mary's case, her giving birth. The point in this example is that the 30 years will continue to remain completed after Jesus suffered.

Another source is the apocryphal text known as the *Acts of Thomas* which was written between 200 and 225 AD:

> Now when the king heard these things from the bridegroom and the bride, he rent his clothes and said unto them that stood by him: Go forth quickly and go about the whole city, and take and bring me that man that is a sorcerer who by ill fortune came unto this city; for with mine own hands I brought him into this house, and I told him to pray over this mine ill-starred daughter; and whoso findeth and bringeth him to me, I will give him

---

[1] Clement of Alexandria, *Stromateis*, 1.21

> whatsoever he asketh of me. They went, therefore and went about seeking him, and found him not; for he had set sail. They went also unto the inn where he had lodged and found there the flute-girl weeping and afflicted because he had not taken her with him. And when they told her the matter that had befallen with the young people she was exceeding glad at hearing it, and put away her grief and said: Now have I also found rest here. And she rose up and went unto them, and was with them a long time, until [*heos hou*] they had instructed the king also. And many of the brethren also gathered there until they heard the report of the apostle, that he was come unto the cities of India and was teaching there: and they departed and joined themselves unto him. (*Acts of Thomas*, 16)

In this instance, at the very least, there is no mention of the flute-girl departing from the men's presence once they had informed the king. It is more than likely that she stayed with them at least some time after the king was informed.

3) Another instance is:

> And when they had journeyed a little way he dismissed the colts, saying: I say unto you the inhabiters of the desert, depart unto your pastures, for if I had had need of all, ye would all have gone with me; but now go unto your place wherein ye dwell. And they departed quietly until [*heos hou*] they were no more seen. (*Acts of Thomas*, 70)

The colts will continue to depart even after they were no longer seen.

4) Further on in the same text:

> And the king seeing the abundance of water said to Judas: Ask thy God that he deliver me from this death, that I perish not in the flood. And the apostle prayed and said: Thou that didst bind this element (nature) and gather it into one place and send it forth into divers lands; that didst bring disorder into order, that grantest mighty works and great wonders by the hands of Judas thy servant; that hast mercy on my soul, that I may always receive

> thy brightness; that givest wages unto them that have laboured; thou saviour of my soul, restoring it unto its own nature that it may have no fellowship with hurtful things; that hast always been the occasion of life: do thou restrain this element that it lift not up itself to destroy; for there are some of them that stand here who shall believe on thee and live. And when he had prayed, the water was swallowed up by little and little, and the place became dry. And when Misdaeus saw it he commanded him to be taken to the prison: Until [*heos hou*] I shall consider how he must be used. (*Acts of Thomas*, 141)

Judas might very well remain in prison even after consideration is given to his plight. The use of *heos hou* here does not imply any cessation of the action of the main clause.

5) Finally, we can consider:

> My mouth sufficeth not to praise thee, neither am I able to conceive the care and providence (carefulness) which hath been about me from thee which thou hast had for me). For I desired to gain riches, but thou by a vision didst show me that they are full of loss and injury to them that gain them and I believed thy showing, and continued in the poverty of the world until [*heos hou*] thou, the true riches wert revealed unto me, who didst fill both me and the rest that were worthy of thee with thine own riches and set free thine own from care and anxiety. I have therefore fulfilled thy commandments, O Lord, and accomplished thy will, and become poor and needy and a stranger and a bondman and set at nought and a prisoner and hungry and thirsty and nalied and unshod, and I have toiled for thy sake, that my confidence might not perish and my hope that is in thee might not be confounded and my much labour might not be in vain and my weariness not be counted for nought: let not my prayers and my continual fastings perish, and my great zeal toward thee; let not my seed of wheat be changed for tares out of thy land, let not the enemy carry it away and mingle his own tares therewith; for thy land verily receiveth not his tares, neither indeed can they be laid up in thine houses. (*Acts of Thomas*, 145)

Did he not continue in the poverty of the world after the Lord, the true riches, was revealed to him? Yes, most certainly.

Since we are discussing how Greek speakers working with the LXX as their current and official text of the Old Testament, we can return to St John Chrysostom. The great bishop cites the verse using *heos hou*, but in asking the question (of why the Scripture uses the phrase), the word he uses for "until" is *heos* alone, showing that for him there was no difference in the meaning between these two expressions.

As a result, it seems that Svendsen must argue that the particular nuance he is excluding in the test period did exist right up to his cut-off date, then disappeared without a trace within his target period, only to re-emerge immediately afterwards.

xi. Conclusion

The evidence presented here on *heos hou* refutes the novel thesis proposed by Svendsen. No determination of the meaning of *heos* and related forms can be made without the context of the passage being involved. The decision on whether *heos* terminates or continues the action of the main verb depends on several factors, including whether one or the other makes logical sense; agrees with the context; agrees with the grammatical construction of the passage; does not contradict other known facts; etc. In conclusion, two things can be asserted regarding *heos* and *heos hou*:

(1) that *heos* and *heos hou* do not always terminate the action in the main clause;

and

(2) that *heos* and *heos hou* are not used differently in Greek grammar.

My own conclusion[1] is that *hou* is indeed found in the original Matthew (notwithstanding the variants) and probably used **for emphasis**. To be precise, the emphasis is on the negative: there was no intercourse during the betrothal and pregnancy, before the birth, hence the use of the imperfect tense, which is unique to Matthew 1:25 (in the New Testament). The choice of the end point (birth, rather than "their purification" as in Luke 2:22) further strengthens this interpretation.

In view of the totality of the data presented in this comprehensive survey, we can maintain that Mary's virginity is not compromised by the use of *heos hou* in Matthew 1:25.

d) Criticism and rebuttal

The Helvidian view has become widely accepted, not only among Evangelical Protestants but also among Protestants of historic denominations, as well as several well-known Roman Catholic scholars. We have seen that taking the *adelphoi* to be the children of Joseph and Mary born after Jesus has the advantage to let the modern reader read the text (Matthew 1:25; Luke 2:7; the passages referring to the "brothers and sisters") in what seems to be the most obvious and natural sense.

A related aspect of this approach is that Helvidian Christians tend to read the story of Joseph and Mary (Matthew 1 and Luke 1) as follows:

> **It is the story of two young people who are (hopefully) in love: Joseph is maybe 22-25 and Mary 15-18. They are excited to get married as all young people are, when an unexpected situation develops: Mary is just then chosen by God to facilitate the incarnation and accepts to be**

---

[1] Cleenewerck's, noting again that this entire section is taken (with permission and minor modifications) from the excellent research done by John Pacheco of Catholic Legate.

> pregnant with Jesus. Joseph learns of the news and wants to put Mary away. He is probably less than happy because his plans are quite upset, but well, he still marries Mary as the angel tells him, but he does (cannot) have marital intercourse during the pregnancy. Finally, Jesus is born! After getting settled, they can continue with their original plans and have a normal life and many other children.

Even a Roman Catholic influenced movie such as Jesus of Nazareth (by Zeffirelli), in which Joseph is a young man, tends to corroborate this narrative. The celebrated Roman Catholic Archbishop Fulton Sheen offered the following description:

> Joseph was probably a young man, strong, virile, athletic, handsome, chaste, and disciplined, the kind of man one sees ... working at a carpenter's bench. Instead of being a man incapable of loving, he must have been on fire with love... Young girls in those days, like Mary, took vows to love God uniquely, and so did young men, of whom Joseph was one so preeminent as to be called the 'just.' Instead then of being dried fruit to be served on the table of the King, he was rather a blossom filled with promise and power. He was not in the evening of life, but in its morning, bubbling over with energy, strength, and controlled passion.[1]

Now, this may seem perfectly sensible to many Christians, while others may sense that something is not quite right with this narrative.

What is certain is that the Epiphanian/Orthodox account is quite different:

> **It is the story of two holy people chosen by God in the fullness of time: Joseph is a widower of a 'certain age' (at least 55) and Mary a virgin who was raised in the Temple,**

---

[1] Fulton Sheen, *The World's First Love*, 77-78. This is an early text, written before Sheen discovered and in fact attached himself to the Eastern Rite (with its Epiphanian tradition).

begin 14-15 at that time, now outside the Temple and commissioned to take part in the weaving of the great curtain. During their arranged betrothal, an unexpected situation does develop: Mary is chosen by God and conceives a child by the overshadowing of the Spirit. Joseph, who is historically and mystically called "Son of Jacob" and "Son of David" learns of the pregnancy from Mary herself, and even though he believes in the miracle, he is afraid to take her into his house as wife (as planned), precisely because he responds like Jacob of old:

"Jacob was afraid: and he feareth, and saith, 'How fearful {is} this place; this is nothing but a house of God, and this a gate of the heavens.'" (Gen 28:17)

But the angel instructs Joseph the Just not to be overwhelmed, but to take Mary into his house, yet without marital relations. Joseph accepts this and also accepts to adopt Jesus as his own son and into his own clan. Finally, Jesus is born! After getting settled, Joseph will live another 25 years (or so) and die a blessed death in the embrace of Jesus and Mary. She then become a widow but continues to belong to Joseph's clan which includes Joseph's children as well as cousins, uncles and aunts.

Admittedly, these are different stories and almost a different cast of characters. The Epiphanian criticism against the Helvidian story is that it projects and imposes modern linguistic and cultural ideas on an ancient text. After all, Orthodox Christians have never had any issues with James and other being called "the brothers of the Lord," because this is how they have been remembered and celebrated in the Eastern Churches. What is puzzling for the 'Epiphanians' is how glibly this ancient majority view is dismissed in favor of an interpretation that create a host of other biblical difficulties. Why, it may be asked, do Protestants rely on the wisdom and integrity of Eusebius and Athanasius for Christian history and the canon, and also rely on what can only be called 'the Greek Orthodox tradition' for their manuscripts, and yet appear so intent on seeing Joseph and Mary engage in the sexual act?

At the popular level, the answer may well be that Evangelical Protestants have no idea that there is such a thing as the Epiphanian view, or who Eusebius might be. At the level of apologetics, we often observe a lack of scholarly rigor, as in the following (and rather typical) article:

> The earliest evidence for the teaching that Mary was a perpetual virgin occurs in the writings of the early church father Jerome who was born in AD 347 and died about AD 419. Prior to Jerome there is no evidence that the early church taught anything other than the scriptural record - that Jesus had siblings: flesh and blood brothers and sisters. Some have claimed that Origen was the first early father who wrote that Mary was a perpetual virgin, but a close examination of his statement reveals that is not true.[1]

This is tragically misinformed and ultimately deceptive. Also, at the level of apologetics, the fact that the Orthodox voice is rarely heard does not help, and the main purpose of this book is to fill this void. As a result, Evangelical Protestants generally interact with Roman Catholic apologists and their preference for the Hieronymian view. In the process, several robust arguments (see our own presentation of these arguments in this book) are never addressed.

Often, Evangelical Protestants are content to conclude that *adelphoi* cannot mean "cousin" and that the idea of Mary's perpetual virginity is a Roman Catholic myth related to the 'obnoxious' (in their view) discipline of clerical celibacy. Another problem is when Helvidians readily accept the view that the *Protevangelium of James* (and similar sources) are in fact heretical (docetic) writings with no historical or theological value, as in one typical comment:

---

[1] Never Thirsty, accessed at http://www.neverthirsty.org/pp/bible-questions/answer01028.html

> The "Epiphanian" position is based on the apocryphal and heretical (Docetic) work, the Protevangelium of James.[1]

In a similar vein, Ben Witherington (otherwise a respected scholar) writes:

> The Protoevangelium of James from the 2nd century AD is a classic example of the effect of a later Christian ascetical movement on the representation of Mary and Joseph.[2]

This type of statement, sadly, tends to be accepted at face value, even though we are dealing with the post-apostolic age, a time of persecutions, during which the churches are recognized as having preserved and authenticated our sacred Scriptures.

Further, the fact that prominent Roman Catholic scholars such as Meier (and more cautiously Brown) have embraced the Helvidian view[3] has given further comfort to our Helvidian friends.

In my view, the challenge for Orthodox/Epiphanian Christians is that arguing on individual points may not be enough. What is needed here is a transformation of one's reception of the entire biblical corpus, to become a 'spiritual Israelite in whom there is no deceit.' Speaking as an educator who has taught introductory courses in Relativity and Quantum Physics, the comparison comes to mind that replacing the old mindset with the more advanced one is indeed an effort as well as an eye (and mind) opening experience. The explanatory power of these modern theories overwhelms

---

[1] Discussion accessed at
http://www.beliefnet.com/columnists/bibleandculture/2009/07/the-dead-shall-have-their-say-more-on-the-james-ossuary.html

[2] Ben Witherington, *Did Jesus found a Dynasty--- James Tabor's new book*, accessed at http://benwitherington.blogspot.com/2006/04/did-jesus-found-dynasty-ja_114493136136345584.html

[3] Both of them priests remaining in good standing with Rome

classical physics and is required for advanced applications and data interpretation.

Likewise, it is in the liturgical life of the Church which is the place of the Spirit where biblical interpretation takes places, can one perceive the beauty and wholeness of the divine tapestry. As Irenaeus once wrote:

> Their manner of acting is just as if one, when a beautiful image of a king has been constructed by some skilful artist out of precious jewels, should then take this likeness of the man all to pieces, should rearrange the gems, and so fit them together as to make them into the form of a dog or of a fox, and even that but poorly executed; and should then maintain and declare that this was the beautiful image of the king which the skilful artist constructed, pointing to the jewels which had been admirably fitted together by the first artist to form the image of the king, but have been with bad effect transferred by the latter one to the shape of a dog, and by thus exhibiting the jewels, should deceive the ignorant who had no conception what a king's form was like, and persuade them that that miserable likeness of the fox was, in fact, the beautiful image of the king. In like manner do these persons patch together old wives' fables, and then endeavour, by violently drawing away from their proper connection, words, expressions, and parables whenever found, to adapt the oracles of God to their baseless fictions.[1]

e) Recent proponents

If it was useful to make specific mention of recent proponents of the Epiphanian view (since it is little-known in Western Christianity), such is not the case with the Helvidian view. We have already encountered several recent proponents, notably Dr Eric Svendsen (of *heos hou* contribution) and Fr John Meier. Our discussion of the

---

[1] Irenaeus, *Against Heresies*, VIII

Helvidian arguments was an attempt to present the best arguments of recent scholarship (notably *heos hou* in Matthew 1:25 and the meaning of *adelphos* in the New Testament) while providing a robust rebuttal.

In my view, the Helvidian arguments cannot and should not be summarily dismissed, even as we (Epiphanians and Hieronymians) ask those on the opposing side to do likewise. However, even the cumulative effect of these arguments (some stronger than others) must be balanced by the comprehensive biblical, historical and theological framework proposed by the "traditional" side.

4) THE HIERONYMIAN VIEW

a) History

The Hieronymian view is named after St Jerome, since he was indeed the originator of this interpretation of the relationship between Jesus and his *adelphoi*.

It is precisely when Helvidius began promoting his own views that Jerome felt compelled to publish his rebuttal (about 383 AD). However, Jerome did not do so on the basis of the Epiphanian position, in part because he considered the apocryphal sources expounding this view as unworthy of consideration and reliance.[1] Instead, Jerome put forward the view that the *adelphoi* were neither uterine siblings nor adoptive/step siblings, but rather cousins of the Lord through Mary of Clopas.

At the outset, it should be said that even though St Jerome was not the easiest of man, he is honored as a saint and great scholar by Roman Catholics and Eastern Orthodox alike. Orthodox Christians are certainly not forbidden to adopt his view as more likely than the Epiphanian, although it should be noted that the liturgical texts of the Orthodox Church simply assume the Epiphanian view and the overall validity of the account found in the *Protevangelium of James*. Conversely, Catholics (notably Eastern Catholics) may well prefer the Epiphanian view, while noting that the Latin West has historically favored Jerome's view.

St Jerome has a wonderfully witty style, worthy of citation:

> In short, what I want to know is why Joseph refrained until the day of her delivery?

---

[1] St Jerome was open about his extreme preference for virginity and negative view of sexual intercourse.

Helvidius will of course reply, "Because he heard the angel say, 'that which is conceived in her is of the Holy Spirit'" [Matt. 1:20b]. And in turn we rejoin that he had certainly heard him say, "Joseph, you son of David, fear not to take unto you Mary your wife" [Matt. 1:20a]. The reason why he was forbidden to forsake his wife was that he might not think her an adulteress. Is it true then, that he was ordered not to have intercourse with his wife? Is it not plain that the warning was given him that he might not be separated from her? And could the just man dare, he says, to think of approaching her, when he heard that the Son of God was in her womb?

Excellent! We are to believe then that the same man who gave so much credit to a dream that he did not dare to touch his wife, yet afterwards, when he had learnt from the shepherds that the angel of the Lord had come from heaven and said to them, "Be not afraid: for behold I bring you good tidings of great joy which shall be to all people, for there is born to you this day in the city of David a Savior, which is Christ the Lord" [Luke 2:10ff], and when the heavenly host had joined with him in the chorus "Glory to God in the highest, and on earth peace among men of good will" [Luke 2:14], and when he had seen just Simeon embrace the infant and exclaim, "Now let you your servant depart, O Lord, according to your word in peace: for mine eyes have seen your salvation" [Luke 2:29], and when he had seen Anna the prophetess, the Magi, the Star, Herod, the angels; Helvidius, I say, would have us believe that Joseph, though well acquainted with such surprising wonders, dared to touch the temple of God, the abode of the Holy Spirit, the mother of his Lord?[1]

Jerome was a very 'intense' student of the Holy Scriptures, having left the Church of Rome (of which he remained a faithful, if delocalized, presbyter) and therefore the city of Rome (with all its

---

[1] Jerome, *Against Helvidius*

temptations) to move to Palestine, learn the Hebrew language and produce the monumental Vulgate.

It is fair to say that Jerome was a strong proponent of virginity over marriage and would have preferred to avoid portraying St Joseph as a widower with many children of his own. However, other considerations led Jerome to formulate his alternative to the Epiphanian view.

The most relevant passage in Jerome's treatise is as follows:

> Now here we have the explanation of what I am endeavouring to show, how it is that the sons of Mary, the sister of our Lord's mother, who though not formerly believers afterwards did believe, can be called brethren of the Lord. Possibly the case might be that one of the brethren believed immediately while the others did not believe until long after, and that one Mary was the mother of James and Joses, namely, "Mary of Clopas," who is the same as the wife of Alphæus, the other, the mother of James the Less.

Here, St Jerome suggests that James and Joses were the sons of Mary of Clopas who was (as he writes), Mary's sister. In other words, he sees them as maternal cousins, and identifies this James with the Apostle James of Alphaeus.

Let us now consider the details of Jerome's arguments as well as possible variants long the same lines.

b) Clues and Proposal

The Hieronymian view first proposes that the James and Joses/Joseph described as the *adelphoi* of Jesus (Mar 6:3) are the same as "James the younger/the Less and Joses" (Mar 15:40). Their mother Mary is not the mother of Jesus but rather a relative of Mary, being the wife or possibly daughter of Clopas.

According to the strict Hieronymian model (Jerome's own proposal), Mary of Clopas is seen as the sister of Mary (the mother of Jesus), based on a possible reading of John 19:25. This proposal makes James and Joses maternal cousins but introduces the near impossibility of two sisters being given the same name.

If we are going to explore the Hieronymian option seriously, we must recognize that (1) Mary the mother James the Less and Joses cannot be the sister of Mary the mother of Jesus whose sister may simply not be named; and (2) that if Mary's sister is the same as Mary of Clopas, then "sister" (ἀδελφή) must mean close relative rather than blood-sisters, and this would make James and Joses something else than strict cousins; (3) the strongest "cousin" connection may actually exist not on the maternal side but on the paternal side, through Clopas.

This Clopas, according to Hegesippus was Joseph's brother which is why Simon/Symeon, the second bishop of Jerusalem (possibly mentioned in Mark 6:3, but Symeon was a very common name) was in fact Jesus' cousin (via Joseph treated as adoptive father).

In this case, what we have is a different kind of Hieronymian model, which some have called (improperly in my view) the Hegesippian-Hieronymian model.

Also, James the Less (son or grand-son of Clopas?) is often identified with James "the brother of the Lord / James the Just" and with the Apostle James of Alphaeus (of the Twelve, mentioned 4 times in the New Testament).

The reasons advanced for his identification is that James "the brother of the Lord" seems to be identified as an Apostle by St Paul:

> But I did not see any other of the apostles, only James the brother of the Lord. (Gal 1:19)

Finally, Clopas (who may well be identified with the Cleopas of Luke 24:18; alternatively rendered as Cleophas) is identified with Alphaeus for linguistic reasons.

c) Key arguments and hinges

The original view set forth by Jerome relied on the two proposals:

(1) That James and Joses/Joseph of Mark 6:5 are the same as the sons of Mary of Clopas in Mark 15:40.

(2) That there are 3 women in John 19:25: Mary the mother of Jesus | her sister who is also called Mary (of Clopas) | Mary Magdalene.

The identification of this James with the Apostle James of Alphaeus and with James of Jerusalem is important but secondary.

However, (2) is unlikely. A more probable harmonization would be to identify Salome (Mar 15:40) as Mary's sister, which would have the effect of making the Apostles James and John (of Zebedee) the Lord's maternal cousins.

This is why Hegesippus' information that Clopas was the brother of Joseph has the effect of maintaining the cousin relationship but not on the maternal side: whether Mary was the wife or daughter of Clopas is somewhat irrelevant since either way, James the Less and Joses would have been the Lord's paternal cousins. Here, the Epiphanian argument that Joseph was truly the father of Jesus in the full power of the adoptive sense is also relevant.

We can also ask what would be the implication of Joseph having died prior to the beginning of the Lord's ministry, which very few scholars would dispute. If indeed Mary was then a widow with an only son (Jesus), it would have been normal for her (and Jesus as well) to be further coopted into the household of Clopas. This would explain why these *adelphoi* were from then on so closely associated with Mary and Jesus.

At this juncture, we must discuss the brother (*adelphos*) versus cousin (*anepsios*) distinction in Greek. A word, however, needs to be said about (1) above, namely the identification of the James and Joses of Mark 6:3 with the James the Less and Joses of Mark 15:40. This is, paradoxically, both the great strength and weakness of the Hieronymian view. It is certainly tempting to conclude that these people are the same, because 'James and Joses' appear as a pair only twice in the Gospel of Mark. And yet, we must ask why Mark is qualifying the James of 15:40 as "James the Less." We have already discussed this problem with Jewish first names (deploring in passing the non-existence of last names): some first names were extremely common (James being one of them) and some people had two names. In the Gospels, we seem to have 4 or 5 individual named "James," which makes our task very complicated indeed. Even the second-century Christian historian Hegesippus noted (bold added):

> James, the brother of the Lord, succeeded to the government of the Church in conjunction with the apostles. He has been called the Just by all from the time of our Saviour to the present day; **for there were many that bore the name of James.**[1]

One way to cut to this Gordian knot is to take into account who the Evangelists were writing for. Mark was quite raw and yet specific in his account, perhaps because he was somewhat in a rush to transcribe St Peter's memories. He was also interested in mentioning those people who might be known by this audience (most probably the Church of Rome).

What is certain is that James the Just, the bishop of Jerusalem, the one famously styled "brother of the Lord" was universally known and respected. The side effect of this premise that Mary of Clopas is unlikely to have been the mother of this James, precisely because this towering figure would not have been referred to as "the Less" and his mother Mary of Clopas simply as "the mother of Joses" (Mar 15:47).

There is also a great difficulty in identifying this James the Just with the Apostle James of Alphaeus, not only because the identification of Clopas with Alphaeus is tenuous at best, but also because the office of Apostle (in the sense of the Twelve) seems different from

---

[1] Cited by Eusebius in *Ecclesiastical History*, II.23

the office of bishop (occupied by James, at the bidding of the risen Lord). Why then does St Paul call this James an Apostle if he was not an Apostle?

> But I saw none of the other apostles except James the Lord's brother. (Gal 1:19)

This is precisely the link that the Hieronymian view detects between James (from Mary of Clopas/Alphaeus), James the Apostle (of Alphaeus) and James of Jerusalem. It is certainly possible that St Paul intended to include James the Lord's brother among the Apostles in the Twelve Apostles. But it is equally plausible that "apostle" is used in the broader sense of those who are sent (including the seventy and missionaries such as Barnabas). Both Acts 6:2 (Luke being closely associated with Paul) and 1 Corinthians 15:5, the Twelve Apostles are simply called "the Twelve." St Paul often used the descriptive term "apostles" for a wider group than the Twelve, and such a group would have included the Lord's *adelphoi*. As Bauckham explains in his superb *Jude and the Relatives of Jesus in the Early Church*:

> It is true that in early Christian literature the brothers of the Lord are never called apostles, which is doubtless because they were known by another term – 'Brothers of the Lord' – which not only described them more closely but also indicated that they ranked with the apostles in status and ministry.[1]

The Hieronymian view, in spite of these challenges, is not without interest in the sense Clopas being the father of Simon (according to Hegesippus) would account not only James and Joses but also for a "Simon" being listed among the *adelphoi* in Mark 6:3. Further, the 'merger' of Joseph's family (Mary and Jesus) after his death with Clopas' family would explain why these cousins could in fact be called *adelphoi* in a Jewish cultural setting. This is important because

---

[1] Bauckham, *Jude and the Relatives of Jesus in the Early Church*, 59

another possible weakness of the Hieronymian view is the fact that cousins could have been systematically referred as *adelphoi* is problematic. In fact, the same Hegesippus who provides the helpful information that Simon was Clopas' son and therefore Jesus' cousin (*anepsios*) always referred to James as *adelphos* rather than as *anepsios*.

This point, however, is not entirely fatal to the Hieronymian viewpoint because we have at least one Scriptural (LXX) instance where *anepsios* and *adelphos* are used interchangeably:

> Then Raguel said to his wife Edna, 'How much the young man resembles my cousin Tobit!' . . . So he said to them, 'Do you know our brother Tobit?' (Tob 7:2-4)

In spite of the above, Meier (as we have seen when discussing his Helvidian arguments) remained convinced that in the New Testament, *adelphoi* cannot possibly mean *cousins*.

Even John McHugh (Roman Catholic Hieronymian) admitted:

> Honesty compels us to admit that this 'interpretation' of the word 'brother' stretches its meaning to the breaking point, and one cannot seriously expect those unconvinced of the perpetual virginity of Mary to accept it.[1]

For this reason, a truly viable Hieronymian view would involve the situation that McHugh suggested (and already mentioned), that the *anepsioi* would have become *adelphoi* when Clopas took over Joseph's family after the death of Jesus' adoptive father. Even then, the *anepsios* / *adelphos* distinction encountered in Hegesippus is not easily resolved, which may explain why Meier is willing to state that both the Helvidian and Epiphanian views are intellectually defensible, but not so the Hieronymian.

---

[1] Mc Hugh, *The Mother of Jesus in the New Testament*, 246

d) Recent proponents

In recent times, the late Fr John McHugh has been the most admired and cited proponent of the modified Hieronymian view. This view remains preferred in the Roman Catholic world (notably among apologists), but there is a growing awareness that the Epiphanian view also exists and that it is not excluded by the Catholic Magisterium.

It should be noted that a few Eastern Christians have embraced the Hieronymian view, for instance (surprisingly in my view) the late Pope Shenouda III (+2012) of the Coptic Orthodox Church.

It has been also debated whether St John Chrysostom (who first alluded to the Epiphanian view in his *Commentary on Matthew*) may have been influenced by St Jerome's treatise to change his former position and embrace the Hieronymian view. This is possible, but less than certain in view of the questionable authenticity of the two passages cited to support this theory. Such a shift on the part of the archbishop of Constantinople remains a possibility, since there is good evidence that his follower Theodoret did prefer the Hieronymian view. This final point leads us to consider the historical data with a particular attention on disputed authorities such as Hegesippus.

Below: Icon of St Jerome (French origin, exact source unknown)

Below: Contemporary Greek Orthodox icon of the flight to Egypt showing James as teenager or young man (Source: unknown)

HISTORICAL DATA

1) SECOND AND THIRD CENTURY WITNESSES

Inasmuch as we have extensively discussed the biblical data (up to the close of the first century), we now focus our attention to the critical (because early) witnesses of the second century.

a) (St) Papias of Hierapolis (c. +110)

The venerable (yet somewhat controversial) bishop of Hierapolis in Asia Minor is sometimes cited as being a witness to this controversy, but the alleged citation from his *Oracles of the Lord* is actually spurious. Svendsen did not seem aware of this and thus cited the passage in question:

> In Papias, *From the Exposition of the Oracles of the Lord (10)*, we read the following identification of the Marys at the foot of the cross in John's gospel:

> Mary the mother of the Lord; Mary the wife of Cleophas or Alphaeus, who was the mother of James the bishop and apostle, and of Simon and Thaddeus, and of one Joseph; Mary Salome, wife of Zebedee, mother of John the evangelist and James; Mary Magdalene. These four are found in the Gospel. James and Judas and Joseph were sons of an aunt of the Lord. James also and John were sons of another aunt of the Lord. Mary, mother of James the Less and Joseph, wife of Alphaeus was the sister of Mary the mother of the Lord, whom John names of Cleophas, either from her father or from the family of the clan, or for some other reason. Mary Salome is called Salome either from her husband or her village. Some affirm that she is the same as Mary of Cleophas, because she had two husbands.[1]

---

[1] Svendsen, 64

Lightfoot, however, had documented the spurious nature of this citation (which is almost self-evident), and there is no need to further discuss the case of Papias.

b) (St) Polycarp of Smyrna (+167)

A disciple of the Apostle John, Polycarp (Bishop of Smyrna in Asia Minor, one of the 7 churches of Revelation) was a contemporary of Papias and the teacher of St Irenaeus of Lyons. Nothing in the extant writings we possess today shed any light on Polycarp's views on the identity of the *adelphoi* of Jesus. In his *Against Helvidius*, St Jerome enrolls St Polycarp among those whom he lists as defenders, with him, of Mary's perpetual virginity:

> Might I not array against you the whole series of ancient writers? Ignatius, Polycarp, Irenæus, Justin Martyr, and many other apostolic and eloquent men, who against Ebion, Theodotus of Byzantium, and Valentinus, held these same views, and wrote volumes replete with wisdom. If you had ever read what they wrote, you would be a wiser man.[1]

However tempted we might be to rely on Jerome's access to a fuller and more perfectly preserved collection of these writings, we must admit that our extant writings of Polycarp do not yield any result on the topic at hand.

c) (St) Ignatius of Antioch (+ 107)

The martyred bishop of Antioch is also enrolled by St Jerome against Helvidius, but as in the case of Polycarp, we cannot confirm Ignatius' position based on our current corpus of Ignatius' letters (in their shorter or longer versions). Citing Ignatius, Origen writes:

> On this subject, I have found a fine observation in a letter of the martyr Ignatius, second bishop of Antioch after Peter, who fought

---

[1] Jerome, *Against Helvidius*, 19

with the wild beasts during the persecution in Rome. Mary's virginity was hidden from the prince of this world, hidden thanks to Joseph and her marriage to him. Her virginity was kept hidden because she was thought to be married.[1]

This text cannot be pressed to absolutely establish that Ignatius believed in Mary's continued virginity. What may be more significant is that Ignatius belongs, like the *Protevangelium of James*, to the overall Antiochian Syrian tradition. This tradition was interested in the Lord's incarnation and which had reasonable connection to the Holy Land to obtain historical information about Jesus' family background. In the end, Ignatius cannot be cited to support a specific position regarding the perpetual virginity of Mary, but he is geographically and historically associated to the documented origin of the Epiphanian view.

d) The *Gospel of Peter* (c 120-150)

The *Gospel of Peter* was a locally popular text in Syria (whose main church was Antioch according to the interesting (but sadly less than comprehensive) record preserved by Eusebius. The Antiochian-Syrian connection is not surprising in view of Peter's association with Antioch which claimed the Chief Apostle as "bishop" prior to relinquishing him to Rome.

Why is this text relevant, in view of the fact that what remains of it does not deal with the *adelphoi* of Jesus? The answer is that the learned Origen mentions that those who defended the perpetual virginity of Mary and the Epiphanian view relied on this text:

> Putting down those who appeared to be His nearest kindred, as people asked, "Is not His mother called Mary, and His brothers, James and Joseph and Simon and Judas? His sisters also, are they not all with us?" People thought, then, that He was the son of

---

[1] Origen, *Homilies on Luke*, 6: 3-4

> Joseph and Mary! However, some say, **basing this on a tradition [found] in the "Gospel according to Peter" (as it is entitled) or on "The Book of James" that the siblings of Jesus were sons of Joseph by a former wife (whom he married before Mary).** Now, those who say so wish to preserve the honor of Mary in virginity to the end, so that that her body which was appointed to minister to the Word... might not know intercourse with a man after that the Holy Spirit came into her and the power from on high overshadowed her. And I think it to be in harmony with reason that [as] Jesus was the first-fruit among men of the purity which consists in chastity, [also] Mary [was] among women, as it would be not be pious to ascribe to any other than to her the first-fruit of virginity.[1]

The most natural reading of the above is that both the *Gospel of Peter* and the *Protevangelium of James* could be used to support the Epiphanian view.

Based on what remains of the text, it appears to be an expansion of the canonical gospels. We also know that this gospel was both popular and controversial in second century Syria, thanks to the testimony preserved for us by Eusebius. There is no question that the *Gospel of Peter* is a very ancient document, probably authored between 100 and 140 AD. When its use by the Church of Rhodus was reported to the Bishop of Antioch, Serapion, he acted as one would expect of what we would now call an archbishop or metropolitan and carefully investigated the matter. Although he noted that the text was indeed associated with the heresy of Docetism, and that it should not be attributed to Peter himself, he nevertheless concluded:

> But we, brethren, gathering to what kind of heresy Marcianus belonged (...) were enabled by others who studied this very Gospel, that is, by the successors of those who began it, whom we

---

[1] Origen, *Commentary on Matthew*

call Docetae (for most of the ideas belong to their teaching) — using [the material supplied] by them, were enabled to go through it and discover that the most part indeed was in accordance with the true teaching of the Saviour, but that some things were added, which also we place below for your benefit.[1]

It seems that the *Gospel of Peter* was a very early (150s?) expansion of the gospel accounts with certain additions and changes that had been introduced to support the viewpoint of those called Docetists (who taught that Jesus only seemed to be human but was really an immaterial spirit of some kind). This heresy would probably influence the concept of virginity *in partu*, but less so an account of Joseph being an older man with children of his own. What is also interesting is that Serapion ultimately concluded that the *Kerygma Petrou* was mostly orthodox.

From the above, we may reasonably infer that the *Gospel of Peter* did indeed include a nativity account, like the *Protevangelium of James*, which portrayed Joseph was as a widower with his own children.

e) The Protevangelium of James (c. 120-150)

i. Importance and reception

There is no doubt that this second century non-canonical text has had a tremendous influence on both Greek and (to an extent) Latin Christendom. The simple reason may well be that PJ is not only a very ancient text but also the only source that provides a theologically credible and acceptable account of what happened before the birth of Jesus.

PJ begins with an elderly couple, Joachim and Anna, who has not been blessed with any offspring, a very classic Biblical theme. These two names are important: even if the Western/Latin tradition

---

[1] Quoted in Eusebius, *Ecclesiastical History*, 6.12.1-6

eventually favored the Hieronymian view over the Epiphanian (which is taken for granted but not elaborated in PJ), the names Joachim and Anna remained.

Indeed, it is striking to reflect on the fact that Joachim and Anna are commemorated by name as the 'ancestors of our God' at *every* service celebrated in the Orthodox Church to this day. For the Eastern-Greek (and modern Orthodox) Churches, the *Protevangelium of James* is not understood as the originator of the Epiphanian view but rather as an acceptable (if uncanonical) exposition of what may well have happened.

Because this text is so important, we must answer several questions:

- What are the origins of the text and of the underlying story?
- Is the *Protevangelium* a historically credible document?
- Is the *Protevangelium* a theologically credible document?
- How does the *Protevangelium* relate with the broader "Epiphanian" tradition?

ii. Origins

The consensus of scholarship is that PJ originates at some point between 110 and 150, somewhere in Syria, in the sphere of influence of the great Church of Antioch. We have already discussed the *Gospel of Peter* as being related to PJ in terms of origins, but as being different in scope. Relying on Origen, we can assume that both 'gospel-type' writings contained a pre-nativity account presenting Joseph as an older man and widower.

Interestingly, PJ does not open with a statement of authorship but rather ends with this statement:

> And I James that wrote this history in Jerusalem, a commotion having arisen when Herod died, withdrew myself to the wilderness until the commotion in Jerusalem ceased, glorifying the Lord God, who had given me the gift and the wisdom to write this history. And grace shall be with those who fear our Lord Jesus Christ, to whom be glory to ages of ages. Amen!

PJ is therefore placed under the authorship or patronage of an unspecified "James" who is otherwise not mentioned in the text, except perhaps in a short allusion:

> [Joseph speaking] "I have sons and am old, while she is young. I will not be ridiculed among the children of Israel... I will register my sons. But this child? What will I do about him? How will I register him?"

This is remarkable to enough to be discussed: PJ mentions that Joseph has sons (daughters are not mentioned) but does not provide any of the names. It would have been very easy for the author of PJ to harmonize these unnamed sons with Mark 6:3, but it is simply not done. In what appears to be a similar phenomenon, PJ suddenly mentions Salome without any indication that she was (as later tradition would have it) Joseph's daughter. Epiphanius, perhaps relying on ancient Palestinian sources, would clarify:

> Joseph begot James when he was somewhere around forty years old. After him he had a son named Joses—then Simeon after him, then Judah, and two daughters, one named Mary and one, Salome; and his wife died.[1]

On this basis, we can assert that PJ does not see itself, and cannot be regarded as *the source* of the Epiphanian view. Rather, the raw family information is narrated in what has been called Christian midrash. It seems taken for granted that Joseph was an older man (and we have seen Scriptural reasons to concur), that James (who needs no qualification) was Joseph's son, and that Salome was Joseph's daughter.

The Orthodox view, then, is that PJ elaborates on historical data already familiar to Christians in Palestine and Syria.

---

[1] Epiphanius, *Panarion*, 78.8.1; 78.9.6; (in Williams, 621) see also *Gospel of Philip*, 59:6-11

Further, if we are to agree that PJ (like the *Gospel of Peter*) has docetic elements, we can see how the insertion of these heretical elements is done in the *Gospel of Peter*, through subtle additions or substitutions superimposed on the historical account. If this is true for the *Gospel of Peter*, the claim that Jesus' birth leaving no mark on Mary (a strong theme in PJ) is docetic does not undermine the overall historicity of the account, on the contrary.

I personally do not see PJ as heretical or docetic in any shape or form: the text teaches that Mary miraculously delivered the baby Jesus, not to deny the reality of Jesus' body, but rather to reflect the theology of Mary as the New Eve and as fulfillment of Isaiah 66.

Regarding the origin and dating of PJ, the perspective offered by Chris Jordan in his scholarly introduction to the text is worth considering:

> However, the canonical gospels could have been written in response to the text of PJ. Since PJ focuses on Herod's pursuit of John the Baptist and how he was dramatically rescued through divine intervention, do not the canonical gospels, as a natural response, place an emphasis on Herod's pursuit of Jesus and his escape into Egypt? Therefore, PJ may be a text that was written during the life of Jesus or at least before the canonical gospels, and the canonical birth accounts of Jesus were written in response to PJ. Resch and Conrady are two nineteenth century scholars who support the thesis that PJ is pre-canonical. Conrady thinks that PJ was used as a source by the authors of the canonical gospels and Resch thinks that the canonical gospels and PJ shared common written sources. PJ might have originally been a part of the canonical gospels, which became separated from the rest of the work at an early period of transmission. Postel suggested in his publication of PJ (1552) that the text of PJ was the missing introduction to Mark's Gospel.[1]

---

[1] Chris Jordan, *Protevangelium Jacobi (PJ): An Introduction*

This viewpoint, which admittedly does not claim to represent a consensus, is remarkable. It contents that PJ may well be a very ancient document, perhaps pre-dating the canonical gospels themselves.

iii. Historicity

This leads us to further examine PJ's claims to being an historical record. Meier (*contra* Bauckham) is a fairly typical instance of a scholar who sees nothing historically valid in PJ:

> The basic question we must put to the PJ is whether it gives indications of being a trustworthy repository of detailed information about the early years of Jesus' life, in particular about his relation to his brothers. In my opinion, anyone who reviews the contents of the PJ must answer in the negative. To substantiate this judgment, I invite the reader to join me in a thorough test of the contents of the PJ. For this test, I suggest that the reader draw three columns on a page and use them to "keep score" as he or she reads through the PJ with me.
>
> In the first column, the reader should note (a) all the material containing mistakes about Palestinian geography, political conditions, or Jewish practices during the Second Temple period, and (b) all the material that confuses or conflates in a maladroit fashion the infancy narratives of Matthew and Luke. Obviously, such material cannot be taken seriously as the source of new historical information about Jesus. In the second column, the reader should note statements that seem to be the product of pious imagination or Christian legend building that flows from a type of "midrash" on OT and NT texts, especially the canonical infancy narratives. In the third column, the reader should note any statement in the PJ that may have a serious claim to represent independent historical information.
>
> Anyone with a fair knowledge of the PJ can guess beforehand the outcome of this test. By the time we finish reading the contents of the PJ--now sorted out in the three columns--we shall find that almost the entire text of the PJ will wind up in columns one and

two; there will be practically nothing in column three. The consequence of this survey for the question of Jesus' brothers is clear. There is no reason to suppose that in the unique case of Jesus' brothers the PJ had access to privileged historical information that it otherwise totally and woefully lacked. This, in brief, is my claim.[1]

Meier goes on to list what items he would place in columns 1 and 2, basically by retelling the PJ story and finding it either the product of imagination or midrashic expansions on both the Old and New Testament.

Clearly, several supernatural events take place in the account of the *Protevangelium*, but certainly no more than in the Gospels themselves. A Christian who is comfortable with the supernatural stories found in the Holy Scriptures should not be disturbed by the miraculous elements found in the *Protevangelium*. These should be placed in a neutral column rather than in Meier's column (a). Compared to the *Infancy Gospel of Thomas* (discussed below) and to the overall corpus of Scriptures (LXX corpus), there is nothing outrageous to be found by the Christian reader in the *Protevangelium*.

If the miraculous is not a disqualification, what about the mistakes found in the text regarding Palestinian geography and second Temple practices?

In my view, these errors (listed below) are much fewer and ambiguous than has been claimed. I will start with a list of alleged errors published by the Evangelical ministry called "Answers in Genesis." The table is preceded by the following statement, which only serves to confirm the crisis of scholarship that exists in many of these ministries:

---

[1] Meier, Op. cit.

The early church father Origen wrote a commentary on Matthew in which he rejected The Protoevangelium of James as spurious and affirmed Mary had other children.[1]

The reader can refer to our discussion of Origen below, but suffice it to state that Origen was not a "father," did not reject as spurious the (sic) "Protoevangelium of James," and certainly did not affirm that "Mary had other children." This did not bode well for the rest of the argument, summarized this table:

Table of some contradictions between The Protoevangelium of James and the Bible:

	Protoevangelium of James	*The Bible*
1	Gabriel is called an archangel (Chapter 9:22), which was a common designation for Gabriel in apocryphal literature written after the first century. (For example, see Revelation of Paul, The Book of John Concerning the Falling Asleep of Mary, and The Apocalypse of the Holy Mother of God.)	The Bible never identifies Gabriel as an archangel, but Michael is described as an archangel in Jude 1:9. The idea of Gabriel as an archangel seems to be a misconception that began in the second century.
2	Mary's response to the angel is different than what is recorded in Scripture. "What! Shall I conceive by the living God, and	Luke 1:34 states, "Then Mary said to the angel, 'How can this be, since I do not know a man?'"

---

[1] Bodie Hodge, *Is the Perpetual Virginity of Mary a Biblical View?*, accessed at https://answersingenesis.org/bible-characters/is-the-perpetual-virginity-of-mary-a-biblical-view/

	bring forth as all other women do?" (Chapter 9:12).	
3	Elizabeth fled the Bethlehem region with her son John (the Baptist) to the mountains because of Herod's wrath when he decided to kill all the baby boys around and in Bethlehem (Chapter 16:3).	Concerning John the Baptist, Luke 1:80 states, "So the child grew and became strong in spirit, and was in the deserts till the day of his manifestation to Israel." It was Joseph, Mary, and Jesus who fled from Bethlehem because of Herod (Matthew 2:13–15).
4	Jesus was born in a cave outside the city of Bethlehem (Chapters 12:11–14:31).	Jesus was born in Bethlehem, the town of David, according to Luke 2:4, 11 and Matthew 2:1.
5	The angel of the Lord, when speaking to Joseph in a dream, said to take Mary but does not mention having her as a wife. The priest chastised Joseph and accused him for taking Mary as a wife secretly by the priest. Joseph takes her home but is reluctant to call her his wife when they go to Bethlehem (Chapters 10:17–18, 11:14, 12:2–3).	Matthew 1:19 reveals that Joseph was already Mary's husband (they were betrothed) before the angel visited him in a dream. Matthew 1:24 points out that after the angel visited Joseph, he kept her as his wife.

6	Mary wrapped Jesus in swaddling cloths and hid him in a manger at the inn to keep him from the massacre by Herod's men (Chapter 16:2).	Mary and Joseph were warned of Herod's plot by an angel, and they fled to Egypt (Matthew 2:13–14).
7	Wise men came to Bethlehem and inquired of Herod where the Child was born (Chapter 21:1–2).	Wise men came to Jerusalem to inquire where the child king was (Matthew 2:1).

At close examination, none of these 7 points amounts to serious criticism:

Point 1 is a reminder that sound scholarship takes time (and a decent knowledge of Greek). As a matter of fact, Gabriel is probably not called "archangel" in this text, as some of the best manuscripts indicate.[1] Even if it were the case, the idea that certain angels (seven) are closest to the throne of God and could be called chief-angels[2] is certainly not a contradiction with Michael's exalted status as the archangel in charge of God's people, yet as one described as "one of the chief princes" (Dan 10:13).

Point 2 seems to demand that every single dialogue should be recorded with journalistic accuracy and absolute consistency across all witnesses. But this is not the case in the canonical Scriptures in the first place, and Mary's reply to the annunciation is neither extravagant nor very different than what is found in Luke. This

---

[1] For a comparison of the readings from the best manuscripts, see http://www.sd-editions.com/AnaServer?protevangel+0+start.anv (verse reference is 12:6)
[2] Compare Luk 1:19; Rev 8:2

criterion could not be applied to the canonical gospels themselves, and therefore cannot be imposed here.

Point 3 is an expected complaint that PJ adds 'John the Baptist' centric themes to the account. Indeed, PJ contends that not only Jesus but also John (born 6 months before) was threatened by Herod's desire to kill any recently-born boy with some claim to the throne. If we take Matthew's account as historically valid (which is rarely done by scholars today in view of the difficulty of harmonizing Matthew and Luke), it seems clear that Herod's soldiers would have been on the lookout for any usual births, of which John's would have been known. PJ does not here contradict the New Testament but rather expands on the events surrounding the flight into Egypt.

Point 4 is of particular interest: PJ teaches, as a matter of casual fact, that Jesus was born in a cave, which is not indicated in the New Testament. However, this was a widespread belief. Justin Martyr took it for granted (as somehow announced in the Prophecies) that Jesus was born in a cave, and Origen mentions the discussions in Bethlehem regarding its exact location. The Old Testament does not demand that Jesus would have been born within the city limits (a modern concept). A hint may be found in the fact that the Patriarchs (and their families) were buried in caves:

> And as for me, when I came from Padan, Rachel died by me in the land of Canaan in the way, when yet there was but a little way to come unto Ephrath: and I buried her there in the way of Ephrath; the same is Bethlehem. (Gen 48:7)

It would have been providential indeed if Rachel's cave would have been associated with the cave of the Nativity, so that her weeping would have been offset by the joy of the birth of the Savior.[1]

---

[1] According to Edersheim in *The Life and Times of Jesus the Messiah*, in Book 2, Chapter 6: "This Migdal Edar was not the watchtower for the ordinary flocks that pastured on the

Point 5 reveals a common lack of understanding of the two step process of betrothal and marriage. We have already discussed Matthew 1:24 at length: Joseph does take Mary as his wife, yet with no intention (as is clear from his subsequent behavior) to consummate the union (at the very least until after the birth). At that point in time, Mary is legally Joseph's wife, and yet, it is significant that Luke 2:5 still refers to her as "his betrothed." For this reason, the Orthodox tradition remembers Joseph as "the betrothed" and Mary as the "unwedded bride."

Point 6 is no more difficult to harmonize than many texts within the Holy Scriptures. Chapter 22 is actually not so much concerned about Jesus and Mary than about the fate of John. The flight into Egypt is not mentioned at all and would have to be assumed from the Gospel of Matthew.

Point 7 is caused by a hasty reading of the English text of PJ 21:1-2:

> (1) Now, Joseph was about to depart to Judea when there a great commotion in Bethlehem of Judea. (2) For astrologers had come, saying, "Where is the one who has been born king of the Jews? For we saw his star in the East and came to worship him."

The text does not actually state that the magi came to Bethlehem but rather, in context, to Judea.

iv. Virgins in the Temple?

Another common criticism, even expressed (surprisingly) by a well-known Orthodox priest, concerns the existence of virgins serving in the Temple:

---

barren sheep ground beyond Bethlehem, but it lay close to the town, on the road to Jerusalem. A passage from the Mishnah (Shekelim 7:4) indicates that the flocks which pastured there were destined for Temple sacrifices."

> The author's knowledge of Jewish culture is just as shaky: he assumes that virgins would reside at the Jewish Temple, like the Vestal Virgins resided in the temple of pagan Rome, but this was not the case.[1]

The reader may remember that such a common (but misinformed) viewpoint has already been refuted. In an excellent paper entitled *Mary in the Protevangelium of James: A Jewish Woman in the Temple?*, Megan Nutzman writes:

> Through a careful reexamination of Mary's time in the temple, I will challenge this conventional hypothesis and argue that the author structures his narrative to evoke three groups of Jewish women who were given special privileges in the temple cult.[2]

In the process, Nutzman is careful to analyze other controversial features of PJ, notably Mary's presence in the holy of holies. She writes:

> [The] indication that she lived in the Holy of Holies, which could only be entered by the high priest on the Day of Atonement. While this anomaly finds no justification in Jewish literature of the period, it should be noted that Mary's presence in the Holy of Holies is not found in her arrival at the temple, her life within its precincts, or her removal to Joseph's home. Rather, it was only in retrospect, during Mary's questioning at the hands of Joseph and the high priest, that the author claimed that she lived in the Holy of Holies... The inconsistent textual witness in 19.1 and the silence of the rest of the narrative about the Holy of Holies may indicate that the phrase was the product of a later interpolation.

---

[1] Lawrence Farley, *The Feast of the Entrance and the Protoevangelium of James*, accessed at http://myocn.net/feast-entrance-protoevangelium-james/

[2] Megan Nutzman, *Mary in the Protevangelium of James: A Jewish Woman in the Temple?*, Greek, Roman, and Byzantine Studies 53 (2013), 552

Marian hymnography is perhaps the most likely source for this phrase.[1]

Regarding the sometimes-disputed claim found in PJ that these temple-virgins would have been commissioned to weave the curtain, Nutzman's research is very solid:

> All these sources corroborate the existence of an elite group of young women responsible for weaving the curtains that adorned the temple.[2]

In the process, she makes reference to Malcolm Lowe's research on the geographical terminology and accuracy of PJ, noting his own conclusion that:

> His evaluation of Ἰουδαῖος in PJ placed it firmly within the category of texts originating in Palestine and led to his conclusion that the author was most likely a Palestinian Jew.[3]

The above discussion does not mean that there are no problematic passages or features in the *Protevangelium of James*, but rather that it is important to carefully assess and identify all possible issues.

Another scholar who has recently challenged the prevalent disdain for PJ is Margaret Barker, notably in her excellent *Christmas: the Original Story*. When PJ describes Mary as being fed by an angel, Barker suggests that those familiar with Temple theology would have understood that priests can properly be described as angels (and vice-versa) in the context of the Temple, as can be seen in the book of Revelation.

In my view, the main problem is how PJ treats Zachariah. Farley observes:

---

[1] Idem, 554
[2] Idem, 564
[3] Idem, 556

> For one thing he identifies Zechariah (the father of John the Baptist), the one who presided over the child Mary's entry into the Holy of Holies, as the high-priest. Oops. Anyone reading the Gospel knows that Zechariah was not the high-priest, but a simple priest. That was why he had to draw lots to burn incense in the Temple (Luke 1:8-9). The high-priest did not have to draw lots.

Certainly, PJ (even considering the variants) gives that impression, namely that Zachariah (the father of John the Baptist) is presented as the high priest. However, PJ 10:6-9 also seems to portray Zechariah as distinct from the high priest and refers to high priests in the plural as being equivalent to senior priests (6:6). A carefully reading of the text shows that the high priest involved in the Mary's entrance in the Temple is actually unnamed.

Overall, PJ 8:7 remains the main problem passage, which textual variants cannot explain. However, scholars agree that there may well be two layers in PJ, an older stratum to which additional material and redaction was added during the second century:

> As was shown above, Petersen himself seems to presuppose the existence of redactional activity in the Prot. Jas. by referring to the compositional level of this document, which contains both of the parallels in question, as the "oldest layer" or "oldest stratum." Petersen does not elaborate upon these terms; nor does he pursue their serious implications for the question at hand. At the very least, "oldest layer" and "oldest stratum" imply the existence of substantial earlier material in the Prot. Jas. that predates the final composition of the document which Petersen—following de Strycker—believes to have occurred in the late second century.[1]

If so, the single instance of Zachariah being erroneously portrayed as high priest may well be an editorial alteration inserted in a

---

[1] George Zervos, *Caught in the Act: Mary and the Adulteress*, 24-25

misguided effort to harmonize PJ with itself and Luke as well as other sources.

v. Other criticism

PJ seems to be a dividing-line text for many (especially Protestants, but also other Christians of a modernist bent), because accepting it as a valuable testimony to the contextual history of the birth of Jesus would entail an acceptance of a fundamentally Eastern Orthodox theological worldview. One Evangelical commentator noted:

> It is plainly clear why God chose Mary to bear Christ: she was the most pure of all the undefiled virgins in Israel at the time. The divine initiative isn't based on grace... For in them we see God in the person of Jesus reaching out to miserable undeserving sinners—Zacchaeus, the thief on the cross, etc.—and freely giving them a place in His eternal kingdom. Sadly, I don't get that from the Protoevangelium of James.[1]

One wonders if God should have chosen a prostitute and divorcee to be the New Eve and mother of the Great King. And how inappropriate to have chosen blameless people (Luk 1:6) to be the parents of the Forerunner, when so many sinners could have been set forth a vessels of grace!

vi. Conclusion

The *Protevangelium of James* is an important and controversial text. It is easy (and all too common) to simply reject the story contained in it as a complete fable written by a Syrian Christian betraying his lack of familiarity with the geographical and religious realities of second Temple Israel. It is also convenient to see this account as primarily motivated by the (allegedly misguided) desire to proclaim

---

[1] Quoted from http://nelima.wordpress.com/2012/05/03/reading-the-protoevangelium-of-james/

Mary's perpetual virginity and as the culprit of all subsequent Epiphanian solutions.

However, there are sound reasons to challenge this perspective and reconsider what exactly in the *Protevangelium* may well reflect a preexisting historical narrative or memory. It is argued here that PJ is neither heretical nor an Epiphanian apology. It simply takes it for granted that Joseph was an older man with his own children, that Salome was already widely known as his daughter and that "James" was immediately identified as his son. In spite of a few specific issues discussed here, the *Protevangelium* is a beautifully woven tapestry of themes that are affirmed elsewhere in the theological memory of first and second century Christianity,[1] including the Temple theology background,[2] Mary's Davidic descent and the New Eve[3] theme.

f) The Infancy Gospel of Thomas (c. 120-180)

The *Infancy Gospel of Thomas* is another ancient text that can most probably be assigned to second-century Syria. Compared to the *Protevangelium of James*, the *Infancy Gospel of Thomas* is a rather 'unpleasant' text in that it contains many strange (and improbable) miracles that Jesus is alleged to have performed as a child.

The only element that is relevant to our discussion has already been cited, being the brief story of how the child Jesus once accompanied his older brother James who had been sent by Joseph to gather wood. The best text (Greek) seems clear that Jesus was younger than

---

[1] Compare *Ignatius to the Ephesians*, 19:1; *Odes of Solomon*, 19:8-9; *Ascension of Isaiah*, 11:9-14

[2] See Introduction to the Gospel of John and Revelation in the *Eastern / Greek Orthodox New Testament*

[3] See PJ 13:5

James, which is consistent with the Epiphanian view encountered in similar texts.[1]

This is not a very impressive witness because modern-day Christians readily see this fable as a rather obnoxious attempt to imagine what the child Jesus might have done in the sphere of the miraculous, but the fact that it takes the Epiphanian view for granted is noteworthy.

g) Hegesippus (c. 110-180) and Eusebius

Hegesippus, (sometimes called "the Chronicler") is a somewhat mysterious yet critically important figure of the post-apostolic age. He seemed to have been a Jewish convert to Christianity who was the first to write a history of the faith as well as a refutation of then-common erroneous teachings. It is clear that Eusebius – the great Church historian of the fourth century – heavily relied on Hegesippus and did preserve for us several excepts from these now-lost works. For this reason, we have to treat Hegesippus and Eusebius (the first two historians and archivists of the Church) as a single unit in spite of the century and a half that separated them. Because of the tremendous importance of this early witness, notably in view of his connection with and interest in James 'the Brother of the Lord,' I deem it useful to present hereunder several relevant quotations from Hegesippus as preserved by Eusebius:

> But Hegesippus, who lived immediately after the apostles, gives the most accurate account in the fifth book of his Memoirs. He writes as follows: "James, the brother of the Lord, succeeded to the government of the Church in conjunction with the apostles. He has been called the Just by all from the time of our Savior to the present day; for there were many that bore the name of James. He was holy from his mother's womb; and he drank no wine nor

---

[1] The modern Hieromyan view sees the *adelphoi* as children of Clopas who would have been Joseph's younger brother. In this case, it is less obvious (but not excluded) that they would have been older than Jesus.

strong drink, nor did he eat flesh. No razor came upon his head; he did not anoint himself with oil, and he did not use the bath. He alone was permitted to enter into the holy place; for he wore not woolen but linen garments. And he was in the habit of entering alone into the temple, and was frequently found upon his knees begging forgiveness for the people, so that his knees became hard like those of a camel, in consequence of his constantly bending them in his worship of God, and asking forgiveness for the people. Because of his exceeding great justice he was called the Just, and Oblias, which signifies in Greek, Bulwark of the people' and 'Justice,' in accordance with what the prophets declare concerning him. [Follows the account of the martyrdom of James] These things are related at length by Hegesippus, who is in agreement with Clement.[1]

After the martyrdom of James and the conquest of Jerusalem which immediately followed, it is said that those of the apostles and disciples of the Lord that were still living came together from all directions with those that were related to the Lord according to the flesh (for the majority of them also were still alive) to take counsel as to who was worthy to succeed James. They all with one consent pronounced Symeon, the son of Clopas, of whom the Gospel also makes mention; to be worthy of the episcopal throne of that parish. He was a cousin, as they say, of the Savior. For Hegesippus records that Clopas was a brother of Joseph.[2]

But when this same Domitian had commanded that the descendants of David should be slain, an ancient tradition says that some of the heretics brought accusation against the descendants of Jude (said to have been a brother of the Saviour according to the flesh), on the ground that they were of the lineage of David and were related to Christ himself. Hegesippus relates these facts in the following words:

---

[1] Eusebius, *Ecclesiastical History*, Book II, Chapter XXIII
[2] Idem, Book III, Chapter XI

"Of the family of the Lord there were still 1 living the grandchildren of Jude, who is said to have been the Lord's brother according to the flesh. Information was given that they belonged to the family of David, and they were brought to the Emperor Domitian by the Evocatus. For Domitian feared the coming of Christ as Herod also had feared it… But when they were released they ruled the churches because they were witnesses and were also relatives of the Lord. Peace being established, they lived until the time of Trojan." These things are related by Hegesippus.[1]

It is reported that after the age of Nero and Domitian, under the emperor whose times we are now recording, a persecution was stirred up against us in certain cities in consequence of a popular uprising. In this persecution we have understood that Symeon, the son of Clopas, who, as we have shown, was the second bishop of the church of Jerusalem, suffered martyrdom. Hegesippus, whose words we have already quoted in various places, is a witness to this fact also. Speaking of certain heretics he adds that Symeon was accused by them at this time; and since it was clear that he was a Christian, he was tortured in various ways for many days, and astonished even the judge himself and his attendants in the highest degree, and finally he suffered a death similar to that of our Lord. But there is nothing like hearing the historian himself, who writes as follows: "Certain of these heretics brought accusation against Symeon, the son of Clopas, on the ground that he was a descendant of David and a Christian; and thus he suffered martyrdom, at the age of one hundred and twenty years, while Trajan was emperor and Atticus governor." And the same writer says that his accusers also, when search was made for the descendants of David, were arrested as belonging to that family. And it might be reasonably assumed that Symeon was one of those that saw and heard the Lord, judging from the length of his life, and from the fact that the Gospel makes mention of Mary, the wife of Clopas, who was the father of Symeon, as has been

---

[1] Idem, Book III, Chapter XIX-XX

already shown. The same historian says that there were also others, descended from one of the so-called brothers of the Savior, whose name was Judas, who, after they had borne testimony before Domitian, as has been already recorded, in behalf of faith in Christ, lived until the same reign. He writes as follows: "They came, therefore, and took the lead of every church as witness and as relatives of the Lord. And profound peace being established in every church, they remained until the reign of the Emperor Trajan, and until the above-mentioned Symeon, son of Clopas, an uncle of the Lord, was informed against by the heretics, and was himself in like manner accused for the same cause before the governor Atticus. And after being tortured for many days he suffered martyrdom, and all, including even the proconsul, marveled that, at the age of one hundred and twenty years, he could endure so much.[1]

Hegesippus in the five books of Memoirs which have come down to us has left a most complete record of his own views. In them he states that on a journey to Rome he met a great many bishops, and that he received the same doctrine from all. The same author [Hegesippus] also describes the beginnings of the heresies which arose in his time, in the following words: "And after James the Just had suffered martyrdom, as the Lord had also on the same account, Symeon, the son of the Lord's uncle, Clopas, was appointed the next bishop. All proposed him as second bishop because he was a cousin (*anepsios*) of the Lord.[2]

What can we deduce from the above citations in which Eusebius attempts to preserve the legacy of Hegesippus? To be specific, was Hegesippus Epiphanian, Helvidian, or Hieronymian?

To an extent, we must rely on Eusebius' character as a bishop dedicated to the preservation of the apostolic teaching that could be

---

[1] Ibid, Book III, Chapter XXXII
[2] Ibid, Book IV, Chapter XXII

traced to the earliest successors of the Apostles to make that decision.

Eusebius himself – a self-avowed admirer of Origen and a careful follower of Hegesippus whom he praises so highly – is clearly an Epiphanian. He writes:

> Then James, whom the ancients surnamed the Just on account of the excellence of his virtue, is recorded to have been the first to be made bishop of the church of Jerusalem. This James was called 'the brother of the Lord' because he was known as a son of Joseph, and Joseph was supposed to be the father of Christ, because the Virgin, being betrothed to him, "was found with child by the Holy Ghost before they came together," as the account of the holy Gospels shows.[1]

Eusebius goes on to cite Clement of Alexandria who was also an Epiphanian. On this basis alone, we may infer the following:

- Eusebius takes the Epiphanian view for granted based on the agreement of ancient testimonies (Hegesippus as we may assume, Clement of Alexandria and Origen from their own words).

- Eusebius understands[2] the difference between being "called/styled" "brother of the Lord" and being specifically a cousin (*anepsios*) as in the case of Symeon.

- For Eusebius reading Hegesippus, "brothers according to the flesh" is not understood to mean that James, Jude and Jesus were uterine brothers of Jesus but rather in the sense that this term was used in the sense of actual family

---

[1] Ibid, Book II, Chapter I

[2] As Lightfoot comments: "In this passage the word 'called' [or 'styled'] seems to me to point to the Epiphanian rather than the Helvidian view, the brotherhood of these brethren, like the fatherhood of Joseph, being reputed but not real." (*The Brethren of the Lord*, 30)

connections (as opposed to mere spiritual bonds; as in Act 1:14-15; compare Rom 9:1-3).

This is a very important point, also discussed by Bauckham, to be contrasted with the following (typical) assertion:

> Hegesippus also refers to "the Lord's brother according to the flesh," which indicates in the strongest terms that Jesus and his brothers were related by blood. Also, he distinguishes between brothers and cousins.

However, "related by blood" does not, in the mind of Hegesippus and Eusebius, imply that a uterine relationship is required. Bauckham clarifies:

> In these phrases, 'according to the flesh' designates the realm of merely physical relationships, by contrast with relationships 'according to the spirit' (cf. Rom 1:3-4; Gal 3:23, 29; Philem 16). So, whereas 'the Lord's brother' might indicate a special relationship with Jesus not shared by other Christian leaders, 'the Lord's brother *according to the flesh*' relativizes that relationship as only a natural relationship. It recognizes that to call a natural brother of Jesus *the Lord's* brother really is as inappropriate as to call the one who is David's Lord David's son...[1]

There is also a difference between "styled brother(s) of the Lord" (with reference to the sons of Joseph, possibly compared with the sons of King David) and a cousin of the Lord such as Symeon.

- There is no reason to question Hegesippus' account that Clopas was the Lord's uncle (being the Joseph's younger brother), and we note that that Symeon was specifically described as the Lord's cousin (*anepsios*) but not styled a "brother of the Lord."

---

[1] Jude, 128

In summary, Hegesippus contradicts the Hieronymian view and would seem to belong to the same group as Clement and Eusebius, namely of the Epiphanian view, lest one would wish to argue in favor of the very improbable idea that Eusebius would not have followed his trusted source on the matter of the relationship between Jesus, James and Joseph.

h) (St) Justin Martyr (c. +165)

There is nothing in Justin Martyr that specifically relates to the idea of Mary's perpetual virginity or the identity of Jesus' *adelphoi*. Jerome does, however, enrolled Justin as an early defender of Mary's perpetual virginity, which is certainly worth mentioning.

Justin, like Irenaeus, presents Mary as the New Eve, and we shall further discuss the non-Helvidian implications of this perspective when discussing Irenaeus.

i) (St) Irenaeus of Lyons (c. +202)

Being a disciple of Polycarp of Smyrna who was a disciple of the Evangelist John, Irenaeus was a man of unique authority among the early Churches, from Asia Minor to Gaul. As bishop of Lyons in modern-day France, he was in a position to "rebuke" the bishop of Rome, Victor, during the so-called Quartodeciman controversy.

We have seen that Irenaeus' theology of Mary as the New Eve is quite elaborate and frankly stunning in view of its 'mariological' implications. Yet, Irenaeus (*contra* Jerome), is sometimes listed among the early witnesses to the Helvidian view. Svendsen, for example, contends:

Yet another writer of the second century[1] who shows evidence of the belief that the brothers of Jesus were biological siblings is Irenaeus (*Against Heresies*, 3.21.10):

And as the protoplast himself Adam, had his substance from untilled and *as yet virgin* soil ("for God had not yet sent rain, and man had not tilled the ground"), and was formed by the hand of God, that is, by the Word of God, for "all things were made by Him," and the Lord took dust from the earth and formed man; so did He who is the Word, recapitulating Adam in Himself, rightly receive a birth, enabling him to gather up Adam [into Himself], from Mary, who was *as yet* [or 'still'[2]] a virgin.

The italicized phrases above ("as yet [a] virgin") are clearly intended by Irenaeus to be taken in parallel. Just as the soil of the earth was as yet virgin (but only until shortly thereafter when it was tilled), so also Mary was as yet a virgin before giving birth to Jesus. The direct implication is that she did not remain a virgin thereafter. Although this is not direct proof that Mary bore other children, it seems to be the natural inference. In any case, if this is Irenaeus' meaning, then the perpetual virginity of Mary was unknown to him. Another passage from this same book of Irenaeus (3.22.4) may also offer support for the Helvidian view:

For the one and the same Spirit of God, who proclaimed by the prophets what and of what sort the advent of the Lord should be, did by these elders give a just interpretation of what had been truly prophesied; and He did Himself, by the apostles, announce that the fullness of the times of the adoption had arrived, that the kingdom of heaven had drawn nigh, and that He was dwelling within those who believe on Him who was born Emmanuel of the Virgin. To this effect they testify, [saying,] that before Joseph had come together with Mary, while she therefore remained in virginity, "she was found with child of the Holy Ghost."

---

[1] The previous one cited by Svendsen was Tertullian.

[2] My addition (Cleenewerck)

> Irenaeus' allusion to Matt 1:18, as well as his words of explanation, indicate that he understands the biblical text to mean that Mary remained in a state of virginity only during that time period before she and Joseph "came together" (Meier, 1992:25). It is also clear that he understands the meaning of "come together" to imply much more than mere cohabitation, both in this passage and in another one as well: "To this effect [the prophets, elders, apostles] were [saying,] that before Joseph had come together with Mary, while she therefore remained in virginity, she was found with child of the Holy Ghost" (Against Heresies, 3.21). It is clear from these passages that Irenaeus arrives at the same conclusion that we did in an earlier chapter concerning the phrase, "before they came together"; namely, that it means "before they engaged in marital relations." Moreover, these passages demonstrate Irenaeus' belief that this condition of Mary did not continue after they came together.

I would like to disagree with Svendsen on the above, with the caveat that I do agree with him that "before they came together" does indeed mean "before they had marital intercourse." Svendsen's criticism of McHugh (already mentioned) is quite valid.

However, I am afraid that Svendsen wishes to read in Irenaeus what is simply not there. Irenaeus clearly teaches that there is a parallel between Eve and Mary: Eve was still a virgin when she disobeyed and afterwards ceased to be a virgin, from which she in fact became the mother of the dying. Mary, like Eve, was still a virgin when she chose the path of obedience and effectively undid Eve's transgression. In doing so, she remained a virgin (unlike Eve) while becoming the mother of the living one.

Irenaeus' exercise in parallelism between Eve and Mary does not result in him teaching that Mary ceased to be a virgin. His accurate citation of Matthew 1 does no such thing, any more than Matthew 1 is written to necessitate subsequent reversal. Rather, a sound understanding of Irenaeus' comparison leads to the conclusion that Mary did remain a virgin, precisely because her obedience was the undoing of Eve's tragic and death-creating journey from virginity to non-virginity.

j) Tertullian (c. 225)

When Helvidius began promoting (c. 380) the view that Joseph and Mary did in fact have other children of their own after Jesus, he could only find the lapsed Tertullian and the lesser-known Victorinus as supporting authorities. This, incidentally, affirms our contention that no other ancient sources (especially not Hegesippus) could be enlisted to support what could only be described, in context, as 'an astonishing hypothesis.' Interestingly, Jerome tacitly admitted that Tertullian could indeed be enrolled by Helvidius, but denied that such was the case of Victorinus:

> Of Tertullian I say no more than that he did not belong to the Church. But as regards Victorinus, I assert what has already been proved from the Gospel—that he spoke of the brethren of the Lord not as being sons of Mary, but brethren in the sense I have explained, that is to say, brethren in point of kinship not by nature. We are, however, spending our strength on trifles, and, leaving the fountain of truth, are following the tiny streams of opinion. Might I not array against you the whole series of ancient writers? Ignatius, Polycarp, Irenæus, Justin Martyr, and many other apostolic and eloquent men, who against Ebion, Theodotus of Byzantium, and Valentinus, held these same views, and wrote volumes replete with wisdom.

In order words, only Tertullian could be cited as having taught the Helvidian view prior to Helvidius. Yet, as Lightfoot wrote:

> This assumption, though probable, is not absolutely certain... Elsewhere however, though he does not directly state it, his argument seems to imply that the Lord's brethren were His brothers in the same sense in which Mary was His mother (adv.

Marc. iv. 19, de Cam. Christ. 7). It is therefore highly probable that he held the Helvidian view.[1]

Svendsen, to his credit, takes the time to cite all three passages in which Tertullian is believed to be teaching the Helvidian view:

> [The Marcionites] say that He testifies Himself to His not having been born, when He asks, "Who is my mother, and who are my brethren?" [However,] it could not possibly have been told to Jesus that His mother and His brethren stood outside, desiring to see Him, if He did not have a mother and brothers. For tell me now, does a mother live on contemporaneously with her sons in every case? Do all sons have brothers born for them? Is it not possible for a man not to have fathers and sisters (living), or even no relatives at all? ... [Those] "who were standing outside" really were "His mother and His brethren!" (...) It seems as if Jesus' language amounted to a denial of His family and His birth; but it arose actually from the absolute nature of the case, and the conditional sense in which His words were to be explained. (...) He transferred the names of blood-relationship to others, whom He judged to be more closely related to Him by reason of their faith. Now no one transfers a thing except from him who possesses that which is transferred. If, therefore, He made them "His mother and His brethren" who were not so, how could He deny them these relationships who really had them?[2]

Tertullian seems clear enough in affirming that the Lord's brothers where really his blood brothers. Svendsen understands the argument well enough when he states "an 'adopted' brother cannot be upheld as proof that one was born in the normal way."[3]

---

[1] J. B. Lightfoot, *The Brethren of the Lord*, 31

[2] Svendsen, 66. I have retranslated and edited Tertullian's text for the sake of clarity. See *Against Marcion*, 4.19

[3] Svendsen, 67. Tertullian's *On the Flesh of Christ*, 7 is essentially the same argument.

Tertullian's writing *On Monogamy* is more difficult to interpret with certainty. He writes:

> Behold, there immediately present themselves to us, on the threshold as it were, the two priestesses of Christian sanctity, Monogamy and Continence: one modest, in Zechariah the priest; one absolute, in John the forerunner: one appeasing God; one preaching Christ: one proclaiming a perfect priest; one exhibiting more than a prophet, — him, namely, who has not only preached or personally pointed out, but even baptized Christ. For who was more worthily to perform the initiatory rite on the body of the Lord, than flesh similar in kind to that which conceived and gave birth to that (body)? And indeed it was a virgin, about to marry once for all after her delivery, who gave birth to Christ, in order that each title of sanctity might be fulfilled in Christ's parentage, by means of a mother who was both virgin, and wife of one husband.

On the one hand, it seems that Mary is presented as being a virgin who will only remain a virgin until her marriage. At the same time, she is presented as similar to John the Baptist who is presented as a life-long ("absolute") virgin.

Overall, it seems that Helvidius was justified in his view that Tertullian could be enrolled as a proto-Helvidian. However, Jerome was also in his right to dismiss Tertullian, who had deserted the Church to join the Montanist sect, as ultimately irrelevant.

From an Orthodox perspective, Tertullian is seen as a man who did belong to the Great Church communion but whose lack of cultural and linguistic connection to Apostolic Tradition (of the kind that Eusebius as so careful to document and preserve) was his downfall. The first Latin-writing author of the early Church was a literalist and radical who tended to draw hasty conclusions from the biblical text, for instance his belief that the Patriarch Enoch had actually written the prophecy cited in Jude 1:9.

In the end, Tertullian is the total sum of the assured witness to the Helvidian view in the first three centuries of the Christian era.

k) (St) Clement of Alexandria (C. +215)

In the case of Clement, we have to rely on the testimony of Cassiodorus (c. +585) who preserved the following passage from *Hypotyposis* in Latin:

> Jude, who wrote the Catholic Epistle, being one of the sons of Joseph and [the Lord's] brother, a man of deep piety, though he was aware of his relationship to the Lord, nevertheless did not say he was His brother...[1]

There is little reason to question that Clement was aligned with the common position of the second century Churches, from Syria to Egypt (the Epiphanian view). Supporting this assumption is that Eusebius often quotes from Clement on other points (including related to James) and give no indication that Clement believed anything different than himself. Not only that, but Clement also documents the common belief in Mary's virginity *in partu* (discussed below) which was found in the *Protevangelium* (and/or *Gospel of Peter*).

> Indeed, some say that, after she brought forth, she was found, when examined, to be a virgin. Now such to us are the Scriptures of the Lord ... in the concealment of the mysteries of the truth. 'And she brought forth, and yet brought not forth' says the Scripture; as having conceived of herself and not from conjunction.[2]

It seems that Clement accepted the validity of this account, while also stating that he primarily wanted to support his teachings from the recognized Scriptures.

---

[1] Cited by Cassiadorus in his *Institutiones Divinarum et Saecularium Litterarum*

[2] Clement of Alexandria, *Stromateis*, or *Miscellanies*

l) Origen (c. +254)

Origen cannot be called a saint in the formal sense (for complex personal and historical reasons), but the Coptic custom of referring to him as "Master Origen" is quite fitting.

This giant of a man had travelled extensively and was very keen to preserve the apostolic deposit not only of his own Church (at Alexandria) but also of the 'common union.'

We have already encountered Origen's reference to the *Gospel of Peter* and the *Protevangelium of James* as sources of the Epiphanian view, for which he indicated measured support. In his *Commentary on John*, Origen further confirms his support to the doctrine of the perpetual virginity of Mary. He writes:

> For if Mary, as those declare who with sound mind extol her, had no other son but Jesus, and yet Jesus says to His mother, Woman, behold thy son,' and not Behold you have this son also,' then He virtually said to her, Lo, this is Jesus, whom thou didst bear.' Is it not the case that everyone who is perfect lives himself no longer, but Christ lives in him; and if Christ lives in him, then it is said of him to Mary, Behold thy son Christ.' What a mind, then, must we have to enable us to interpret in a worthy manner this work, though it be committed to the earthly treasure-house of common speech, of writing which any passer-by can read, and which can be heard when read aloud by anyone who lends to it his bodily ears?[1]

Finally, we have Origen's *Commentary on John* (Fragment 31) in which the Alexandrian Master explicitly endorses the Epiphanian view. Not surprisingly, we see Eusebius and the Cappadocian fathers adopting the same position.

---

[1] Origen, *Commentary on John*, Chapter VI

2) FOURTH CENTURY WITNESSES

a) Eusebius of Caesarea (+340)

We have already discussed the testimony of Eusebius when discussing Hegesippus. Eusebius has been criticized for uncritically accepting ancient sources, but this is actually in favor of his reliability as a witness of the ancient and common tradition of what he called the common union of Churches.

It is sobering to think that when Eusebius was writing, the canon of the New Testament was still a matter of debate. His testimony in this regards has certainly vindicated him *a posteriori*, and the same could well be said of his Epiphanian view.

b) (St) Athanasius of Alexandria (+373)

The great defender of Nicene Orthodoxy (and first proclaimer of the New Testament canon in his Festal Letter of 367) is often cited as having used the Greek term *aiparthenos* (ever-virgin) in his *Discourse against the Arians*:

> Let those, therefore, who deny that the Son is by nature from the Father and proper to his essence deny also that He took true human flesh from the ever-virgin Mary.[1]

Admittedly, not all scholars concur that the use of *aiparthenos* (ever-virgin) by Athanasius is original.[2] We also have another text, which has sometimes been ascribed to a Pseudo-Athanasius, which is why its authenticity is here deemed probable but not entirely certain:

> If Mary would have had another son, the Savior would not have neglected her nor would he have confided his mother to another

---

[1] Athanasius of Alexandria, *Discourses against the Arians*, 2:70
[2] Cf. Tim S. Perry, Daniel Kendall, *The Blessed Virgin Mary*, 26, notably footnote 27

person, indeed she had not become the mother of another. Mary, moreover, would not have abandoned her own sons to live with another, for she fully realized a mother never abandons her spouse nor her children. And since she continued to remain a virgin even after the birth of the Lord, he gave her as mother to the disciple, even though she was not his mother; he confided her to John because of his great purity of conscience and because of her intact virginity.

Overall, we can only be disappointed that Athanasius left us such a limited (and verifiable) record on the matter. His successor, the controversial St Cyril of Alexandria (+444), clearly supported the Epiphanian view, and so did his friend Hilary, which is why we could safely conclude that Athanasius not only assumed the ever-virginity of Mary but also the Epiphanian view. However, J. G. Lightfoot is to be admired for his caution in this regards, since he opted not to list Athanasius in any particular camp.

c) (St) Hilary of Poitiers (+367)

Hilary was the bishop of relatively faraway Poitiers, in what is now France, but he seems to have been acquainted with several Eastern (and Greek-speaking) bishops, notably St Athanasius.

He is on the record as endorsing the Epiphanian view:

> If they [the brethren of the Lord] had been Mary's sons and not those taken from Joseph's former marriage, she would never have been given over in the moment of the passion [crucifixion] to the apostle John as his mother, the Lord saying to each, 'Woman, behold your son,' and to John, 'Behold your mother' [John 19:26–27), as he bequeathed filial love to a disciple as a consolation to the one desolate.[1]

---

[1] Hilary of Poitiers, *Commentary on Matthew*, 1:4

d) (St) Basil of Caesarea (+379)

It is safe to assume that Basil's view would simply be aligned with Origen and his predecessor as bishop of Caesarea, the historian Eusebius. There is a sermon ascribed to him[1] that cannot be absolutely authenticated, but that should be mentioned, in which St Basil would have declared:

> [The opinion that Mary bore several children after Christ] ... is not against the faith; for virginity was imposed on Mary as a necessity only up to the time that she served as an instrument for the Incarnation. On the other hand, her subsequent virginity was not essential to the mystery of the Incarnation.

Basil was well-aware that Matthew 1:25 could be interpreted (or as he would have put it, 'misinterpreted') as indicating that Joseph reversed his abstinence after the birth of Jesus. In the same homily, he states:

> [The passage] "he had no intercourse with Mary until her son was born" (Mat 1:25) does indeed afford a certain ground for thinking that Mary, after acting in all sanctity as the instrument of the Lord's birth (which was brought about by the Holy Spirit), did not refuse to her husband the customary privileges of marriage. But as for ourselves, even though this view does no violence to rational piety (...) yet [we state that] the friends of Christ cannot bear to hear that the Theotokos ever ceased to be a virgin..."[2]

In this homily, Basil refutes a number of 'standard' Helvidian arguments based on Matthew 1, and noted:

---

[1] For an excellent discussion of this homily, see Mark DelCogliano, *Tradition and Polemic in Basil of Caesarea's Homily on the Theophany* (Vigiliae Christianae 66 (2012) 30-55), accessed at https://stthomas.academia.edu/MarkDelCogliano

[2] St Basil, *Homilia in sanctam Christi generationem*, PG 31:1468

> There is an account, and it has been handed down to us from the tradition, that Zechariah entrusted Mary to the place for the virgins after conceiving the Lord.

Clearly, Basil is referring here to the account found in the *Protevangelium of James* which he accepts as traditional and valid.

Overall, St Basil is consistent: he accepts the Epiphanian tradition as reliable, and interprets the Scriptures in a manner that is consistent with the reading of the ancient fathers. However, he does not raise this interpretative tradition to the level of dogma.

e) (St) Gregory of Nyssa (c. +395)

St Gregory of Nyssa (Basil's younger brother) seems to have personally met St Jerome, but never discusses (in whatever writings are extant) the relative merits of the Epiphanian and Hieronymian views, as if he was unaware of the latter.

We may safely assume that Gregory, like Basil, was an Epiphanian. Echoing our own reflection on the implications of Mary being the New Eve and the Mother of the Living One, he writes:

> This life, then, which is stronger than the power of death, is, to those who think, the preferable one. The physical bringing of children into the world— I speak without wishing to offend— is as much a starting-point of death as of life; because from the moment of birth the process of dying commences. But those who by virginity have desisted from this process have drawn within themselves the boundary line of death, and by their own deed have checked his advance; they have made themselves, in fact, a frontier between life and death, and a barrier too, which thwarts him. If, then, death cannot pass beyond virginity, but finds his power checked and shattered there, it is demonstrated that virginity is a stronger thing than death; and that body is rightly named undying which does not lend its service to a dying world, nor brook to become the instrument of a succession of dying creatures. In such a body the long unbroken career of decay and death, which has intervened between the first man and the lives of

> virginity which have been led, is interrupted. It could not be indeed that death should cease working as long as the human race by marriage was working too; he walked the path of life with all preceding generations; he started with every new-born child and accompanied it to the end: but he found in virginity a barrier, to pass which was an impossible feat. Just as, in the age of Mary the Theotokos, he who had reigned from Adam to her time found, when he came to her and dashed his forces against the fruit of her virginity as against a rock, that he was shattered to pieces upon her, so in every soul which passes through this life in the flesh under the protection of virginity, the strength of death is in a manner broken and annulled, for he does not find the places upon which he may fix his sting.[1]

In spite of his adoption of the Epiphanian view, St Gregory also offered an unlikely speculation on the identity of Mary the mother of James the Less (and Joses) as being Mary the mother of Jesus, but only in an adoptive sense.[2] This strange theory is also found in the *History of Joseph the Carpenter*:

> And Mary found James the Less in his father's house, broken-hearted and sad on account of the loss of his mother, and she brought him up. Hence Mary was called the mother of James.[3]

f) (St) John Chrysostom (+407)

With John Chrysostom, we are leaving the 'age of Nicene transition' and entering the age of established orthodoxy (or Orthodoxy). Coming from Antioch but ending up in Constantinople, the famed and fiery preacher of the imperial capital is on the record for defending Mary's perpetual virginity against those who would have used Matthew 1:25 to impose a Helvidian interpretation on this

---

[1] Gregory of Nyssa, *On Virginity*, 13
[2] See Lightfoot, *The Brethren of the Lord*, 38-39
[3] The *History of Joseph the Carpenter*, 4

text. Chrysostom's *Commentary on Matthew* is an early text in which the Epiphanian view is implied:

> How then, one may say, are James and the others called His brethren? In the same kind of way as Joseph himself was supposed to be husband of Mary. For many were the veils provided, that the birth, being such as it was, might be for a time screened.[1]

It his *Commentary on Galatians* which can be dated several years after the *Commentary on Matthew*, Chrysostom appears to have adopted the Hieronymian view since he describes James the Lord's brother as a son of Clopas (Cleophas) identified as Alphaeus:

> But observe how honorably he mentions him, he says not James merely, but adds this illustrious title, so free is he from all envy. Had he only wished to point out whom he meant, he might have shown this by another appellation, and called him the son of Cleophas, as the Evangelist does. But as he considered that he had a share in the august titles of the Apostles, he exalts himself by honoring James; and this he does by calling him the Lord's brother, although he was not by birth His brother, but only so reputed.[2]

It is possible that Chrysostom's frequent interactions with the West would have led him to encounter and adopt Jerome's explanation. Indeed, his disciple Theodoret was the other case of a Hieronymian in the East.

g) (St) Jerome (+420)

St Jerome is the originator of the Hieronymian view (which he considered to be the biblical view), and we have already cited significant portions of his treatise Against Helvidius.

Jerome revisited the issue in his *Commentary on Matthew*:

---

[1] Chrysostom, *Homily 5 on Matthew*
[2] Chrysostom, *Homily 1 on Galatians*

> Some surmise that the brothers of the Lord are sons of Joseph by another wife. They follow apocryphal nonsense, fabricating some little woman named Escha. But as the book that we have written against Helvidius shows, we understand the brothers of the Lord to be not sons of Joseph, but first cousins of the Savior. They are children of the Mary who was the Lord's aunt, who is said to be the mother of James the Less and of Joses and Jude.[1]

It is important to realize that the original (maternal) Hieronymian view is rarely adopted as such today. Those who think that Jerome's identification of James and Joses in Mark 6:3 and Mark 15:40 is valid generally really on the paternal relationship (Joseph and Clopas being brothers) rather than the maternal hypothesis (two sisters named Mary).

The "apocryphal nonsense" Jerome is alluding to does not refer to the *Protevangelium of James* which does not give the name Escha to Joseph's first wife.

Whatever writing or writings he had in mind, Jerome felt that the identification between the James and Joses of Mark 6:3 and 15:40 was quite certain and never gave any sign of interest in the Epiphanian view.

After St Jerome, St Augustine also adopted the Hieronymian view, as Lightfoot documented:

> In his commentary on the Galatians indeed (i. 19), written about 394 while he was still a presbyter, he offers the alternative of the Hieronymian and Epiphanian accounts. But in his later works he consistently maintains the view put forward by Jerome in the treatise against Helvidius (In Joh. Evang. x, HI. 2. p. 368, ib. xxviii, in. 2. p. 508; Enarr. in Ps. cxxvii, IV. 2. p. 1443; Contr. Faust, xxii. 35, vm. p. 383; comp. Quaest. X VII in Matth., HI. 2. p. 285)... Thus supported, it won its way to general acceptance

---

[1] Jerome, *Commentary on Matthew*, 14

in Western the Latin Church; and the Western Services recognise only one James besides the son of Zebedee, thus identifying the Lord's brother with the son of Alphaeus.

h) (St) Epiphanius of Salamis (+403)

Although St Epiphanius was not the last to die among the fourth century fathers discussed so far, it seems fitting to end with him and discuss the perceived officialization of the position that bears his name.

It is useful to recall certain important details regarding Epiphanius, notably the generally accepted conclusion that he was indeed of Jewish origin. Epiphanius was himself from Palestine and someone with a great deal of critical freedom. He is remembered for the Epiphanian view (of course, as discussed in his famous *Panarion*, or 'medicine chest' against heresies), his anti-Origenism, his ascetical leanings, a possible iconophobic position.

Even though we can be sure that Epiphanius was a conservative, we have to deal with the fact that he rarely cited his sources. In particular, we cannot tell if he is relying on Hegesippus, Eusebius or some other ancient authority. In the case of Mary's death (dormition), Epiphanius is careful not to make anything up but rather to report what he was factually aware of, namely that he was aware of no record available to him at that time. He also repudiates the worship of Mary and seems to have tried to discourage the increasingly widespread use of icons, all of which indicate a very conservative mindset.

Here, it may be said that reading Epiphanius' *Panarion* (in Frank Williams' excellent edition) is a rewarding experience. The great bishop of Salamis engages the biblical text with competence and preserves countless traditional accounts (for instance the names and deeds of the 70/72 disciples).

There is no question, however, that Epiphanius' interest in chronology and the relative age of Joseph, James and Jesus stretches our credulity. Epiphanius tells us that Joseph was 80 years old when betrothed to Mary, having already 6 sons and 2 daughters. This provokes a "sic" from the otherwise restrained editor of the *Panarion*, and indeed, this is not a scenario that I have used in this book. It is, however, generally consistent with the proposition that Joseph died at the ripe old age of 111, and that James was 40 when Jesus was born, and 96 at his death in 62 AD. Helvidian author Ben Witherington criticizes:

> But Epiphanius failed to do his math. By this reckoning, James would have been over seventy years old when Jesus died in A.D. 30 and well over a hundred when he himself died in 62.[1]

This is not quite correct, although the numbers don't perfectly align. Epiphanius has James dying in 62 at age 96, which is consistent with his contention that he was about 40 when Jesus was born. And to his credit, Epiphanius admits that this lifespan is indeed "many years" and yet sticks to his story, however without reference to his sources (Hegesippus, PJ, Eusebius, etc).

Epiphanius is certainly not the inventor of the Epiphanian view, but he certainly provided a lengthy discussion of the matter in his energetic refutation of the "antidicomarian heresy."

i) Conclusion

Considering 367[2] and 381[3] as turning points during the fourth century, what we see is the crystallization of a consensus regarding the question of Mary's perpetual virginity and *adelphoi* that we can only compare to the crystallization of the New Testament canon.

---

[1] Witherington, *The Brother of Jesus*, 207

[2] Festal letter of St Athanasius which is the first proclamation of the finalized New Testament canon

[3] Council of Constantinople, and proclamation of Christianity as official religion of the Roman Empire

St Jerome stands on his own as the (usual) odd man out, although he concurs with the rest (indeed more stridently) that Mary always remained a virgin. His theory, which hinges on two plausible identifications, cannot be entirely dismissed, as John McHugh forcefully argued.

Anyone who is intimately familiar with the 4th century Fathers and the liturgical life passed on as traditions from James the Just to St Cyril of Jerusalem is perfectly at home with the picture of Mary, Joseph and James (as well as Jesus) interiorized by the great churches during those critical years. The Helvidian-alternative, so attractive to the modern mind, is actually incomprehensible for Orthodox Christians for whom the life of Jesus is understood as a grand theological tapestry in which Mary is not just a temporary means-to-an-end but rather a holy sanctuary and the Mother of the Great King. It may well be true that one has to be a spiritual Israelite to perceive the connection between Eve, the Ark, the Gate facing East, the sons of David pledging allegiance to Solomon, Joseph's age at the time of his death or the incongruity of a 30-year old James becoming the Church's first bishop.

From the fourth century onward, the prevalent and accepted view is that Mary always remained a virgin, although with some ongoing discussions and speculations as to the exact relationships between the relatives of Jesus "according to the flesh." We can tell from Basil and Epiphanius that there were always those who believed that the *adelphoi* where the children of Joseph and Mary, and we see that both bishops dealt with this viewpoint somewhat differently. For Basil, the Helvidian position was unpleasant and at odd with received tradition, but it was not strictly speaking a heresy. For the more rigorist and polemical Epiphanius, the same viewpoint was clearly identified (called "antidicomarian") and condemned as heresy with a language so strong that it is almost amusing:

> Who will choose, from self-inflicted insanity, to cast a blasphemous suspicion [on her], raise his voice, give free rein to

> his tongue, flap his mouth with evil intent, invent insults instead of hymns and glory, hurl abuse at the holy Virgin, and deny honor to the precious Vessel?[1]

In this regards, we have concluded that 'popular scholarship' – this may well be an oxymoron– is completely unreliable, as in:

> The teaching of the "perpetual virginity" is simply not found in the New Testament and it is not part of the earliest Christian creeds. The first official mention of the idea does not come until 374 AD from a Christian theologian named Epiphanius. Most of our early Christian writings before the later 4th century AD take for granted that the brothers and sisters of Jesus were the natural born children of Joseph and Mary.[2]

Hopefully, the reader is now equipped to refute such a statement by relying on the primary sources, and by ever being mindful that the very concept of "New Testament" is only meaningful as 4th century development.

---

[1] Epiphanius, *Panarion*, in the Williams edition, 625
[2] James Tabor, *Sorting out the Jesus Family: Mother, Fathers, Brothers & Sisters*, accessed at http://jamestabor.com/2012/12/27/sorting-out-the-jesus-family-mother-fathers-brothers-sisters

VIRGINITY 'IN PARTU'

Many Christians (Evangelicals of course but also Orthodox and Catholic) are surprisingly **unaware** of the teaching of virginity *in partu* of the Blessed Virgin Mary.

In plain words, there are two ways to believe that Mary remained ever-virgin: the first is simply that she never engaged in sexual intercourse with anyone throughout her life; the second includes the first, but adds that even in the act of giving birth, her physical integrity was preserved. This teaching, which is part and parcel of both Orthodox and Catholic theology, is (to the modern mind) hard to understand, even for the faithful of both Churches. The *Protevangelium of James* conveys this belief in this way:

> And the midwife cried out, and said: This is a great day to me, because I have seen this strange sight. And the midwife went forth out of the cave, and Salome met her. And she said to her: "Salome, Salome, I have a strange sight to relate to you: a virgin has brought forth— a thing which her nature admits not of." Then Salome said: "As the Lord my God lives, unless I thrust in my finger, and search the parts, I will not believe that a virgin has brought forth!"[1]

Orthodox Christians who attend Vespers will often hear the following hymn called a *dogmatikon* (which refers to a theological teaching about the Mother of the Lord):

> In times past, the image of the unwedded Bride was inscribed in the Red Sea. There, Moses parted the waters; here, Gabriel took part in the miracle. Then, Israel rode dry-shod through the deep; now the Virgin has without seed given birth to Christ. After the passing of Israel, the sea remained impassible, after the birth of Emmanuel, the blameless Virgin remained incorrupt. You, O

---

[1] *Protevangelium of James*, 19

God, who are, have forever been and have appeared as man, have mercy on us.[1]

This is typological imagery applied (in rather classic Christian manner) to the birth of Christ. We find this particular teaching clearly explained by St Gregory of Nyssa:

> As the Son has been given to us without a father, so the Child has been born without a birth. As the Virgin herself did not know how the body that received divinity was formed in her own body, so neither did she notice the birth. Even the prophet Isaiah affirms that her giving birth was without pain, when he says: 'Before the pangs of birth arrived, a male child came forth and was born' (Isa 66:7)… Just as she who introduced death into nature by her sin was condemned to bear children in suffering and travail, it was necessary that the Mother of life, after having conceived in joy, should give birth in joy as well. No wonder that the angel said to her, 'Rejoice, O full of grace!' (Luk 1:28). With these words he took from her the burden of that sorrow which, from the beginning of creation, has been imposed on birth because of sin.[2]

This teaching of the Cappadocian father – and we have no reason to believe that Basil and the other Gregory did not agree with this – has become part and parcel of the Orthodox understanding of what God had accomplished in Mary the Theotokos. St Basil had also specifically addressed the matter in his commentaries on Genesis:

> Note and retain, I pray you, this point in the history of birds; and if ever you see any one laugh at our mystery, as if it were impossible and contrary to nature that a virgin should become a mother without losing the purity of her virginity, bethink you that He who would save the faithful by the foolishness of

---

[1] Dogmatikon of the Stichera of Vespers, in tone 2
[2] Gregory of Nyssa, *On the Song of Songs*, 13; (PG 44), as quoted in Gambero, *Mary and the Fathers of the Church*, 158

preaching, has given us beforehand in nature a thousand reasons for believing in the marvellous.[1]

St Gregory of Nazianzus, likewise, leaves no doubt regarding his own convictions:

> Believe that the Son of God, the Eternal Word, Who was begotten of the Father before all time and without body, was in these latter days for your sake made also Son of Man, born of the Virgin Mary ineffably and stainlessly (for nothing can be stained where God is, and by which salvation comes)...[2]

The other Cappadocian, Gregory of Nyssa, tells us that this belief (very explicitly taught in the *Protevangelium of James*) was also, and perhaps primarily, an attempt to do justice to the Scriptural data, notably Isaiah 66. It is probably beyond the scope of this essay to discuss this particular chapter of Isaiah verse by verse and in context, and so it suffices to cite the relevant text:

> Before she was in labor she gave birth; before her pain came upon her she was delivered of a son (Isa 66:7)

This is a not only a critically important prophecy (Isaiah's scroll) but certainly an important chapter:

> Thus says the LORD: "Heaven is my throne and the earth is my footstool; what is the house which you would build for me, and what is the place of my rest? All these things my hand has made, and so all these things are mine, says the LORD. But this is the man to whom I will look, he that is humble and contrite in spirit, and trembles at my word. "He who slaughters an ox is like him who kills a man; he who sacrifices a lamb, like him who breaks a dog's neck; he who presents a cereal offering, like him who offers swine's blood; he who makes a memorial offering of frankincense, like him who blesses an idol. These

---

[1] Basil of Caesarea, *Hexaemeron*, Homily 8

[2] Gregory Nazianzen, *The Oration on Holy Baptism* (40), Preached at Constantinople on January 6, 381 (this was the day when both Nativity and Theophany were celebrated).

have chosen their own ways, and their soul delights in their abominations; I also will choose affliction for them, and bring their fears upon them; because, when I called, no one answered, when I spoke they did not listen; but they did what was evil in my eyes, and chose that in which I did not delight." (Isa 66:1-4)

All Christians believe (or should believe) that the same Lord Sabbaoth who appeared to Isaiah in chapter 6 is no other than the Word of God who took flesh from the Virgin Mary. He who shared in the Father's glory before the ages became 'circumscribed' in the womb of his mother who became "a house built for me and a place for my rest" (like the Ark and Temple). The righteous man described in this passage may well be Joseph, but this is undoubtedly reading back into the text. It is not surprising, however, that Christians would have pondered how verse 7 of Isaiah's prophecy could have been fulfilled, especially in light of Matthew's application of Isaiah 7:14.

Indeed, it is not only the Virgin who conceived, but also the Virgin who gives birth. Quite practically, we have seen that this meant no marital intercourse for Mary and Joseph during the pregnancy, which is generally a point of agreement among all Christians. However, the parallel between Mary and Eve (as "the New Eve") also bore the implication that Eve's curse (Gen 3:16) would have been lifted in Mary's birth-giving. Subsequent apologists would notice an unusual detail in the "first-born" text of Luke 2:

> And she gave birth to her first-born son and **[she] wrapped him in swaddling cloths**, and laid him in a manger, because there was no place for them in the inn. (Luk 2:7)

Unexpectedly, Mary was in condition to take care of the newborn Jesus, which may be taken by some as an indication that the delivery was unexpectedly easy.

For those who believe in Christ's supernatural incarnation – nothing more or less than the historical Christian view that see him as fully human and fully divine – the issue is not whether the Lord could have entered into the world without altering his mother's virginity. Of course, it could be done. The question is more: is there any biblical or historical evidence that this was the case?

Clearly, Isaiah 66:7 is only going to convince those who start with sympathy for the idea, and this would typically be those Christians who already embrace the conviction (strongly defended in this essay) that Mary did in fact remain a perpetual virgin. Irenaeus, on account of his spiritual connection to John (and Mary) via Polycarp, is a powerful early witness to a reasonable association of Isaiah 7:14-17 with 66:7:

> With regard to his [Christ's] birth the same prophet says in another place: "Before she came to labor, she gave birth; before the pains came upon her, she delivered a male child" [Is. 66:7], thus proclaiming the unexpected and wondrous character of the birth from the Virgin.[1]

Even more than the virginity *post-partu*, Mary's virginity *in partu* requires an act of faith, and with it a willingness to see these prophecies fulfilled in Mary. For those who trust in the historic succession of presbyters and bishops as a sure guarantee of truth (as Irenaeus did)[2] this is nothing extraordinary.

Ultimately, then, our acceptance or rejection of these particular Marian doctrines is intimately connected with our relationship with the Church (itself foreshadowed by Mary in Revelation 12).

For those who believe that the Holy Spirit has providentially guided the Church into all truth, notably during the decisive years of

---

[1] Irenaeus, *Proof of the Apostolic Preaching*

[2] "It is within the power of all, therefore, in every Church, who may wish to see the truth, to contemplate clearly the tradition of the apostles manifested throughout the whole world; and we are in a position to reckon up those who were by the apostles instituted bishops in the Churches, and [to demonstrate] the succession of these men to our own times; those who neither taught nor knew of anything like what these [heretics] rave about." (*Against Heresies*, Book III, Chapter 3)

'canon discerning' and 'heresy repelling,' it is quite easy to side with the likes of Clement of Alexandria or Gregory of Nyssa. For those however who approach the Scriptures from a purely modernistic mind, it is understandable that the Virgin's virginity *in partu* may be a mystery too great to contemplate and accept. Yet, the Lord himself would use the imagery Isaiah 66 (the prophecy's last words) as great warning:

> Who has heard such a thing? Who has seen such things? (66:8) And they shall go forth and look on the dead bodies of the men that have rebelled against me; for their worm shall not die, their fire shall not be quenched, and they will be loathsome to all mankind. (66:24; compare Mark 9:48)

One thing is certain: belief in Mary's virginity *in partu* is not motivated by heretical Docetism: the connection between Isaiah 7 and 66 was made by the same Irenaeus who understood Mary as the New Eve and who, as a successor of Polycarp, had a unique spiritual lineage to Mary.

Below: Icon of St Epiphanius of Salamis (Granica Monastery, Serbia)

CONCLUSION

We have concluded our exploration of the still-controversial (perhaps increasingly controversial) teaching of historical Christianity that Mary remained a virgin her entire life, and that those who are called the *adelphoi* of Jesus were not in fact uterine siblings.

There is no question that the very terms *adelphoi* (used in several passages) combined with Matthew 1:25 and Luke 2:7 has given rise to the conviction among many that the 'uterine sibling interpretation' is simply obvious and should be held as the default position, the burden of proof being placed on the competing theories.

However, Orthodox Christians believe that the burden of proof should rest squarely on the shoulder of those who would challenge the teachings of the near-unanimity of the ancient Fathers, and further argue that the Helvidian view, in spite of its appearance of being the 'natural reading' of the text, presents significant issues that cannot be ignored.

The Helvidian view does offer a simple reading of Matthew 1 and Mark 6 (with similar texts mentioning "brothers / sisters") but from a theological perspective, the picture that emerges is quite different and atrophied. James Tabor (controversial opponent of the traditional views) writes:

> Once one insists that "the blessed Virgin Mary" was "ever-virgin," with no sexual experience whatsoever, then the brothers and sisters have to be explained away. I say this with no disrespect for those who hold such views of Mary. Yet it is important to understand when, how, and why these ideas developed. Good history never needs to be the enemy of devoted faith. The conflict arises when later forms of ascetic piety and assumptions about "holiness" are imposed on a culture for dogmatic or political reasons. What is lost is the historical reality of who Mary truly was as a Jewish married woman of her time. What we lose is Mary herself!

However, the same can be said, in reverse. By imagining a Mary who after giving birth to the Living One and a Joseph who utterly fails to perceive that his betrothed is a consecrated vessel, we would lose Mary herself as well.

There is a furious desire on the part of many to interpret the early Church's (and I have argued New Testament) enthusiasm for virginity and continence as some kind of quasi-heretical aberration, from which sprung the contrived story of an older Joseph already with children. This is an underlying issue that needs to be understood and addressed, as Epiphanius had aptly done:

> God's holy church holds marriage sacred and honors married persons, for "Marriage is honorable and the bed undefiled." <But> it regards continence as the most admirable, and commends it because it is engaged in the contest and has despised the world, as being still more powerful [than the world].[1]

> Is marriage unholy, after all? Is the marriage bed profane? Isn't "the bed undefiled?" Is marriage debased? But prophets and high priests refrain from it because their service is for a higher purpose.[2]

In addition, the Helvidian view poses the problem of trusting the Fathers for their providential task of preserving and discerning the canon of the New Testament, while rejecting their conviction regarding Mary's perpetual virginity and the identity of the *adelphoi*. As Protestant scholar Lee McDonald expressed with lucidity:

> Those who would argue for the infallibility or the inerrancy of scripture logically should also claim the same infallibility for the churches in the fourth and fifth centuries, whose decisions and historical circumstances have left us with our present Bible. This is apparently what would be required if we were to acknowledge

---

[1] In Williams, 118
[2] In Williams, 628

only the twenty-seven NT books that were set forth by the church in that context. Was the church in the Nicene and post-Nicene eras infallible in its decisions or not?[1]

All in all, Orthodox Christians have the advantage to approach the matter of Mary's perpetual virginity without having to be inconsistent, as Meier aptly stated, to renounce their intellectual integrity. Making sense of the totality of the Scriptural treasure-chest is not something to be taken lightly, and we can hardly do better than cite Origen's advice to St Gregory the Wonderworker and bishop of Neocaesarea:

> Do you then, my son, diligently apply yourself to the reading of the sacred Scriptures. Apply yourself, I say! For we who read the things of God need much application, lest we should say or think anything too rashly about them. And applying yourself thus to the study of the things of God, with faithful prejudgments such as are well pleasing to God, knock at its locked door, and it will be opened to you by the porter, of whom Jesus says, To him the porter opens. And applying yourself thus to the divine study, seek aright, and with unwavering trust in God, the meaning of the Holy Scriptures, which so many have missed. Be not satisfied with knocking and seeking; for prayer is of all things indispensable to the knowledge of the things of God. For to this the Saviour exhorted, and said not only, Knock, and it shall be opened to you; and seek, and you shall find, but also, Ask, and it shall be given unto you. My fatherly love to you has made me thus bold; but whether my boldness be good, God will know, and His Christ, and all partakers of the Spirit of God and the Spirit of Christ. May you also be a partaker, and be ever increasing your inheritance, that you may say not only, "We have become partakers of Christ," but also partakers of God.

---

[1] Lee McDonald, *The Formation of the Christian Biblical Canon*, 255-256

APPENDICES

1) THE HOLY LAND CIRCA 30 AD

2) EPIPHANIAN CHRONOLOGY

a) From St Epiphanius

c. 83 BC	Joseph is born
c. 43 BC	James is born
c. 4 BC	Joseph (80) betrothed to Mary
c. 4/3 BC	Jesus is born
c. 22 AD	Joseph dies
c. 30 AD	Jesus' death crucifixion, James (about 72) becomes bishop of Jerusalem)
c. 62 AD	James dies (96)

b) Alternative proposal

c. 60 BC	Joseph is born
c. 18 BC	James is born
c. 4 BC	Joseph (55/56) betrothed to Mary
c. 4/3 BC	Jesus is born
c. 22 AD	Joseph (84) dies
c. 30 AD	Jesus' death crucifixion, James (about 47) becomes bishop of Jerusalem)
c. 62 AD	James dies (79)

c) Compare Helvidian view

c. 30 BC	Joseph is born
c. 4 BC	Joseph (28) betrothed to Mary
c. 4/3 BC	Jesus is born
c. 1 AD	James is born

c. 22 AD   Joseph (54) dies

c. 30 AD   Jesus' death crucifixion, James (about 30) becomes bishop of Jerusalem)

c. 62 AD   James dies (62)

3) EPIPHANIAN FAMILY TREE

The following family tree appears to be based on: Richard J. Bauckham, *All in the Family: Identifying Jesus Relatives*, in The Burial of Jesus, Biblical Archaeology Society, p. 49

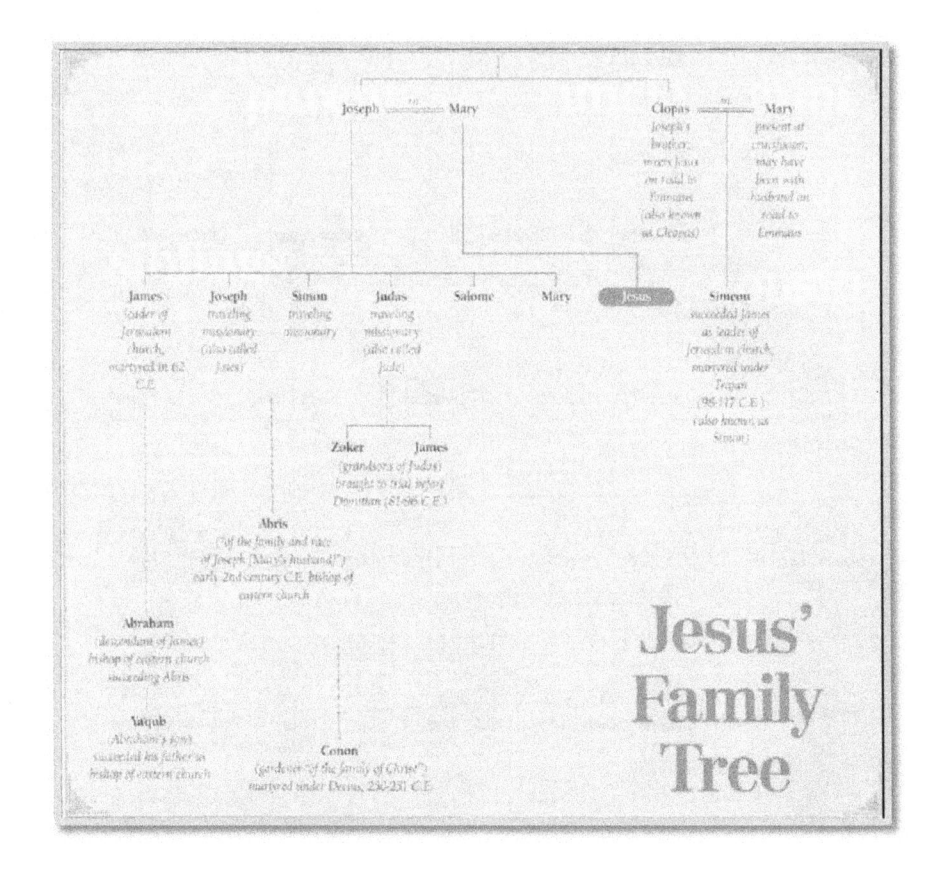

Aiparthenos | Ever-Virgin? Page 244

The following family tree is reconstructed based on the Orthodox Prologue of Ohrid:

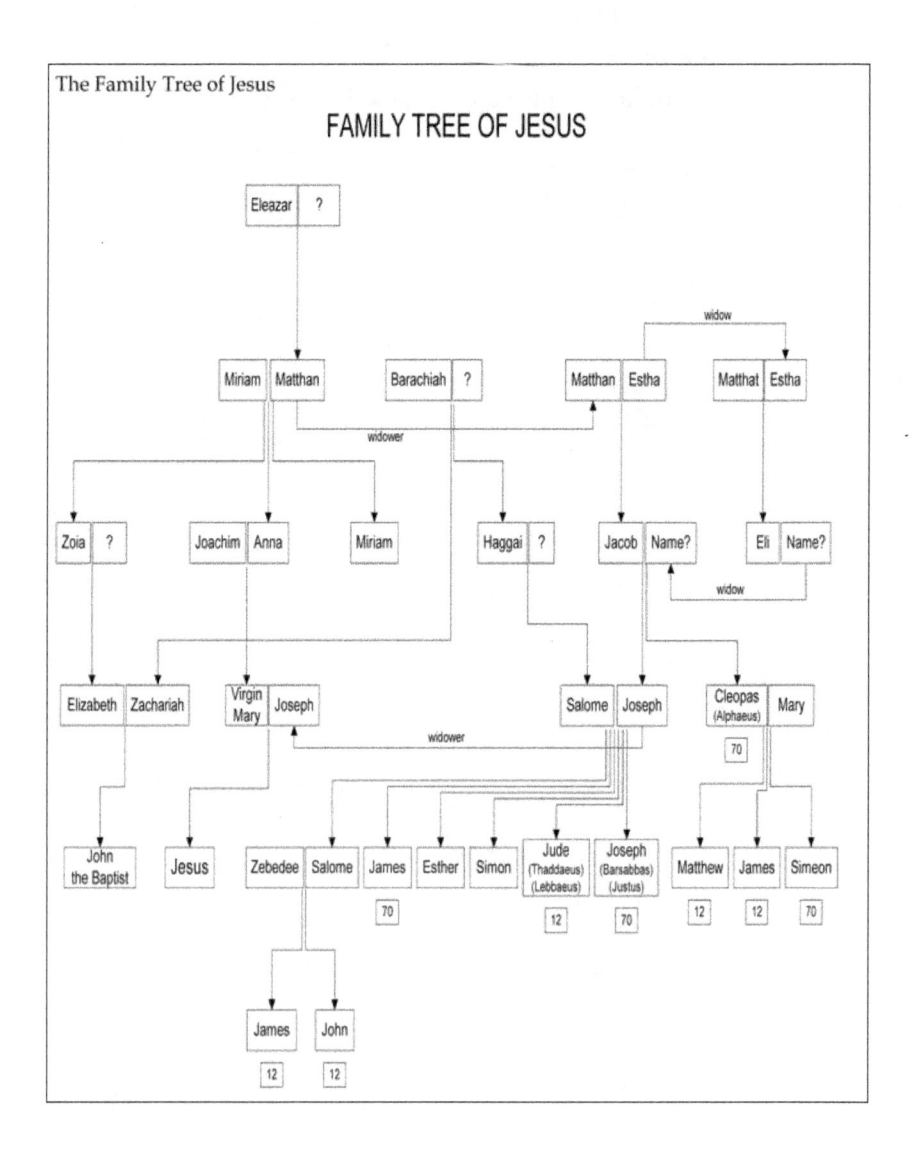

The Family Tree of Jesus

FAMILY TREE OF JESUS

- Eleazar — ?
  - Miriam — Matthan (widower); Barachiah — ?; Matthan — Estha; Matthat — Estha (widow)
    - Zoia — ?
      - Elizabeth — Zachariah
        - John the Baptist
    - Joachim — Anna
      - Virgin Mary — Joseph (widower)
        - Jesus
    - Miriam
      - Zebedee — Salome
        - James [12], John [12]
    - Haggai — ?
      - Salome — Joseph
        - James [70], Esther, Simon, Jude (Thaddaeus) (Lebbaeus) [12], Joseph (Barsabbas) (Justus) [70]
    - Jacob — Name?
    - Eli — Name? (widow)
      - Cleopas (Alphaeus) [70] — Mary
        - Matthew [12], James [12], Simeon [70]

4) LIGHTFOOT'S SUMMARY

This page from J. B. Lightfoot's still relevant *The Brethren of the Lord (Dissertations on the Apostolic Age)* presents a summary of 'who taught what' among the ancient authors and fathers:

THE BRETHREN OF THE LORD. 45

A. *Sons of Joseph and Mary.*
- Tertullian,
- Helvidius,
- Bonosus,
- Jovinianus (?),
- Antidicomarianites.

B. *Sons of Joseph by a former wife.*
- Gospel of Peter,
- Protevangelium etc.,
- Clement of Alex.,
- Origen,
- Eusebius,
- Hilary of Poitiers,
- Ambrosiaster,
- Gregory of Nyssa,
- Epiphanius,
- Ambrose,
- [Chrysostom],
- Cyril of Alex.,
- Eastern services (Greek, Syrian, and Coptic),
- Later Greek writers.

C. *Sons of the Virgin's sister.*
- Jerome,
- Pelagius,
- Augustine,
- [Chrysostom],
- Theodoret,
- Western services,
- Later Latin writers.

A. or B. '*Brethren*' *in a strict sense. James the Just not one of the Twelve.*
- Early versions,
- Clementine Homilies (?),
- Ascents of James,
- Hegesippus,
- Apost. Constit.,
- Cyril of Jerusalem (?),
- Victorinus the Philosopher.

B. or C. *Perpetual virginity of Mary.*
- Basil,
- Catholic writers generally.

Uncertain. Hebrew gospel, Victorinus Petavionensis.
Levirate. Theophylact.

5) THE PROTEVANGELIUM OF JAMES

Chapter 1

1 In the records of the twelve tribes of Israel, Joachim was a very rich man. 2 He always brought a double offering to the Lord, 3 saying to himself, "My offering for all the people is from my surplus and my own offering to the Lord God is for forgiveness, to atone for my sins." 4 As the great day of the Lord (Yom Kippur) was drawing near and the children of Israel were bringing their offerings, however, 5 Reubel stood in his way, saying, "You cannot offer your gifts first because you have not conceived a child in Israel."

6 And Joachim became extremely frustrated and went away to the history of the twelve tribes of his people, saying to himself, "I will look in the records of the twelve tribes of Israel and see whether I am the only one who has not conceived a child in Israel." 7 And he searched and found that all the righteous people had raised children in Israel. 8 And he reminded himself about the patriarch Abraham and that the Lord God gave his son Isaac to him in his last days.

9 Then, Joachim was extremely distraught and did not appear to his wife, but gave himself to the desert and pitched his tent there. 10 He fasted forty days and forty nights. 11 All the while, Joachim was saying to himself, "I will not go down for food or drink until the Lord my God visits me; prayer will be my food and drink."

Chapter 2

1 Then, his wife Anna mourned and lamented greatly for two reasons, saying, "I lament that I am a widow and I lament that I am childless."

2 When the great day of the Lord was drawing near, 3 her servant Juthine said to her, "How long are you going to humble yourself? Do you not see that the great day of the Lord is approaching? You are not allowed to mourn. 4 Take this headband which the leader of the activity gave me. I am not allowed to tie it because I am your slave and it has a royal mark."

5 Then, Anna said, "Get away from me. I did not cause these things, even though the Lord God has humbled me greatly. Perhaps a crafty person has given this to you and you have come to cause me to partake of your sin."

6 So her servant Juthine said, "Should I invoke a curse on you because you did not hear my voice? The Lord God has shut your womb and he will not give you offspring in Israel."

7 At this, Anna also became extremely frustrated and removed her mourning garment, washed her head and clothed herself with her wedding dress. 8 Around the ninth hour, she went down to her garden to walk around. She saw a laurel tree and sat down under it. 9 And after a rest, she petitioned the Lord, saying, "God of my ancestors, bless me and hear my prayer, just as you blessed our mother Sarah and gave her son Isaac to her."

Chapter 3

1 And Anna looked up to the heavens and saw a nest of sparrows in the laurel tree. 2 Immediately, Anna cried out mournfully, saying to herself,

"Woe unto me, who gave birth to me? What womb caused me to grow? 3 For I was born cursed in front of the children of Israel. I am reviled and they treat me with contempt and cast me out of the temple of the Lord my God.

4 "Woe unto me, what am I like? I am not like the birds of the sky, for the birds of the sky are fruitful before you, Lord.

5 "Woe unto me, what am I like? I am not like the domestic animals, for the domestic animals are fruitful before you, Lord.

6 "Woe unto me, what am I like? I am not like the wild animals of the earth, for the wild animals of the earth are fruitful before you, Lord.

7 "Woe unto me, what am I like? I am not like these waters, for these waters are fruitful before you, Lord.

8 "Woe unto me, what am I like? I am not like this earth, for the earth produces its fruit in season and blesses you, Lord."

Chapter 4

1 Suddenly, an angel of the Lord stood in front of her, saying, "Anna, Anna, the Lord God has heard your prayer. You will conceive and give birth and your child will be spoken of everywhere people live."

2 And Anna said, "As the Lord God lives, whether I give birth to either a male or a female child, I will bring it as an offering to the Lord my God and it will be a servant to him all the days of its life."

3 Next, two angels came, saying to her, "Look your husband Joachim is coming with his flocks." 4 For an angel of the Lord had gone down to Joachim, saying, "Joachim, Joachim, the Lord God has heard your prayer. Go down from here. Look, your wife Anna has conceived in her womb."

5 Immediately, Joachim went down and called the shepherds, telling them, "Bring ten lambs without spot or blemish here to me; the ten lambs will be for the Lord God. 6 Bring twelve tender calves; the twelve calves will be for the priests and the elders. 7 And bring one hundred male goats; the one hundred male goats will be for all the people."

8 Then, Joachim came with his flocks. Anna was standing at the gate. 9 When she saw Joachim coming with his flocks, Anna ran and wrapped herself around his neck, saying, "Now I know that the Lord God has blessed me greatly. See, the widow is no longer a widow and the childless woman has conceived in her womb."

10 And Joachim rested for the first day he was home.

Chapter 5

1 The next day, when he was presenting his offerings, he said to himself, "If the Lord God will be reconciled to me, he will make it clear to me with the priest's metal disc." 2 And Joachim presented his offerings and paid attention to the priest's metal disc until he went up to the altar of the Lord. And he saw no sin in it. 3 Joachim said, "Now, I know that the Lord God has been reconciled to me and has sent all my great sins away for me." 4 And having been justified, he departed from the temple and went to his house.

5 And his wife's pregnancy came to term. After nine months, Anna gave birth 6 and she said to the midwife, "What is it?"

7 The midwife said, "A girl."

8 Anna said, "My soul exalts this day." And she put her baby to bed.

9 After her days were completed, Anna cleansed her menstrual flow 10 and gave her breast to the child and gave her the name Mary.

Chapter 6

1 Day by day, the child grew stronger. 2 When she was six months old, her mother set her on the ground to test whether she could stand. And after walking seven steps, she came to her mother's breast. 3 And her mother picked her up, saying, "As the Lord my God lives, you will not walk on this earth again until I take you to the temple of the Lord."

4 And she made a sanctuary in her bedroom and would not permit anything common or impure to pass through it. 5 And she called the pure daughters of the Hebrews and they played with her.

6 When the child's first birthday came, Joachim held a great celebration. He invited the high priests and the priests and the Sanhedrin and the whole nation of Israel. 7 And Joachim brought the child to the priests and they blessed her, saying, "God of our ancestors, bless this child and give her name eternal fame among all generations."

8 And all the people said, "Let it happen, amen."

9 And he brought the child to the high priests and they blessed her, saying, "Exalted God, look upon this child and give her a final blessing which will not be succeeded."

10 And her mother took her up to the bedroom-sanctuary and gave her breast to the child. 11 And Anna composed a song for the Lord God, saying, "I will sing a holy song to the Lord my God because he has examined me and removed my horrible disgrace from me. 12 And the Lord God gave me the fruit of his righteousness, of one nature, but manifold before him. 13 Who will proclaim to the sons of Reubel that Anna nurses a child? Do you hear? Hear this, twelve tribes of Israel: Anna nurses a child!"

14 And she gave the child rest in the bedroom-sanctuary and went out and served them. 15 When dinner was completed, they departed feeling good and glorified the God of Israel.

Chapter 7

1 She cared for the child for months. When the child turned two years old, Joachim said, "Let's take her to the temple of the Lord so we can relate the message we were given."

2 And Anna said, "Let's wait until the third year, so that she will not seek her father or mother."

3 And Joachim said, "Let's wait."

4 When the child turned three, Joachim said, "Let's call the pure women of the Hebrews. 5 Let them take up lamps and light them so that the child will not turn back and her heart will never be led away from the temple of the Lord." 6 And they did these things until they went up to the temple of the Lord.

7 And the priest welcomed her. Kissing her, he blessed her and said, "The Lord God has magnified your name for all generations; 8 through you the Lord will reveal deliverance to the children of Israel in the last days."

9 And he set her down on the third step of the altar and the Lord God poured grace upon her. 10 She danced triumphantly with her drinks and every house in Israel loved her.

Chapter 8

1 And her parents went down, marveling at and praising and glorifying the Lord God because the child had not turned back to look at them. 2 While Mary was in the temple of the Lord, she was fed like a dove and received food from the hand of an angel.

3 When she turned twelve, a group of priests took counsel together, saying, "Look, Mary has been in the temple of the Lord twelve years. 4 What should we do about her now, so that she does not defile the sanctuary of the Lord our God?" 5 And they said to the high priest, "You have stood at the altar of the Lord. Go in and pray about her. And if the Lord God reveals anything to you, we will do it."

6 And the priest went in taking the vestment with twelve bells into the holy of holies and prayed about her. Suddenly, an angel of the Lord stood before him, saying, "Zachariah, Zachariah, depart from here and gather the widowers of the people and let each one carry a staff. 8 And the one whom the Lord God points out with a sign, she will be his wife." 9 So the

heralds went out to the whole surrounding area of Judea and the trumpet of the Lord rang out and all the men rushed in.

Chapter 9

1 Throwing down his ax, Joseph went out to meet them. 2 And after they had gathered together with their rods, they went to the high priest. 3 After receiving everyone's rod, the high priest went into the temple and prayed. 4 When he was finished with the prayer, he took the rods and went out and gave them to each man, 5 but there was no sign among them. Finally, Joseph took his rod. 6 Suddenly, a dove came out of the rod and stood on Joseph's head. 7 And the high priest said, "Joseph! Joseph! You have been chosen by lot to take the virgin into your own keeping."

8 And Joseph replied, saying, "I have sons and am old, while she is young. I will not be ridiculed among the children of Israel."

9 And the high priest said, "Joseph, fear the Lord your God and remember what God did to Dathan and Abiron and Kore, how the earth split open and swallowed them because of their rebellion. 10 Now fear God, Joseph, so that these things do not happen in your house."

11 Fearing God, Joseph took her into his own possession. 12 And he said to her, "Mary, I took you from the temple of the Lord and now I bring you into my house. I am going out to build houses, but I will come back to you. The Lord will protect you."

Chapter 10

1 Meanwhile, the priests were meeting together, saying, "Let us make a curtain for the temple of the Lord."

2 And the high priest said, "Call the pure virgins from the tribe of David to me." 3 And the servants went out and sought and found seven virgins. 4 And the high priest remembered that the child Mary was from the tribe of David and was pure before God. 5 So the servants went out and got her.

6 And they brought the women into the temple of the Lord. 7 And the high priest said, "Cast lots to see who will spin the gold and the pure and the linen and the silk and the violet and the scarlet and the true purple threads."

8 And Mary was appointed by lot to the true purple and scarlet threads. And taking them, she went to her house. 9 This was at the same time Zachariah fell silent and Samuel replaced him until Zachariah could speak again. 10 Mary was spinning the scarlet thread which she had taken.

Chapter 11

1 And she took the cup and went out to fill it with water. 2 Suddenly, a voice said to her, "Rejoice, blessed one. The Lord is with you. You are blessed among women." 3 And Mary looked around to the right and the left to see where this voice came from. 4 And trembling she went into her house. Setting down the cup, she took the purple thread and sat down on the chair and spun it.

5 Suddenly, an angel stood before her saying, "Do not be afraid Mary. You have found grace before the Lord of all. You will conceive from his word."

6 Upon hearing this, however, Mary was distraught, saying to herself, "If I conceive from the Lord God who lives, will I also conceive as all women conceive?"

7 And the Angel of the Lord said, "Not like that, Mary. For the power of God will come over you. Thus, the holy one who is born will be called son of the most high. 8 And you will call his name Jesus, for he will save his people from their sins."

9 And Mary said, "See, I am the servant of the Lord before him. Let it happen to me according to what you say."

Chapter 12

1 And she made the purple and the scarlet thread and carried it to the high priest. 2 And taking it, the high priest blessed her and said, "Mary, God has magnified your name. You will be called blessed among all the generations of the earth."

3 Then, Mary went gladly to her cousin Elizabeth. 4 And she knocked at the door and when Elizabeth heard, she threw down her scarlet thread and ran to the door and opened it for her. 5 And she blessed her and said, "Where have you come to me from? Why should the mother of my Lord come to me? See how the child in me leaps and blesses you."

6 But Mary had forgotten the mysteries which the angel Gabriel had told her. And looking into heaven she said, "Who am I, Lord, that all the generations of the earth will bless me?"

7 She spent three months with Elizabeth. 8 Day after day, her womb swelled and she was afraid to go to her house and hid herself from the children of Israel. 9 Mary was sixteen years old when these mysterious things happened to her.

Chapter 13

1 In the sixth month of her pregnancy, Joseph came from his house-building and went into the house to find her swelling. 2 And he struck his face and threw himself on the ground in sackcloth and wept bitterly, "How can I look to the Lord God? What will I pray about her, for I took her as a virgin from the temple of the Lord and did not guard her? 4 Who has set this trap for me? Who did this evil in my house? Who stole the virgin from me and defiled her. 5 Has not the story of Adam been repeated with me? For while Adam was glorifying God, the serpent came and found Eve alone and deceived her and defiled her - so it has also happened to me."

6 And Joseph got up from his sackcloth and called her and said to her, "After having been cared for by God, what have you done? 7 Did you forget the Lord your God? You who were raised in the holy of holies, you who received from the hand of an angel, do you know how much you have humiliated yourself?"

8 Then, she wept bitterly, saying, "I am pure and I did not know a man."

9 And Joseph said to her, "Where did this thing in your womb come from then?"

10 But she said, "As the Lord my God lives, I do not know where it came from."

Chapter 14

1 Then, Joseph was extremely frightened and kept quiet about her, pondering what he should do. 2 And Joseph said to himself, "If I hide her sin, I will be rebelling against the law of the Lord. 3 And if I expose her to the children of Israel . . . well, I am afraid that the child in her might be

angelic and I will be betraying innocent blood to a judgment of death. 4 What then will I do about her? I will send her away from me secretly."

5 And night overtook him. And suddenly an angel of the Lord appeared to him in a dream, saying, "Do not fear this child. For the child in her is from the Holy Spirit. 6 She will bear a son for you and you will call his name Jesus. For he will save his people from their sins."

7 And Joseph arose from his sleep and glorified the God of Israel who had given grace to him. 8 And he guarded the child.

Chapter 15

1 Then, Annas the scribe came to him and said to him, "Joseph, why have you not appeared to our traveling group?"

2 And he said to him, "Because I was worn out from the trip and rested my first day back."

3 And Annas turned and saw Mary pregnant.

4 And he ran off at top speed to the high priest and said to him, "Look at Joseph, the one you bear witness for. He has broken the law badly."

5 And the high priest said, "What is this?"

6 And he said, "The virgin which Joseph received from the temple of the Lord, he defiled her and has stolen her wedding festivities and has not revealed it to the children of Israel."

7 And he said to him, "Has Joseph done these things?"

8 And he said to him, "Send a servant and he will find the virgin pregnant."

9 And the servants went and found her just as he said and they led her with Joseph to the law court.

10 And the high priest said to her, "Mary, what is this? How have you humiliated yourself? 11 Did you forget the Lord your God, you who were raised in the holy of holies and received from the hand of an angel? 12 You who heard their songs and danced before them, what is this?"

13 And she wept bitterly, saying, "As the Lord God lives, I am pure before him and I did not know a man."

14 And the high priest said, "Joseph, what is this?"

15 But Joseph said, "As the Lord lives, I am pure from her."

16 And the high priest said, "Do not lie, but speak the truth. You stole your wedding festivities and did not reveal it to the children of Israel 17 and you did not bow your head before the mighty hand that it should bless your seed."

18 Joseph was silent.

Chapter 16

1 And the high priest said, "Return the virgin which you took from the temple of the Lord."

2 And Joseph cried [...]

3 The high priest said, "I will give you the water of the Lord's wrath to drink and it will make your sin clear in your eyes." 4 And taking the water, the high priest gave it to Joseph to drink and sent him out into the desert. And he returned unharmed.

5 And he made the young girl drink also and sent her out into the desert. And she came back unharmed. 6 And all the people were astonished that their sins were not revealed. 7 And the high priest said, "If the Lord God has not revealed your sins, I will not judge you either." And he released them. 8 And Joseph took Mary and went away to his house, rejoicing and praising the God of Israel.

Chapter 17

1 Then, there was an order from the Emperor Augustus to register how many people were in Bethlehem of Judea. 2 And Joseph said, "I will register my sons. But this child? What will I do about him? How will I register him? 3 And my wife? Oh, I am ashamed. Should I register her as my daughter? The children of Israel know that she is not my daughter. 4 This day, I will do as the Lord wants."

5 And he saddled his donkey and sat her on it and his son led and Samuel followed. 6 And they arrived at the third mile and Joseph turned and saw that she was sad. 7 And he said to himself, "Perhaps the child within her is troubling her." 8 And again Joseph turned around and saw her laughing

and said to her, "Mary, what is with you? First your face appears happy and then sad?"

9 And she said, "Joseph, it is because I see two people with my eyes, one crying and being afflicted, one rejoicing and being extremely happy."

10 When they came to the middle of the journey, Mary said to him, "Joseph, take me off the donkey, the child pushing from within me to let him come out."

11 So he took her off the donkey and said to her, "Where will I take you and shelter you in your awkwardness? This area is a desert."

Chapter 18

1 And he found a cave and led her there and stationed his sons to watch her, 2 while he went to a find a Hebrew midwife in the land of Bethlehem.

3 Then, Joseph wandered, but he did not wander. 4 And I looked up to the peak of the sky and saw it standing still and I looked up into the air. With utter astonishment I saw it, even the birds of the sky were not moving. 5 And I looked at the ground and saw a bowl lying there and workers reclining. And their hands were in the bowl. 6 And chewing, they were not chewing. And picking food up, they were not picking it up. And putting food in their mouths, they were not putting it in their mouths. 7 Rather, all their faces were looking up.

8 And I saw sheep being driven, but the sheep were standing still. 9 And the shepherd lifted up his hand to strike them, but his hand remained above them. 10 And I saw the rushing current of the river and I saw goats and their mouths resting in the water, but they were not drinking. 11 And suddenly everything was replaced by the ordinary course of events.

Chapter 19

1 And I saw a woman coming down from the mountain and she said to me, "Man, where are you going?"

2 And I said, "I am seeking a Hebrew midwife."

3 Replying, she said to me, "Are you from Israel?"

4 And I said to her, "Yes."

5 Then, she said, "And who is giving birth in the cave?"

6 And I said, "The one who has pledged to be married to me."

7 And she said to me, "She is not your wife?"

8 And I said to her, "She is Mary, the one who was raised in the temple. I won her by lot to be my wife. 9 She is not yet my wife, but has a fetus from the Holy Spirit."

10 And the midwife said, "Really?"

11 And Joseph said to her, "Come and see."

12 So the midwife went with him. 13 And they stood near the cave and a dark cloud was hovering over the cave. 14 And the midwife said, "My soul glorifies this day, for today my eyes have seen a miracle: salvation has come to Israel."

15 And immediately, the cloud withdrew from the cave and a great light appeared in the cave so that their eyes could not bear it. 16 And a little while later the same light withdrew until an infant appeared. And he came and took the breast of his mother, Mary.

17 And the midwife cried out and said, "How great this day is for me, for I have seen this new miracle."

18 And the midwife departed from the cave and met Salome and said to her, "Salome, Salome, I have to describe this new miracle for you. A virgin has given birth, although her body does not allow it."

19 And Salome said, "As the Lord my God lives, unless I insert my finger and investigate her, I will not believe that a virgin has given birth."

Chapter 20

1 And the midwife went in and said, "Mary, position yourself, for not a small test concerning you is about to take place."

2 When Mary heard these things, she positioned herself. And Salome inserted her finger into her body. 3 And Salome cried out and said, "Woe for my lawlessness and the unbelief that made me test the living God. Look, my hand is falling away from me and being consumed in fire."

5 And Salome dropped to her knees before the Lord, saying, "God of Abraham and Isaac and Jacob, 6 do not expose me to the children of Israel, but give me back to the poor. 7 For you know, Lord, that I have performed service and received my wage from you."

8 Suddenly, an angel of the Lord appeared, saying to her, "Salome, Salome, the Lord of all has heard your entreaty. 9 Stretch out your hand to the child and lift him up and he will be salvation and joy for you."

10 And Salome went to the child and lifted him up, saying, "I worship him because he has been born a king to Israel." 11 And at once Salome was healed and left the cave justified.

12 Suddenly, there was a voice saying, "Salome, Salome, do not proclaim what a miracle you have seen until the child comes to Jerusalem."

Chapter 21

1 Now, Joseph was about to depart to Judea when there a great commotion in Bethlehem of Judea. 2 For astrologers had come, saying, "Where is the one who has been born king of the Jews? For we saw his star in the East and came to worship him."

3 And when Herod heard, he was shaken up and sent servants to the astrologers. 4 And he also sent for the high priests and questioned them in his palace, saying to them, "What has been written about the messiah? Where will he be born?"

5 They said to him, "In Bethlehem of Judea, for so it has been written." 6 And he let them go.

7 And he questioned the astrologers, saying to them, "What sign did you see about the one who has been born king?"

8 And the astrologers said, "We saw a star shining with incredible brilliance amidst the constellations and making them seem dim. And so we knew that the king had been born in Israel and we came to worship him."

9 And Herod said to them, "Go and search. If you find him, report to me so that I also may come and worship him."

10 And the wise men departed. Then, the star which they had seen in the east led them until they came to the cave and stood over the head of the

child. 11 And when the astrologers saw him with his mother Mary, they took gifts out of their bags: gold, frankincense, and myrrh.

12 And having been warned by the angel not to go into Judea, they returned to their country by another road.

Chapter 22

1 When Herod saw that he had been tricked by the astrologers, he flew into a rage 2 and sent his executioners, telling them to destroy all the infants that were two years old or younger.

3 And when Mary heard that all the children were being destroyed, she was afraid and took the child and wrapped him up and put him in a stall of cows.

5 And when Elizabeth heard that John was being sought, she took him and headed for the hills. And she looked around to find where she could hide him, but there was not any good place. 7 Then, as Elizabeth sighed, she said with a loud voice, "Mountain of God, take me, a mother with her child." For Elizabeth was too afraid to go up higher. 8 And at once, the mountain split open and received her. And there was light shining through the mountain to her. 9 For an angel of the Lord was with them, guarding them.

Chapter 23

1 But Herod continued seeking John. 2 And he sent his servants to Zachariah at the altar, saying to him, "Where did you hide your son?"

3 But he replied, saying to them, "I am here as a servant of God and am serving in his temple. How should I know where my son is?"

4 And his servants departed and reported to him all these things. Outraged, Herod said, "Is his son destined to rule Israel?"

5 And he sent his servants again, saying to him, "Tell me the truth? Where is your son? Do you know that your blood is under my hand?"

6 And the servants departed and reported these things to him.

7 And replying, Zachariah said, "I am a witness of God. Have my blood. 8 The Lord will receive my spirit because you are shedding innocent blood at the entrance of the temple of the Lord."

9 And around daybreak, Zachariah was murdered, even though the children of Israel did not know that he had been murdered.

Chapter 24

1 Then, at the hour of greeting, the priests departed and the blessing of Zachariah did not greet them as usual. 2 Expecting Zachariah, the priests waited to welcome him with prayer and to praise the Most High God.

3 When he failed to come, they were all afraid. 4 One of them courageously went into the sanctuary and saw hardened blood next to the altar of the Lord 5 and heard a loud voice saying, "Zachariah has been murdered and his blood will not be wiped away until vengeance comes."

6 When he heard these words, he was afraid and went out and told the priest what he had seen and heard. 7 And gathering up their courage, they went in and saw what had happened. 8 And as the panels of the temple cried out, they ripped their robes from the top down. 9 And they did not find the corpse, but they found his blood which had turned to stone. 10 And fearing, they went out and reported to the people that Zachariah had been murdered. 11 And all the tribes of the people heard and they mourned and wept for three days and three nights.

12 Then, after three days, the priests deliberated about who they should appoint to take the place of Zachariah. 13 And the lot went to Simeon. 14 For he was the one to whom it had been revealed by the Holy Spirit that he would not see death until he saw the messiah in the flesh.

Chapter 25

1 I, James, wrote this history when there was unrest in Jerusalem, at the time Herod died. 2 I took myself into the desert until the unrest in Jerusalem ceased. 3 All the while, I was glorifying God who gave me the wisdom to write this history.

4 And grace will be with all who fear the Lord. Amen. Birth of Mary. Revelation of James. Peace to the writer and the reader.

6) ORTHODOX LITURGICAL TEXTS

a) From the Feast of the Entrance of the Theotokos into the Temple (November 21)[1]

Let us believers exchange glad tidings, singing to the Lord with psalms and songs of praise, honoring His holy tabernacle, the living ark who contained the uncontainable Word; for in a supernatural manner is she offered to God as a babe. And Zachariah the great High Priest receiveth her rejoicing since she is God's abode.

Today the living temple of holy glory, the glory of Christ our God, Who alone is blessed and undefiled, is presented in the Mosaic Temple, to live in its holy precincts. Wherefore, Joachim and Anna rejoice now with her in spirit, and the ranks of virgins praise the Lord with songs honoring His Mother.

Verse 1. Virgins shall be brought to the King after her: her companions shall be brought unto Thee.

Having openly enjoyed the divine grace, Anna, rejoicing, presenteth the pure ever-virgin one in the Temple, calling the maidens to present her, as they carry lamps, saying, Go forth, my daughter, to Him Who gave thee to me. Be thou to Him a vow, an incense of sweet odor. Enter thou unto the veiled ones and learn the mysteries. Prepare thyself to become a delightful abode unto Jesus Who granteth the world the Great Mercy.

Verse 2. With gladness and rejoicing shall they be brought: they shall be brought into the temple of the King.

The all-holy Virgin, the temple that contained the Godhead, is placed in the Temple of God. And the maidens, going before her,

---

[1] At Great Vespers, the readings are from Exodus. (40:1-5, 9-11, 16, 34-35), 1 Kings (7:51-8:11) and Ezekiel (43:27-44:4).

carry lamps. Wherefore, her parents, Joachim and Anna, rejoice and exchange glad tidings; for they gave birth to the all-blameless one who gave birth to the Creator, who, as she resided in the heavenly abodes, fed by the angel's hand, was manifest as Mother of Christ, Who granteth the world the Great Mercy.

b) From the minor Feast of the Conception of the Theotokos by Joachim and Anna (December 9)

Kathismata:

> Behold, at the almighty behest of the Lord God, in Anna's holy womb the new heaven is fashioned, from which hath shone forth the bright-beaming Sun that doth never set, Who hath lightened all the world with rays of His Godhead in the tenderness of His exceeding compassion, the only Lover of mankind.

> David, raise thy voice and cry: What is it God hath sworn to thee? What he swore to me, saith he, behold, He likewise hath fulfilled: for as the fruit of my loins, He bestowed the Virgin. From her, the Fashioner and the new Adam, Christ, hath been born a King to sit upon my throne; and as a king today He reigneth, Who hath a Kingdom unshakeable. The barren beareth the Theotokos, the nourisher of our Life

c) From the Feast of St James of Jerusalem, the Brother of the Lord (October 23)

Doxasticon of Vespers:

> With the blood of martyrdom didst thou embellish the priesthood, O Hieromartyr and Apostle; for while standing on the pinnacle of the Temple, thou didst proclaim God the Word to be the Creator of all. Wherefore, when thou wast hurled down by the Jews, thou wast deemed worthy of the heavenly bridal chambers. O James, Adelphotheos, entreat Christ our God that our souls may be saved!

> Distinguished among the Apostles as the brother and successor of Christ the Chief Shepherd, thou didst love death for His sake,

and wast not ashamed of martyrdom, O glorious James. Entreat Him unceasingly that our souls may be saved!

Enlightened with the fiery brightness of the Divine Spirit, thou didst prove to be a divine zealot of piety, O James, Brother of God. Wherefore, He that in His compassion received thee as a brother, clothed thee like Aaron of old, but with raiment more venerable than that of the priesthood of the Law. O thou who art glorious among the Apostles, entreat Christ that our souls be saved.

Synaxarion:

James is called the Brother of the Lord and 'adelphotheos' because he was the son of the righteous Joseph, the betrothed of the Most-holy Theotokos. When the righteous Joseph was near death, he divided his estate among his sons, and wanted to leave a portion to the Lord Jesus, the son of the Most-holy Virgin, but all the other brothers opposed this, not regarding Jesus as their brother. James greatly loved Jesus and declared that he would include Jesus in his share. According to tradition, James traveled to Egypt with the Most-holy Virgin and Joseph, when Herod sought to slay the newborn King. Later, as soon as he heard Christ's teaching, James lived by it. The Lord numbered him among His Seventy Apostles. James was Bishop of Jerusalem for thirty years and zealously governed the Church of God. At the instruction of the Lord, James compiled the first Liturgy. He converted many Jews and Greeks to the Christian Faith, and even the unbelieving Jews were amazed at his righteousness, referring to him as "James the Just." When Ananias became High Priest, he and other Jewish elders determined to kill James. Once, during the feast of Passover, when many people had gathered in Jerusalem, the elders forced James to climb onto the roof of the Temple, and tried to make him speak against Christ. He climbed up and spoke to the people of Christ as the Son of God and the true Messiah, of His Resurrection and His eternal glory in the heavens. The infuriated priests and elders pushed him off the roof; he fell and was severely injured, but was still alive. Then, one man ran up and struck him on the head with a fuller's club with such force that his brains spilled out. Thus, this most glorious apostle of Christ died a martyr's death.

From Othros:

> The wise Apostles' assembly elected thee, O James, to serve in holy Zion as her first hierarch in Christ our Benefactor, since thou, because of His birth in the flesh, wast shown forth to be His very brother and tried fellow traveler, who with love didst follow in His steps.

d) From the cycle of Vespers (Tone 1)

> In times past, the image of the unwedded Bride was inscribed in the Red Sea. There, Moses parted the waters; here, Gabriel took part in the miracle. Then, Israel rode dry-shod through the deep; now the Virgin has without seed given birth to Christ. After the passing of Israel, the sea remained impassible, after the birth of Emmanuel, the blameless Virgin remained incorrupt. You, O God, who are, have forever been and have appeared as man, have mercy on us.

INDEX

Alphaeus, 38, 79, 172, 173, 174, 175, 176, 182, 221, 223

Ark, 76, 86, 87, 88, 89, 90, 92, 99, 225, 231

Athanasius, 62, 89, 97, 103, 165, 216, 217, 224

Augustine, 91, 222

Basil, 40, 41, 42, 63, 112, 218, 219, 225, 229, 230, 233

Bauckham, 20, 56, 59, 69, 98, 106, 110, 112, 122, 123, 124, 129, 140, 176, 190, 207, 243

Chrysostom, 115, 116, 134, 162, 178, 220, 221, 233

Clopas, 37, 57, 81, 82, 96, 128, 129, 130, 170, 172, 173, 174, 175, 176, 177, 202, 203, 204, 205, 207, 221, 222

Dogma, 40

Epiphanius, 44, 52, 53, 54, 55, 56, 57, 77, 121, 129, 188, 223, 224, 225, 226, 237, 241

Eusebius, 49, 55, 63, 70, 112, 165, 166, 175, 184, 185, 186, 202, 203, 205, 206, 207, 208, 213, 214, 215, 216, 218, 223, 224

First-born, 119

Geisler, 45, 124, 125, 126, 132

Gospel of Peter, 184, 185, 186, 187, 189, 214, 215

Gregory of Nazianzus, 230

Gregory of Nyssa, 63, 80, 83, 84, 219, 220, 229, 230

Hegesippus, 55, 81, 130, 133, 173, 174, 175, 176, 177, 178, 202, 203, 204, 205, 206, 207, 208, 211, 216, 223, 224

Helvidius, 52, 62, 113, 128, 133, 170, 171, 183, 211, 213, 221, 222

Heos hou, 137, 142, 151

Hilary, 63, 112, 217

Irenaeus, 63, 93, 94, 113, 132, 133, 168, 183, 208, 209, 210, 232, 233

James, 1, 4, 16, 18, 19, 20, 21, 30, 31, 38, 46, 48, 49, 50, 53, 54, 55, 56, 57, 58, 61, 62, 66, 77, 78, 79, 80, 81, 82, 96, 97, 98, 103, 107, 110, 111, 126, 128, 129, 130, 132, 156, 165,

166, 167, 170, 172, 173, 174, 175, 176, 182, 184, 185, 186, 187, 188, 192, 197, 198, 200, 201, 202, 203, 205, 206, 208, 214, 215, 219, 220, 221, 222, 223, 224, 225, 226, 228, 230, 236, 241, 242, 246, 260, 262, 263, 264

Jerome, 52, 106, 113, 121, 128, 166, 170, 171, 172, 173, 178, 183, 208, 211, 213, 219, 221, 222, 225

Joseph, 18, 19, 20, 26, 28, 29, 31, 32, 33, 34, 35, 37, 40, 44, 45, 46, 50, 53, 54, 55, 56, 57, 58, 59, 60, 61, 64, 69, 70, 71, 72, 73, 74, 75, 76, 77, 78, 80, 81, 82, 83, 84, 85, 89, 94, 95, 96, 102, 103, 104, 105, 107, 110, 111, 113, 114, 115, 118, 120, 122, 123, 124, 125, 126, 128, 129, 130, 132, 135, 139, 156, 163, 164, 165, 166, 167, 170, 171, 172, 173, 174, 176, 177, 182, 184, 186, 187, 188, 193, 194, 196, 197, 201, 202, 203, 206, 207, 208, 209, 210, 211, 214, 217, 218, 220, 221, 222, 223, 225, 226, 231, 237, 241, 242, 251, 253, 254, 255, 256, 257, 258, 263

Justin Martyr, 63, 93, 109, 133, 183, 195, 208, 211

Luke 2

5, 113, 118, 196

Mark 15

40, 80, 82, 83, 174, 222

Mark 6

3, 58, 59, 61, 80, 83, 106, 174, 176, 188, 222

Matthew 1

25, 73, 74, 110, 113, 117, 118, 119, 120, 125, 133, 134, 135, 137, 143, 148, 155, 159, 163, 169, 218, 220, 236

McHugh, 20, 31, 74, 75, 114, 177, 178, 210, 225

Meier, 21, 22, 56, 60, 102, 106, 110, 111, 121, 122, 123, 124, 140, 167, 168, 177, 190, 191, 210, 238

Origen, 54, 63, 109, 110, 112, 117, 134, 166, 183, 184, 185, 187, 192, 195, 206, 215, 218, 238

Pacheco, 133, 163

Protevangelium, 16, 54, 56, 62, 107, 109, 129, 166,

167, 170, 184, 185, 186, 187, 189, 191, 197, 198, 200, 201, 214, 215, 219, 222, 228, 230, 246

Salome, 54, 80, 81, 128, 129, 174, 182, 188, 201, 228, 257, 258

Svendsen, 20, 21, 46, 47, 102, 110, 111, 114, 116, 117, 128, 133, 134, 135, 136, 138, 139, 141, 142, 143, 144, 146, 148, 149, 150, 151, 152, 153, 154, 155, 156, 157, 158, 159, 162, 168, 182, 208, 209, 210, 212

Symeon, 173, 203, 204, 205, 206, 207

Tertullian, 62, 63, 113, 126, 133, 209, 211, 212, 213

Witherington, 50, 125, 167, 224

Below: Icon of the Crucifixion showing four women at the cross

SHORT BIBLIOGRAPHY

Behold Your Mother - A Biblical and Historical Defense of the Marian Doctrines [Book] / auth. Staples Tim. - [s.l.] : Catholic Answers, 2014.

Christmas, The Original Story [Book] / auth. Barker Margaret. - The Society for Promoting Christian Knowledge : [s.n.], 2008.

James (New Testament Readings) [Book] / auth. Bauckham Richard. - [s.l.] : Routledge, 1999.

James the Brother of Jesus: The Key to Unlocking the Secrets of Early Christianity and the Dead Sea Scrolls [Book] / auth. Eisenman Robert. - [s.l.] : Penguin Books, 1998.

Jesus the Virgin-Born [Book] / auth. Nutt Edgar Alan. - [s.l.] : Xulon Press, 2007.

Jude and the Relatives of Jesus in the Early Church [Book] / auth. Bauckham Richard. - [s.l.] : Bloomsbury T&T Clark, 2004.

Just James: The Brother of Jesus in History and Tradition [Book] / auth. Painter John. - [s.l.] : University of South Carolina, 2004.

Mary and the Fathers of the Church: The Blessed Virgin Mary in Patristic Thought [Book] / auth. Gambero Luigi. - [s.l.] : Ignatius Press, 2006.

Mary in the Protevangelium of James: A Jewish Woman in the Temple? [Journal] / auth. Nutzman Megan. - [s.l.] : Greek, Roman, and Byzantine Studies, 2013. - Vol. 53.

On retrojecting later questions from later texts: A reply to Richard Bauckham [Journal] / auth. Meier Paul // Catholic Biblical Quarterly. - [s.l.] : Catholic Biblical Quarterly, 1997. - 3 : Vol. 59. - p. 511.

Roman Catholics and Evangelicals: Agreements and Differences [Book] / auth. McKenzie Norman Geisler and Ralph. - [s.l.] : Baker Academic, 1995.

The Brother of Jesus and the Lost Teachings of Christianity
[Book] / auth. Bütz Jeffrey. - [s.l.] : Inner Tradition, 2005.

The Brother of Jesus: James the Just and His Mission [Book] / auth. Neusner Jacob et al. - [s.l.] : Westminster John Knox Press, 2001.

The brothers and sisters of Jesus in ecumenical perspective [Journal] / auth. Meier John. - [s.l.] : Catholic Biblical Quarterly, 1992. - 1 : Vol. 54.

The brothers and sisters of Jesus: An Epiphanian response to John P. Meier [Journal] / auth. Bauckham Richard. - [s.l.] : Catholic Biblical Quarterly, 1994. - 4 : Vol. 56.

The mother of Jesus in the New Testament [Book] / auth. McHugh John. - [s.l.] : Doubleday, 1975.

Theotokos : a theological encyclopedia of the blessed Virgin Mary [Book] / auth. O' Caroll Michael. - [s.l.] : Clarentians, 1982.

Who Is My Mother? : The Role and Status of the Mother of Jesus in the. New Testament and Roman Catholicism [Book] / auth. Svendsen Eric. - [s.l.] : North-West University, 2001.